AUGUSTINE *and the*

FUNDAMENTALIST'S

DAUGHTER

AUGUSTINE *and the* FUNDAMENTALIST'S DAUGHTER

Margaret R. Miles

CASCADE *Books* • Eugene, Oregon

AUGUSTINE AND THE FUNDAMENTALIST'S DAUGHTER

Copyright © 2011 Margaret R. Miles. All rights reserved. Except for brief quotations in critical publications or reviews, no part of this book may be reproduced in any manner without prior written permission from the publisher. Write: Permissions, Wipf and Stock Publishers, 199 W. 8th Ave., Suite 3, Eugene, OR 97401.

Cascade Books
An Imprint of Wipf and Stock Publishers
199 W. 8th Ave., Suite 3
Eugene, OR 97401

www.wipfandstock.com

ISBN 13: 978-1-60899-759-6

Cataloging-in-Publication data:

Miles, Margaret R. (Margaret Ruth), 1937–

    Augustine and the fundamentalist's daughter / Margaret R. Miles

    viii + 228 p. ; 23 cm. — Includes bibliographical references.

    ISBN 13: 978-1-60899-759-6

    1. Miles, Margaret R. (Margaret Ruth), 1937– 2. Historians—United States—Biography.

BX4827.M55 A94 2011

Manufactured in the U.S.A.

For Mary Lillian Brown Miles

1908–1986

Contents

Introduction 1

1 Disorder and Early Sorrow 15
2 Learning How to Live 42
3 Laziness and Inertia 57
4 Beyond the Pleasure Principle 69
5 Staying Is Nowhere 89
6 Mothers and Sons, Mothers and Daughters 100
7 Relaxing from Myself—a Little 116
8 Conversion and Conversions 130
9 Parents or Fellow Pilgrims? 146
10 The Difficulty of Beautiful Things 159
11 The One Thing 172
12 A Sharp Quick Sense of Life 190
13 The Weight of Love 201

Epilogue 219

Bibliography 223

Introduction

All the genuine deep delight in life is in showing people
the mud pies you have made: and life is at its best when
we confidingly recommend our mud pies to each other's
sympathetic consideration.
  —J. M. THORNBURN[1]

Nothing we ever do is in direct opposition to our family's
example: somehow we always manage to replicate some
form of the pattern we're trying to escape.
  —ROXANNA ROBINSON[2]

MY PAPERBACK COPY OF AN English translation of Augustine's *Confessions* (Rex Warner's translation for Mentor-Omega Books), which I first read in 1964, is so tattered that I carry it around in a cut-to-fit box. As I open it now, a small shower of confetti from its dry and brittle pages litters the floor. For the last forty years I have reread St. Augustine's *Confessions* every few years, astonished that reading the same text with different experience and questions made a different text pop into my eyes. Each time I read it I noticed themes, preoccupations, and habits of mind—Augustine's, and mine—that I had not noticed before. Rereading is good for self-knowledge. A book, perhaps not just any book, but

---

1. Susanne Langer, quoting J. M. Thorburn, at the end of the preface to *Philosophy in a New Key*.

2. Robinson, "Truro Accord," 7.

a book similar in richness to the *Confessions*, can become a palimpsest that maps its reader's interests and stages of understanding. The astonishing richness of Augustine's *Confessions* supports an apparently infinite number of readings.

The *Confessions* I read when I was thirty is not the same *Confessions* that I read now, at seventy. Moreover, the circumstances in which I read have a great deal to do with what I notice. Over the years I have read the *Confessions* in preparation for classes I was taking or teaching, or on vacation on a Greek island. Now, writing my own confessions, bringing my experiences to Augustine's text, makes his *Confessions* new again.

Like Scripture, Augustine's *Confessions* is good to think with. *Augustine and the Fundamentalist's Daughter* is not a commentary; rather, I take Augustine's *Confessions* as my model; I think with the *Confessions* as Augustine thought with Scripture. I seek to identify the intellectual and emotional events and ideas that have been as formative for me as his were for him. My memories, observations, and reflections are stimulated by, and interwoven with, those of Augustine, reflecting the many years I have conversed in my mind with his *Confessions*.

Augustine believed that the understanding and exposition of Scripture was a preacher's central task.[3] Shortly after his appointment to the priesthood he requested a leave for the purpose of studying Scripture; he wrote: *I am still a weakling spiritually, and need the medicine of scripture. This I must study at all costs, though hitherto I have lacked the time.*[4] Evidently, he put to good use the months granted him for the study of Scripture, for the definitive demonstration of his knowledge was his ability to *think with* scriptural language, to weave it throughout his own memories, reflections, and observations in the *Confessions*.[5]

Augustine forged a new and distinctly Christian language by alternating his own narrative, prayer, and scriptural phrases. For example,

> Why then do I ask you [God] to enter into me? I could not exist, my God, were it not for your existence in me. Or would it be truer to say that I could not exist unless I existed in you, of whom are

---

3. Brown, *Augustine of Hippo*, 249.
4. Augustine *Epistula* 21.
5. Italicized phrases in the text are quoted from Augustine's *Confessions*. Citations in parentheses are from the *Confessions*.

all things, by whom are all things, in whom are all things? *So it is, my Lord, so it is.* (1.2)

The new understanding of Scripture Augustine acquired coincided with his fascination with a new reading practice. In Book 6 he recounts his amazement at finding Bishop Ambrose of Milan reading silently when he and his mother visited him. In North Africa the (few) literate always read aloud in order to benefit the (many) illiterate. Augustine and Monnica sat in silence and observed Ambrose for some time, during which Augustine speculated about his reasons for reading silently. Later, he developed his own practice of silent reading for the purpose of exercising and cultivating a subjective self, lingering on phrases and passages that excited him without the immediate urgency of communicating to others by preaching or teaching (9.4).

To tell a long story briefly, this reading practice later developed into medieval monks' *lectio divina,* combining the inwardness of silent reading with reading aloud, so that the precious words could be seen on the page, heard, and spiritually digested. Later still, the sixteenth-century Protestant reformations stimulated literacy by emphasizing the practice and habit of individual Bible-reading. Daily individual Bible-reading was the primary devotional practice of the fundamentalists of my childhood. The origin of this practice were those fourth-century moments in which Augustine watched Bishop Ambrose read and became intrigued by what silent reading could produce. Practicing it himself he discovered both a new intimacy with Scripture and a new configuration and articulation of the self.

Augustine and the Fundamentalist's Daughter seeks to demonstrate that rereading the same text—the right text—across a lifetime can give form and articulation to ideas and experiences that would otherwise seem to be *spilled and scattered* without meaning or significance (11.29). When one brings the question of *oneself* to reading, rereading, rethinking, reinterpreting the same text at different ages, in different circumstances, and with different heated interests, new understandings occur—especially, gradually, the understanding that the missing self was always right there, right here.

New understandings directly affected Augustine's feelings. Describing his youthful excitement in reading Cicero's *Hortensius,* he says that the book *altered my way of feeling,* filling him with *passionate zeal* to love and seek and obtain and embrace and hold fast wisdom itself (3.4). And he *felt* ideas physically. Throughout the *Confessions* he describes the physical and emotional feelings that accompanied intellectual and emotional events and situations. Perhaps the most famous of these narrations was his description of the intellectual and emotional crisis surrounding his conversion in the garden at Ostia: *My forehead, cheeks, eyes, color of face, and inflection of voice expressed my mind better than the words I used. . . . [I] made many movements of my body . . . I tore my hair, beat my forehead, locked my fingers together, clasped my knee . . . flung myself down on the ground somehow under a fig tree and gave free rein to my tears* (8.8, 12).

Unaffected by Descartes' much later philosophical separation of body and soul, Augustine assumed what philosopher Maxine Sheets-Johnstone calls the "first person body":

> the body that we know directly in the context or process of being alive. . . . The body that emerges alive and kicking is . . . the center and origin of our being in the world. It is, in fact, our first world and reality. The first person body is not a body that we outgrow or even can outgrow; it is only one we can choose to deny or deprecate. It is a body . . . whose biological reality is neither separable from, nor a third-person dimension of its lived and living presence.[6]

The first-person body is alive and intelligent; study of human beings that focuses *only* on biology, or *only* on rationality cannot describe it. Augustine characterized it this way: *[Y]ou gave me when an infant life and a body which, as we see, you have equipped with senses, fitted with limbs, adorned with its due proportion and, for its general good and safety, have implanted in it all the impulses of a living creature* (1.7). He understood that his adult body was extrapolated from, and continuous with, his infant body. The first-person body is, throughout life, the lived body, complete with feeling and intelligence.

Augustine invited his readers to "hear" his ideas of God, the world, and himself, in the context of his experiences.[7] Most philosophers and theologians have presented ideas as if they fell intact from the clouds,

---

6. Sheets-Johnstone, *Corporeal Turn*, 20.

7. Ray Monk's biographies of Ludwig Wittgenstein and Bertrand Russell present the subject's ideas in the context of their lives, events, and experiences; see Monk, *Ludwig Wittgenstein* and *Bertrand Russell*.

with no reference to the circumstances or the intellectual and social environment in which they had effective explanatory power and resonance while other ideas did not. Moreover, we often read the most extraordinary ideas of an age as if they were common ideas. Yet few authors simply reiterate the well established, taken-for-granted assumptions of their particular time and place. Augustine was critical of his society, its customs and its habits.

My affection for the *Confessions* has been accompanied by various irritations in the different times and situations in which I read it. In early readings, I was irritated by what I saw as Augustine's oversensitivity, self-flagellation, and anxiety about sex. Later I found his gender expectations unforgivable, and I thought his assumption that his own experience was universal was egregiously benighted. His rhetorical strategy of narrating his experience as a conversation with God annoyed me. I found his failure to flesh out any character but his own exasperating. My own confessions criticize Augustine's *Confessions*, sometimes implicitly, sometimes explicitly. I do not, for example, use Augustine's annoying rhetorical ruse of *mentioning* sexual experience in order to capture his reader's attention, only to switch immediately to philosophical or theological reflections. I do, however, seek to emulate the rigor and depth with which Augustine thought about his life.

I learned to lay aside second-hand judgments inherited from many modern interpreters, who read him as neurasthenic, dualistic, and monomaniacal. Allowing oneself even briefly to see the world as Augustine saw it can be a life-changing experience. The passionate, even violent, imagery with which he described his search for God challenges all sluggishness. Yet for Augustine, finding the resolution of his anguished search was more like relaxing than like increased struggle: *Cessavi de me paululum—I relaxed a little from myself* (7.14). I recognize that Augustine's rhythm of avid search and grateful acceptance has become the systole and diastole of my own life.

Books 1–9 narrate Augustine's struggle toward Christian faith. Books 10–13 explore the philosophical and theological ideas that furnished the resolution of his struggle. Although Augustine closed what modern readers recognize as his autobiographical narrative in Book 9, the last four books are also autobiographical; they place the details of his individual life in the context of time and space. Augustine wrote his *Confessions* when he was about forty years old and recently established as a bishop in Hippo, North Africa. Similarly, *Augustine and the Fundamentalist's Daughter* concludes when I was about forty and beginning to teach at Harvard Divinity School. The last four books of my account reflect on some major shifts in my thinking and feeling, as do Augustine's last books.

Fundamentalism, as I experienced it as a child, was more than a set of beliefs, more than the insistence that every word of Scripture came from the mouth of God (in the King James Version). Fundamentalism was also a worldview, an acute alertness to wrongdoing, and a particular construction and understanding of "self." The fundamentalist self begins with an especially poignant sense of *lack*, the "quite valid suspicion that *'I am not real'*."[8] The fundamentalist recognizes more vividly than most people that the sense of self is groundless, a mental construction.[9]

No one described the experience of the missing self better than Augustine. Multiple vivid images and metaphors describe his desperation and evisceration: malnutrition, insomnia, itching wounds and scratched scabs, and the feeling of being *wasted and scattered*, distracted and dispersed. *For I have been spilled and scattered among times whose order I do not know; my thoughts, the innermost bowels of my soul, are torn apart with the crowding tumults of variety. And so it will be*, he added, *until all together I can flow into you, purified and molten by the fire of your love. And I shall stand and become set in you, in my mold, in your truth* (11.29). Augustine grounded the self in a personal God who, by watching him, and watching out for him, guaranteed his reality.

Through Augustine I became acquainted with Plotinus, a Platonic philosopher whose ideas are woven throughout the *Confessions*.[10] Augustine learned from—and borrowed from—Plotinus throughout his life.[11] So do I. Most importantly, Plotinus helps me to get over myself,

---

8. Loy, *Lack and Transcendence*, xi.
9. Ibid., 101; quoted by Sheets-Johnstone, *Roots of Morality*, 381.
10. O'Connell, *St. Augustine's Early Theory of Man*, passim.
11. Miles, *Plotinus on Body and Beauty*.

Introduction

relieving Augustine's intense focus on the anxious self. Plotinus became the great scholarly love of my life.

Examples of Plotinus's usefulness in relaxing the anxious self appear throughout this book; here is one example. Plotinus taught that the gifts and pains of the universe circulate without design or address and, inevitably, each person receives some of both. Far from saying "Why me?" when pain occurs, one should, when one hears of another's pain, say "Why *not* me?" Plotinus's universe, ruled by chance and choice, seems to me more real than Augustine's universe, carefully organized and meticulously governed by an omnipotent and omniscient God. In Plotinus's world, chance is ubiquitous, but *choosing* how one will respond is always a human prerogative, even, as Camus said, on the way to the gallows. Plotinus advises that, rather than special pleading for preferential treatment, one "await with confidence and accept with gratitude" the gifts and pains that come one's way.[12]

For much of my life I have been occupied with a strenuous and urgent effort to come to terms with the fundamentalist psyche I inherited. This book describes the complex process of identifying fundamentalist characteristics in myself and deciding whether I want to retain them, adjust them, or discard them. Altering my beliefs was easy compared to changing my assumptions about myself, other people, and the world. Habits of mind and behavior were most difficult to identify and modify. It has been startling to recognize that, in some significant ways, I am still a fundamentalist. For example, I choose to retain a certain suspicion of American society—its social arrangements, media, and consumer orientation—that is highly reminiscent of my parents' religious *and* immigrant perspective. Since I am a scholar, I have learned to call this habitual suspicion a "critical approach." But most importantly, I sought to change my beliefs and values without losing my father's passion.

It is difficult for a fundamentalist to accept complexity and ambiguity. The fundamentalist sorts everything in categories of right or wrong, good or bad; "us" is right, "them" is wrong. These categories are laborsaving devices; it's much easier to label and file than to notice and

12. Dinesen, "Babette's Feast."

puzzle over the irreducible complexity of human beings and human life. Fundamentalists also have the confidence that their judgments are supported by divine fiat, that they enjoy the God's-eye view. They tend to have the answers before the questions have been articulated.

Literalism is another foundation of the fundamentalist psyche. Fundamentalists require themselves actually to *do* what they say they will do. The fundamentalists of my childhood did not talk to "make conversation," and did not understand people who did. We heard everything said to us as if it were a promise. When a nineteen-year-old soldier told me when I was four years old that he was going to wait for me until I grew up and marry me, I took it absolutely literally. Well, children *are* literal, but one can't go through life that way without accumulating disappointments.

A humorous example of fundamentalist literalism: My sister's six-year-old son came home from school one day distressed because the teacher had shown the class a picture of a dissected human heart, and "Jesus was not in it," he said. Having taught her children that Jesus lives in their hearts, my sister had to think quickly. "That's because the heart you saw did not belong to a Christian," she said.

Fundamentalists personalize the universe as Augustine did. They understand everything that happens to them as ordered by a "personal savior" God. Nothing is coincidental or accidental. Augustine interpreted a painful toothache as God *torturing* him to remind him of his sins (9.4). Scripture is God's direct communication to fundamentalists in the particular circumstances of their lives, which, of course, God knows. Generations of Christians have comforted themselves with the belief that God allows nothing to happen to them that is too much for them to bear.[13] This is a performative belief; trusting that it is true, they then go on to bear whatever needs to be borne. They interpret the pains and distresses that come to them either as God's punishment, or as tests of their faith.

Augustine exemplifies the fundamentalist's obsessive fretting over his relationship with God. He was fascinated by restlessness and rest (1.1), by anxiety and relaxation (7.14), because he had so little of the latter. His passionate nature easily tipped into compulsive self-doubt and

13. Tony Morrison, *Jazz*, 99: "'He ain't give you nothing you can't bear, Rose.' But had He? Maybe this one time He had. Had misjudged and misunderstood her particular backbone. This one time. Her particular spine."

relentless pursuit, whether of *honors, marriage, money* (6.6), or of God. Relaxation was, for Augustine, always temporary, a momentary relief that prepared him for the next onslaught of anxiety. Augustine comments on the relief brought by his conversion from professional and sexual pursuits: *Now my face was perfectly calm* (*tranquillo iam vultu*; 8.12). But his intense subjective engagement did not change; the later books of the *Confessions* still worry over minutiae that seem to him to threaten his relationship with God; and he still exhibits intemperate anxiety over such abstract matters as how to explain time (11.22).[14]

The fundamentalist *knows*, exemplifying Plato's "double ignorance." *A bad state to be in*, Augustine said, *not even to know what it is that I do not know!* (11.25–26). The opposite of the fundamentalist psyche is what Augustine called humility, or resolving *not to know what I do not know*. Ironically, the mature Augustine both shows the fundamentalist confidence that he knows a great many things that he could not possibly *know*, and prescribes for this condition: *The way is firstly humility, secondly humility, and thirdly humility*,[15] because we *know* so little.[16] In the words of the Scripture verse Augustine quoted more often than any other verse throughout his career: *We see now through a glass darkly . . .*[17]

~

14. *My soul is on fire to solve this very complicated enigma . . . let my longing penetrate into these things . . . . Grant me what I love; for I do love it and it was you who granted me to love. . . . By Christ, I beg you, in his name, the holy of holies, let no one disturb me* (11.22). It is striking that this impassioned outburst occurs in Augustine's description of his struggle to understand time, a topic that, by his own admission, he did not need to understand: *What, then, is time? I know what it is if no one asks me what it is, but if I want to explain it to someone who has asked me, I find that I do not know* (11.14).

15. Augustine *Epistula* 118.

16. Freud put it this way: "The unconscious is the true psychic reality; in its inner nature it is just as much unknown to us as the reality of the external world, and it is just as imperfectly communicated by the reports of our sense organs." *Interpretation of Dreams*, VII:383.

17. 1 Cor 13:12; Davidson wrote: "If we want to know what we know, we must give up what we suppose about our individuality, our self, [and] our subject position." *Emergence of Sexuality*, 91.

Augustine's *Confessions* is dappled with longing, as sunlight through woods. Every few sentences it bursts forth in an impassioned cry to God. Open the book anywhere and you will find sentences like this: *I was on fire then, my God, I was on fire to leave earthly things behind and fly back to you* (3.4). And: *O beauty of all things beautiful. O truth, truth, how I panted for you even then deep down in the marrow of my soul* (3.6). Similarly, the fundamentalists I knew as a child had a strong sense that "this world is not my home," a deep longing for the heaven they believed awaited them. As my father lay dying he longed to go "home." Longing was not, however, specific to particular situations, but a way of life.

In his treatise on fasting, Augustine described the precise purpose of longing: *Longing makes the heart deep (desiderium sinus cordis)*. Longing, balanced with gratitude, stretches the heart's capacity. For the converted Augustine, longing was not directed to some future time or place. It was, rather, a discipline in which past and future collapse into the present moment, the moment in which God *is*. Physical hunger brings body to the soul's project, enabling the whole person to *feel* longing.

I must clarify my agenda in this book: First, not all fundamentalists are alike. I know people who hold fundamentalist religious beliefs, but who are more loving than judgmental, more accepting of others whose beliefs differ from their own than my father, and who evidence more joy than was characteristic of my home. Second, my agenda is not to demonstrate that Augustine was a fundamentalist in any contemporary sense of the term. While Augustine's *Confessions* demonstrate a number of fundamentalist traits, Augustine and my father did not have identical, or even similar, psyches. Differences matter, and I will point them out as they appear. One of the most important differences is Augustine's attitude toward scriptural interpretation. As discussed in subsequent chapters, he found great relief in Ambrose's advice that Scripture is not to be taken literally; rather, the spiritual meaning must be sought. Moreover, Augustine professed to tolerate, even to appreciate, multiple interpretations of Scripture, as long as they did not violate Christian doctrine.

Introduction

> Can you not see how foolish it is out of all that abundance of perfectly true meanings which can be extracted from those words rashly to assert that one particular meaning was the one that Moses had chiefly in mind, and thereby in one's pernicious quarrelsomeness to offend charity herself? (12.25)

My father did not tolerate multiple interpretations of Scripture! For him, there was a right way—his—and a wrong way—yours.

Biographies in late antiquity presented their subjects through narration of their ideal traits, that is, as heroes. Episodes were an "interaction of fact and fantasy," selected in order to highlight what the biographer considered the inner meaning of the subject's life.[18] Augustine's *Confessions* must have startled an audience accustomed to this genre, for rather than presenting himself as heroic, Augustine allowed himself to be remarkable for nothing but his wrongheaded passion. He introduced the young Augustine briefly and without pretension: *I lived and I felt* (1.20).

Augustine's *Confessions* is an intellectual autobiography in the fullest sense of the term, describing the development of his ideas and values alongside, and in sync with, his experiences and feelings. Augustine wrote about books and teachers, but the vividness and accuracy of autobiography depends on showing how, in the exceedingly complex mixture of family, friends, and experiences, the author's ideas were built, bit by bit. For we do not "have" ideas; we make them and, in turn, the ideas we make, make us. Autobiography is truthful, not by meticulous exposure of all the details of one's life, but by insight. Augustine's *Confessions* is a model of achieving a balance between description of experience and reflection on it.

Autobiography is also necessarily the biography of one's body and one's culture. Our physical pains and joys, and our interpretations of and responses to them, are formative. And we belong to, and are shaped by, the great social, political, and economic conditions of our time. The idiosyncratic combination of family and events that we think of as

---

18. Cox, *Biography in Late Antiquity*, 134.

informing our unique individuality are not as decisive as our social, historical, and cultural location.

Augustine was not comfortable writing autobiographically. Neither am I. He formally addressed God, who was, he assumed, perennially ready to forgive and forget his flaws and faults. But he was also vividly aware of a more immediate and critical audience. It is probably safe to say that he did not picture readers who lived fifteen hundred years after his own time, but he did realize that his contemporaries would be interested in reading his memoirs. *To whom am I relating this? Not to you, my God. But I am telling these things in your presence to my own kind, to that portion of mankind, however small it may be, which may chance to read these writings of mine* (2.3).

He was terrified of the possibility that his contemporaries would laugh at him, repeatedly specifying his desired reader to be one who *will not laugh*. Endeavoring to overcome this fear, he blustered: *Let proud-hearted men laugh at me, and those who have not yet, for their own health, been struck down and crushed by you, my God* (4.1). His parents' laughter at the punishments inflicted on him by his childhood schoolmasters still haunted the middle-aged Augustine (1.9). Rather than laughter, the reader-response he sought was smiling indulgence: *I know that your spiritual ones will be smiling at me, though kindly and lovingly, if they read the story of these confusions of mind* (5.10).

My hesitations regarding autobiographical writing are not quite the same as Augustine's. I fear self-deception. I fear failures of self-knowledge and the inevitable omissions and distortions emerging from a single perspective. Events and conversations are inevitably shared with others, each of whom saw, felt, and remembered differently. Reports that rely only on one perspective have an irreducible and unavoidable fictional component; they do not tell the whole story.

I also recognize that I do not possess a "naked eye," but have instead a conditioned eye, exquisitely attuned to noticing some things while blatantly ignoring others. I cannot simply "tell it as it was," but only as I saw and experienced it. In this, as Bob Dylan's song goes, I am "not so unique." Theologian David Brown has described limitation of perspective as an essential human characteristic. He suggests that it is, therefore, a limitation that even Jesus, in being fully human, must have shared. To be human is to see "through a glass, darkly."

Introduction

Autobiographical reflections may be prompted by various motivations. Perhaps the author wants to convince his reader of his integrity, honesty, and commitment to worthy causes. For example, Leni Riefenstahl, filmmaker for the Nazis, wrote her *Memoirs* primarily from an overriding concern with self-justification. Augustine of Hippo wrote his *Confessions* in order to gather his life about him, to remember, in the words of Deuteronomy, "all the ways by which the Lord your God has led you through this wildness." *I confess that I attempt to be one of those who write because they have made some progress, and who, by means of writing, make further progress.*[19] I write, quite simply, to know what I think.

Theological language came more naturally to Augustine than it does to me. For Augustine, theological language was a fresh language of discovery. In my youth, religious language was always present, on hand to interpret every nuance of experience, precluding thinking for myself, and preventing freshness of experience and thought. So I resist the temptation to know as much about God and God's activity in the world as Augustine claimed to know.

Someone has remarked that the *only* character in the *Confessions*, the only actor, the only protagonist, is God. I, on the other hand, do not see an all-knowing, all-caring God leading, shaping, and directing my life. But I do see a certain grace and beauty active in the painful and joyful moments that constitute my life. Perhaps that gracefulness and omnipresent beauty *is* what Augustine called God. For Augustine and Plotinus, it was absolutely essential to learn to *see* both the visible world and the life that animates it *as beauty*. Plotinus said that "the one who attains the vision of the incomprehensible beauty is happy . . . and the one who fails to attain it has failed utterly."[20]

Augustine was judgmental of his youthful self. He remarked elsewhere that if a person is to be able to "love the neighbor as oneself," she must first love herself, but he strongly condemned his youthful self. Unlike Augustine, I am as grateful for my frustrations, losses, and bad choices

---

19. Augustine *Epistula* 143.2.
20. *Ennead* 1.6.7.

as I am for the privilege I have received. Augustine called his accomplishments and successes *mere smoke and wind* (1.17), but is one grateful for smoke and wind? I prefer to see the coincidences, luck, and hard work involved in a rewarding career as gifts, to which the appropriate response is gratitude. Mistakes and fortunate choices together create the vividly textured pattern of a life; the beauty is in the whole, not in selected fragments. It's the richness of the mixture that produces feelings of gratitude.

⁓

"Suffer me not to be separate": T. S. Eliot's cry at the end of "Ash Wednesday" articulates my longing. Not to be isolated in a small corner of the life of the universe, but to fling the empty self into the great beauty. My part is infinitesimally small, yet part of the whole, and sometimes I experience that reality in physical, emotional, and intellectual ecstasy. I cannot personalize the great life, beauty, and love in which we all participate, as Augustine did, but my consanguinity with the whole is not an abstraction. It is as concrete a reality as I know. Despite anecdotal evidence to the contrary, I believe that the central reality of the universe is life, beauty, and love. At my best I live in gratitude.

In his thirteen books, Augustine *spelled out* his engagement in the world. He said that no matter what we do, no matter how ultimately self-destructive our behavior may be, we all seek to be happy.[21] He used the image of God gently but firmly turning his head (*fovisti caput*) as the hidden yet, in hindsight, manifest trajectory of his life.[22] He explored the dissonance between his conscious intention of seeking happiness and his youthful pursuit of riches, honors, and sex. But the concept of happiness is complex for Augustine, as will be discussed in subsequent chapters, and finally, he described his engagement in the world as oriented, not to happiness, but to *being loving*: *My weight is my love; by it I am carried wherever I am carried* (13.9).

---

21. Philip Roth remarked that happiness consists of the following: "one achieves, one is productive, and there's pleasure and ease in all of it." *Exit Ghost*, 250.

22. O'Connell, *Early Theory*, 65–86, *passim*.

1 *Disorder and Early Sorrow*[1]

I lived and I felt. . . . I looked for pleasure, exaltations, truths not in God, but in God's creatures (myself and the rest), and so I fell straight into sorrows, confusions, and mistakes. (1.20)

We come to expect love in the forms we first knew it.
—GEORGE MAKARI[2]

OUR HEARTS ARE RESTLESS UNTIL *they rest in you* (1.1). Augustine's memoirs begin with the evanescent self, guaranteed nothing but mortality. Created *ex nihilo*, nothingness remains with us as lack, void, restlessness, the "suspicion that 'I' am not real."[3] He proceeds quickly to prayer, to re-collection of the scattered self in which the self is placed, stabilized, and secured in God: *I could not exist therefore, my God, were it not for your existence in me. Or would it be more accurate to say that I could not exist unless I existed in you?* (1.2). The missing self, the lack, has been filled with the ultimate security, the God *who fills all things and are wholly present in everything you fill* (1.3). Having established his own existence, he begins to trace his life from the womb forward.

---

1. The title of this chapter is borrowed from a short story by Thomas Mann in *Death in Venice*.
2. Makari, *Revolution in Mind*, 332.
3. Loy, *Lack and Transcendence*, xiii.

Handicapped by inability to observe his own infant behavior, Augustine was forced to rely on the report of others and on observation of another infant, perhaps his son. At first the infant is nothing but "life and a body" (1.7). Instinctively he sucks nourishment from a woman's breast, nourishment that is generously provided, he specifies, not by the nurse herself, but by God. Augustine remarked that he must have smiled *first when I was asleep, and later when I was awake* (1.6). He implies that the infant's waking smile is simply extrapolated from the biological sleeping grimace. Had he lingered to explore the infant's first smile (at approximately three months of age, as later studies show) and its implications, he might have revised his teaching that the infant's first intentional act—what is "original" to the infant—is sin. For, according to modern researchers, the smile is an affectively charged movement, "a sign of openness toward another, sign of friendliness and warmth, a social interaction."[4]

Psychiatrist René Spitz, who studied the smiling response, analyzed the infant's disposition to smile as a "manifestation of pleasure experienced when beholding the presence of a human partner."[5] From extensive experimental studies, Spitz concludes that the infant's smile is intentional, "the first natural sign of recognition of another that, in its gesture of amiability, carries with it a natural moral tone: to be open and friendly toward others . . . . [It is] a spontaneous individual kinetic act, and precisely not legislated or taught."[6] Similarly, psychiatrist Melanie Klein, studying infant behavior at the breast, observed that within a few weeks after birth, an infant who has learned that she will be fed when she is hungry is then more interested in the mother's face than in the nourishment she offers.[7]

Answering the objection that the infant's smile merely imitates the smiling face it sees, Maxine Sheets-Johnstone argues that the infant's smile is not only intentional, but it is also "an *initiatory* act," not a response.[8] Interpreting the smile as the infant's original intentional and

4. Sheets-Johnstone, *Roots of Morality*, 350.

5. Spitz, *First Year of Life*, 100.

6. Sheets-Johnstone, *Roots of Morality*, 352.

7. A 1609 painting by Artemesia Gentileschi, *Madonna and Child*, perfectly illustrates Klein's statement. The Madonna holds her nipple toward the Child, who, ignoring the nipple, gazes at her face; Miles, *A Complex Delight*, 136.

8. Ibid., 305.

initiatory act is conclusively supported by research showing that *blind babies smile*.[9]

However, what Augustine noticed as he observed infant behavior was that the infant's first intentional act is sinful.[10] He asks, *Who can recall to me the sin I did in my infancy*? Observing *a baby who was envious; it could not yet speak but it turned pale and looked bitterly at another baby sharing its milk*, he declared that *infants are harmless because of physical weakness, not because of any innocence of mind* (1.7). For a fundamentalist, the essential statement of *selfhood* is: I *am* a sinner.[11] Although this acknowledgement might appear to license sinning, fundamentalists strain every nerve not to *appear* sinful.

G. K. Chesterton once said that original sin is the *only* Christian doctrine that is fully documented; any newspaper, any day, will give ample testimony to the perversity of human nature. This is not the place for an exposition on the doctrine of original sin, but a clarification is necessary. The doctrine is not based on the claim that the infant's first intentional act was/is sinful, but on St. Paul's claim that Adam's sin made all humans sinners. Augustine developed Tertullian's idea of the existence of an original weakness (*vitium originalis*) into the doctrine of original sin (*peccatum originalis*). In his treatise, *Ad Simplicianum*, written shortly before his *Confessions*, "we meet the epoch-making phrase *originale peccatum*, meaning a sinful quality which is born with us and is inherent in our constitution."[12] Furthermore, *originale peccatum* includes not only the possibility of sin, but also "original guilt."[13] Augustine also volunteered the innovation that original sin is transmitted through sex at the moment of conception. His experience of helpless *concupiscentia* was confirmed for him by his observation that the infant's first intentional act already shows the effects of original sin.

---

9. On this point, Sheets-Johnstone cites the findings of two researchers, T. G. R. Bower, *Human Development* (1979), and Selma Fraiberg, *Selected Writings of Selma Freiberg* (1987); See *Roots of Morality*, 305.

10. Augustine's doctrine of original sin was "mildly phrased but already complete in essential outline in the first book of the treatise *De diversis quaestionibus ad Simplicianum*," written in 397 CE, shortly before he wrote the *Confessions* in 401 CE; Williams, *Ideas of the Fall and of Original Sin*, 327.

11. In the words of Psalm 51, "I am a sinner from my mother's womb."

12. Williams, *Ideas*, 327.

13. Ibid., 328.

Ontogeny recapitulates phylogeny; individuals reiterate the experience of the species. Moreover, Augustine's often repeated principle that any good in the individual is directly attributed to God makes it imperative and obvious that the infant's first *intentional* act must be sinful. The *only* way to be a self is to be a sinner.

༄

Augustine assumed that the subjects one studies are silent until one approaches them with the right question. He brought to his interpretation of the infant his predilection for noticing sin. The question he brought to observation of the infant was, *What, then, was my sin? Was it that I cried for more as I hung upon the breast?* The jealous infant suggests a possibility to Augustine; perhaps his sin was envy: *Can one really describe as 'innocence' the conduct of one who, when there is a fountain of milk flowing richly and abundantly, will not allow another child to have his share of it?* (1.7). Infant's inarticulateness insures that they and their behavior become helpless victims of adult projections!

Augustine's interpretation of the infant's body language is reminiscent of a discussion I had with my mother some years ago. In defense of her anti-abortion position, Mother told me that she saw an anti-abortion advertisement that showed a fetus in the womb shrinking from a knife that came towards it. "But Mother," I said, "my granddaughter (then six months old) would not know enough to shrink from a knife." She had to acknowledge that the ad depended either on trick photography or on coincidence, and in either case, on projection.

The studies of modern psychiatrists and psychologists from an ontogenetic perspective indicate that pleasure and openness to another's presence precedes the frustration and rage Augustine understood as fundamental to human nature. Infantile fear responses develop from the so-called startle reflex (at about two months, to sudden loud noise or loss of support), to "stranger anxiety." Stranger anxiety is the infant's first antisocial behavior. In other words, fear responses originate in reaction to environmental stimuli and are not extrapolated to social stimuli until the infant is approximately nine months old.[14] From an ontogenetic perspective, Augustine was wrong, but influentially wrong.

14. Sheets-Johnstone argues that stranger anxiety does not disappear as the child

Disorder and Early Sorrow

Throughout the history of the West, sweeping conclusions about "human nature" have been drawn from Augustine's doctrine of original sin. Theologians such as Martin Luther and Jean Calvin have based their theologies on the belief that humans are fundamentally sinful. My mother agreed. On days when I had a cold, was out of sorts or otherwise crabby, she said, "That's your real self coming out!" Later I had a friend whose mother, in similar circumstances, said, "You're not yourself today, dear."

Even Sigmund Freud, the father of psychoanalysis, who disagreed dramatically with Augustine on almost everything else, found the roots of repression and neurosis in infantile life.[15] Freud and Augustine share a bleak and disrespectful view of children.[16] "Freud's child is a humiliated creature, driven by discomfort, dread, and shame."[17] He is anxious, grasping, ignorant, and insecure, cravenly seeking protection, reassurance, love. Augustine's child is greedy, disobedient, lying, lazy, jealous, and unhappy.

> *And when people did not do what I wanted, either because I could not make myself understood or because what I wanted was bad for me, then I would become angry with my elders for not being subservient to me, and with responsible people for not acting as though they were my slaves, and I would avenge myself on them by bursting into tears.* (1.6–7)

Moreover, Augustine saw in the infant's behavior the source and paradigm of lifelong aggression and acquisitiveness: *For it is just these same sins which, as the years pass by, become related no longer to tutors, schoolmasters, footballs, nuts, and pet sparrows, but magistrates and kings, gold, estates, and slaves* (1.19).

---

grows to adulthood. Rather, stranger anxiety is the foundation of, and is extrapolated into, xenophobia; *Roots of Morality*, 363ff.

15. Freud said that repression "is the cornerstone on which the whole theory of psychoanalysis rests"; *On Narcissism* (1914), 399. However, Alan Bass has shown that in his later years, Freud "began to rethink the centrality of repression in favor of a theory based on disavowal"; *Difference and Disavowal*, 7.

16. Similarly Lacan disparaged infants and their abilities; see Sheets-Johnstone, *Roots of Power*, 161–62.

17. Neiman, *Evil in Modern Thought*, 320.

Clearly, Augustine did not regard infancy with rose-colored glasses. It is important, and only fair, however, to notice that although "sin" is a judgmental word in our contemporary usage, Augustine insisted that the appropriate attitude toward sin is not condemnation but sympathy: *And no one is sorry for the children; no one is sorry for the older people; no one is sorry for both of them* (1.9). He was acutely and intimately aware of the misery of "sin."

Augustine did not remember his childhood as happy. He (and his readers) blame his parents for being amused when the child Augustine was beaten (1.9). He was terrified of beatings, which he remembered as occurring rather often, prompting his first desperate prayers. His teachers and parents condoned corporal punishment, considering it necessary to curb the child's curiosity and love of play. As a middle-aged man, he wrote, "Is there anyone who, faced with the choice between death and a second childhood, would not shrink in dread from the later prospect and choose to die?"[18] Is this egregious exaggeration, or Augustine's honest memory of childhood?

A tee shirt I once saw announced a gathering of people who had happy childhoods—it was to be held in a phone booth. Undoubtedly, people who acknowledge happy childhoods are rare. But is a happy childhood as valuable as those think who did not have one? I know a few people who had happy childhoods, and they seem to be perpetually disappointed in adulthood. Since childhood, nothing has felt quite as wonderful as their parents' loving attention and provision. Perhaps it is more productive of a happy adulthood to have a happy *enough* childhood: no abuse, no beatings, no deprivations, but the ordinary discomforts, awkwardness, and insecurities of a body that is growing and thus unpredictably different from one day to the next, parents that become tired and exasperated, and playmates that abandon one for other friendships. These childhood disappointments make the child notice that there are other people with their own perspectives and projects in the world. Indeed, this begins to be apparent to the infant at the mother's breast, when nourishment is not immediately forthcoming or is in

---

18. Augustine *City of God* 21.14.

insufficient supply; the infant slowly recognizes that the mother is not an extension of his/her body, but *another person*.¹⁹

∽

When I was two years old Mother told me not to stray into the neighbor's yard. I replied triumphantly, "You say no, I say les [*sic*]!" This was my first, and almost my last, forthright statement of independence. My parents, however, did not recognize this defiance as a valiant effort to construct a self. The word they used for it was "will," or better, "willfulness." And they responded to evidence of my "will" as Lutheran catechisms had advised centuries earlier:

> Use the knife of God's Word to cut off the branches of their [children's] contumacious will. Raise them in the fear of God. And when their wild nature comes up again—as weeds always will—and the old Adam sins in them again, kill it and bury it deep in the ground, lest the newly grown good nature once again revert to its wild state.²⁰

I was not beaten as a child, but I was spanked. I recall one spanking, at age seven, because I cut a piece of my hair to create bangs. A pretty little girl at school had bangs, and I wanted them too. Then I tried to hide the cut hair—as if it couldn't be noticed that my hair looked different!—and probably also lied about cutting it. The worst of the spankings was that they were not immediate but "wait till your father gets home." I don't remember the spankings as very painful, but the anticipation was. Each time I was told that I was being spanked "because we love you so much." I translate: my parents saw it as their duty not to "spare the rod and spoil the child." Later, as a parent I believed that one should *only* strike a child in anger. A swift hit on the child's bottom because he has irritated you beyond tolerance is more honest than a deferred and premeditated, cool-headed punishment.

My parents inherited Augustine's belief that the original, self-defining, intentional act of the infant was sinful through the further

---

19. Benjamin, *Bonds of Love*, 45; Benjamin argues that it is highly important to the child's development that, beyond her attentiveness to the child's needs and wants, the mother insists on *mutual recognition*.

20. Quoted by Strauss, *Luther's House of Learning*, 291.

elaborations of historical Christian authors like Martin Luther. Beginning in the 1520s, Lutheran catechisms for children articulated the practical meaning of original sin. Children were instructed to memorize catechisms such as the following from as early an age as possible.

> Question: What have you learned from the Ten Commandments? Answer: I have learned the knowledge of our damnable sinful life. For the Ten Commandments are a book of vices to us in which we read clearly what we are before God without Grace, namely: idol worshippers, miscreants, blasphemers and despisers of God's divine name, cursed robbers of his holy temple, and renegades to his eternal word. We are disobedient abusers of our fathers, we are child murderers and envious dogs, killers, whoremongers, adulterers, thieves and rogues, deceivers, dissemblers, liars, perjuring tale bearers, false witnesses, insolent misers. In sum, we are wild insatiable beasts against whose evil nature God erects the commandments as if they were high walls and locked gates.[21]

Augustine's suggestion that the appropriate response to sin is sorrow and sympathy seems to have been lost in transmission by subsequent authors who translated the doctrine of original sin into childrearing practices. Children's catechisms were intended to create in the child a psychic "place" of despair in order to prepare them for the assurances of God's grace and mercy to the "miserable offenders." Reformation historian Gerald Strauss writes: "[God's] love is always evoked at emotionally powerful junctures . . . when the bereft forlorn human victim of his own wrong instincts sees the restoration of divine love as the *only* remaining hope of comfort, peace, and solace."[22]

Ah! So my parents should have followed up the message that I was a "miserable sinner" with "assurances of God's love and forgiveness," but I do not recall that this happened. Perhaps because I did not confess voluntarily, but had to be caught and punished, my "sin" did not seem to invite forgiveness, but rather increased distrust and watchfulness on my parents' part. After the "You say no, I say les" and the haircutting incidents, I do not recall other defiant moments. I had learned my lesson. I found ways of getting around the cycle of disobedience and

21. Caspar of Aquila, Superintendent in Saxony, 1538; quoted in ibid.
22. Ibid.

punishment. What I had learned, and learned well, was not to defy, but to lie and sneak.

The message that I, when I am "me," am a sinner—that it is my sin that defines me, my *self*—has been nearly impossible to eradicate. Similarly, throughout his *Confessions,* before and after his conversions/conversion, Augustine defined himself by his sins, alternatively scrutinizing, accusing, and condemning himself. Any goodness he has, and any happiness, is from God.

"Shoulds" and "shouldn't's" are a staple of fundamentalist child rearing. I still occasionally catch myself thinking in these terms. I wonder what my life would be like without them, without large and small shoulds and shouldn'ts. Some things I do because I think I "should" are actually things I want to do. So I *could* do them because I want to, rather than because I tell myself I "should." If I did this, the arena of shoulds would shrink and I could be happier and more honest, thus overcoming childhood training that says I *should* only do something because I *should* do it, not because I want to, or because it gives me pleasure.

Somebody wise has said that each of us is our own favorite character in fiction. We tell ourselves, in constant interior self-talk, a story about who we are that helps us get by, or flourish, or that limits or even destroys us as we set out to prove that the story we tell ourselves is an accurate story. Any psychiatrist will verify that many of us care more about being right, in the story we tell ourselves about ourselves, than about changing our story in order to be happy. Martha Nussbaum has carried this observation further by suggesting that those we love are also characters in fiction. "We love made-up people, people we have made up to be people we can love."[23]

Here come my people.

---

23. Nussbaum, *Love's Knowledge*, 326.

Augustine and the Fundamentalist's Daughter

In the 1880s Henry, not then my grandfather, visited Martha, not then my grandmother but a young and sheltered English girl, daughter of a customs officer, living in a suburb of London. Henry tells of it in a letter to his daughter, my mother, dated August 3, 1947.

> My dearest Mollie,
>
> I completed 71 years yesterday and it is a serious reflection that I am now within what is most likely to be the last decade of my earthly life; not that this troubles me, but I realize that within a measurable distance now I shall cease to be anything more than a memory and only that to a very limited number like yourself.
>
> Dear Mother is quite frail; it would take little to bring her earthly life to a close. I have her portrait before me as I write, and I marvel at the change time has wrought. I fell in love with her the first moment I met her and I remember so well her dark hair and eyes, so expressive, and her quick nervous temperament and musical ability. It seemed a hopeless thing for me to let my heart go out to her but I prayed about it and the answer was given, and there came a night when I visited her home to say goodbye to leave for a distant city. I knew I had to get an answer from her or say farewell forever and the first hope was when I found the three sisters were alone, but how to get *her* alone was the problem. In desperation I proposed taking all three for a walk on the Downs, a wide open heath with some brush, close to the suspension bridge. Then her two sisters declined the offer and she accepted, so I knew my great chance had come and

within an hour very hesitatingly I told her I loved her and asked if she could care enough about me to marry me some day when I could offer her a home and an income, and while we sat there with the future of half a century being decided a band played in the distance an air of which the words run

> Glory of flowers and fairyland around us
> Over my life the joyous sunlight falls,
> So is my dear whose charms so fast have bound me,
> Bound like a bird within these crimson walls.
> Dream oh my darling till we meet once more,
> Dream of a happiness for us in store,
> Dream of a future that our fate may hold
> Lost in the wonderland of love untold.

Then I said goodbye but I had your mother's promise to marry me and four years later she came out to Johannesburg and fulfilled it.

I must close now, with very much love from Daddy.

He gave her a ring engraved with the word "mispah." "The Lord watch between me and thee while we are absent one from the other"—a Hebrew blessing (originally a curse uttered by warring brothers). She had not seen him in the four years since he asked her to marry him, but she gathered her belongings, had a wedding dress made, and sailed to South Africa. Their wedding was brief; due to the distance, neither of their families attended. When the minister held out his hand for the ring, Henry, nervously misunderstanding, shook it.

> Did they have a happy marriage?
> I don't even know whether it makes sense to speak of the
> happiness of their marriage or whether they ever thought
> about it. They lived a life together, took the good with the
> bad, respected each other, relied on each other. I never
> once saw them have a serious argument, though they often
> teased and even poked fun at each other. They took pleasure
> in being together . . .[24]

Perhaps gambling is such a major preoccupation for Americans because we no longer gamble with our lives as Henry and Martha did. Those of us who are able create every possible emotional and financial security for ourselves. We live together before we marry, and even then we consider our commitments rescindable. What we gain in security, we forfeit in excitement. Then we head for the nearest casino.

24. Schlink, *Homecoming*, 19.

Disorder and Early Sorrow

Grandpa was a stern man with high expectations of himself and others. He was also intransigent about religion. He was deeply prejudiced against Catholics. The most precious possession of his family was a "britches" Bible, so called because of the Genesis passage in which Adam and Eve, ashamed of their nakedness, sew "britches" with which to cover themselves. This Bible had a burned corner; it had been thrown into a fire, and retrieved only partially burned, in one of the sixteenth-century persecutions of English Protestants. Grandpa's daughter, my aunt, became a Catholic in her twenties. From the day he was told this until the day he died, my grandfather refused to see her.

Despite his Calvinist pessimism about the world, and his struggle with depression, Grandpa Brown had a sense of humor. Once Mother said to me, "Your sense of humor is just like Grandpa Brown's; he also thought things were funny that nobody else thought were funny."

Dad's family were farmers in Eastern Ontario. His father became wealthy because "the Lord blessed him" for growing strawberries in rich soil in which everyone else grew tobacco. A large percentage of his money went to "the missionaries" when he died. Dad's family were simple rural people with few wants, generous spirits, and ungrammatical English. Dad left the farm, went to the city, and became a speech teacher and a preacher. He prided himself on flawless English and he read the dictionary in search of interesting words. Over his desk hung a plaque that read "Thy speech maketh thee known" (Matt 26:73). He corrected his children's speech constantly—over dinner, in the car, anywhere and everywhere. After I had been teaching at Harvard for several years, he once corrected my grammar, remarking, "You have been among people who damaged your grammar."

My father's fundamentalism was founded on his passionate love for God and Scripture, most evident when he preached. With his well-thumbed and underlined Bible in hand, he clearly relished exploration and interpretation of God's word. His delight was palpable and communicable. Dad's capacity for rich delight was his greatest gift to me. When I sometimes felt myself immersed in, and excited by, the beauty of the texts I was teaching, I recognized that this ability to lose himself in delight was what he experienced in preaching; "he wist not that his face shone."[25]

Confidence that he accurately apprehended God's character and commands authorized my father to pursue his mission with persistence and fervor. He wrote several tracts presenting and passionately advocating the "way of salvation." To neglect to point sinners to God at every opportunity would, in his view, have been the most reprehensible cowardice and laziness. Repeatedly throughout his life, people complained of his aggressive "witnessing." While he was on a rare vacation in Hawaii, a young man remarked to him in a friendly way, "Hot as hell today, isn't it!" Father replied, "Young man, I hope you never find out how hot hell is!" In old age the manager of the retirement facility where he lived scolded him for "preaching to too many people." A woman in a convalescent home where he played his violin and preached actually hit him, saying, "Go home and play your violin!" But "persecution" was nothing more than evidence that he was "doing the Lord's work."

25. Exodus 34:29.

However, his most painful persecution came upon him through his children. The physical and emotional troubles caused, or exacerbated, by the pressures emanating from a fundamentalist worldview and childrearing methods might have prompted a less confident man to examine his own part in creating these problems. To Dad they demonstrated simply that one who does "the Lord's work" may expect the devil to use every possible means to undermine, harm, and destroy him. It was all about him.

Mary my mother, daughter of her intrepid parents, was pious, neurasthenic, and beautiful. As a young woman she dropped out of nurse's training because of "nerves." After experiencing what she described as a "purely sexual attraction," which she denied herself, she met my father. Her attraction to him was "intellectual," thus acceptable. Days of awkwardness followed her timid request to her father to marry this young, fervent minister who came from a farm in Ontario, Canada. Mary's father maintained his silence on the matter until the strain—and Kenneth's urgent letters—forced her to ask him again. "Go and get the calendar," he said. She did, and he studied it for several minutes before saying mildly, "Perhaps it would be nice to be married on your mother's birthday." So August 21, 1936, it was. Her father's only further utterance on the subject was, "Perhaps you can make a man of him."

One afternoon when Mother was dying, my sister, who had come to visit her, was dozing on the twin bed in her room. The night before had not been a good one and both were exhausted. Suddenly Mother said, "I'm happy." Startled, because none of us had ever heard her say such a thing before and because she had not been talking coherently for several weeks, Marilyn repeated, "You're happy, Mother?" Again mother said, "I'm happy." Persisting, Marilyn asked, "*Why* are you happy, Mother?" Mother replied with some irritation, "I'm happy because I'm happy." Not until now, dying.

Their wedding in Vancouver, British Columbia, was small, attended by a few family friends; because of the distance, Kenneth's family was unable to attend. Then came the wedding trip. Money was scarce, so they went to a rough hotel in the Canadian northwest where the rooms were divided only by curtains. In the morning, the other lodgers, having heard that there was a honeymooning couple there, shouted and teased them to come down for breakfast. Mary absolutely refused, so Kenneth went down, checked them out, and hurried her to a hotel with more privacy.

My parents' world was an idyll, a private, carefully sheltered, unrealistic and frayed idyll, but an idyll nevertheless. It was "us," immigrants from Canada to American society, and "them," a society permeated with "Hollywood" values. Idylls aren't all bad. An idyll is a constructed world, a world *over against* the common social world of values and practices. It is an illusory world, but so is the social world. But incredible strength is required to sustain an idyll. The dead weight of the "commonsensical" social world is difficult to resist, supported as it is at myriad tiny points by assumptions, language, and practices. That's why idylls tend to collapse, not because they are illusory, but because the energy they require for maintenance is based on resistance to the social world. And the social world is inevitably stronger than private worlds.

Disorder and Early Sorrow

My own susceptibility for idylls is one of the most subtle but persistent of my parents' legacies.

A photograph taken on their wedding day, August 21, 1936, shows a thin man and woman with sweet, shy smiles. The woman slouches a little, so as not to appear taller than the man. The solemnity of the occasion was apparently stronger for them than the happiness. They took themselves, and eventually their four children, with the utmost seriousness, as a "solemn trust from God," souls given to them temporarily to mold and shape. But this is ahead of the story. I arrived nine months after the wedding. By the time Mother wrote her autobiography in old age, my birth had become a satisfying, even euphoric, event in her mind.

Not so with sex. After I had been married for several years, Mother told me that sex was "the cross [she] always had to bear." Father, a passionate man, no doubt suffered too. Yet mutual resentment is not the whole picture. In the last week of her life, my father leaned over her bed and said, "I love you, Molly." He didn't expect an answer—she hadn't spoken for days—but she replied, "I love you too, Kenny"—her last words.

Mother often quoted Elizabeth Barrett Browning to the effect that life is "uphill all the way. All the way? Yes, all the way." Leonard Wolff, Virginia's husband, when he was depressed, said that life is "downhill all the way." These contradictory expressions reveal a great deal, not about life, but about what a person is predisposed to see. "Uphill all the way" features struggle—continuing and even increasing in old age. "Downhill all the way" from *this* perspective would mean "easy sledding." But inhabiting a "downhill all the way" perspective, one notices futility, defeat, sinking, a slipping-down life.

Religious xenophobia did not end with Grandpa's generation. My father wrote virulent anti-Catholic tracts, full of scatological details of the alleged sexual behavior of monks and nuns. He placed them in the "tract-racks" of the Baptist churches where he ministered. These tracts embarrassed Mother, so she covertly took them by the handful and threw them in the trash in the women's restroom. Dad, checking the racks, was delighted to see that they had all been taken and exclaimed, "People love them; I will order more!" And he did. Again they disappeared. And so on.

In his old age, Dad had a heart attack and triple bypass surgery in a Roman Catholic hospital in Seattle. While he was recovering, the chaplain, a nun, came to visit and pray with him. He called me in Boston, his voice full of amazement and excitement, to tell me that "these people love the Lord!" Unfortunately, his conversion was temporary; he soon backslid into his old attitude.

January 6, 1994. Today I fly to Seattle to see my father, who is having triple bypass heart surgery. Multiple and contradictory feelings pour across and through me. Is there time to make things right between us? I have many petty and not-so-petty resentments of his role in my childhood, yet now he is an old man, on the verge of death. Perhaps the time for reconciliation has come and gone; perhaps it could never have been satisfactorily addressed. He didn't give me the world, as fathers are supposed to do. Instead he made me feel constricted in a narrow space in which I couldn't breath. Claustrophobic; the Latin word *angustiae* means "narrowness, shortness of breath," a physical feeling.

Perhaps the best we can do is this pretense of cordiality. He is fortified in his own rightness, reminding me of Augustine, in whose ear God whispered—he claimed. Yet Dad tells me that he has insomnia over "things" he wishes he'd done differently. He doesn't say what things. Dad died eight years after his bypass surgery, in 2002, three days before his ninety-first birthday, of an accumulation of strokes that progressively destroyed his ability to swallow and to speak. In the last two years of his life, he spoke like a drunk, slurred and almost incomprehensible, no matter how hard he tried to articulate his words. Finally, he reverted to writing. He explained to me laboriously, in writing, that he didn't go to church anymore because it embarrassed him that people couldn't understand his speech.

Every summer from about age eight to twelve or thirteen, I visited my grandparents in Vancouver, British Columbia, for a month. After initial bouts with searing homesickness, I settled in to their daily routine. I picked the beautiful huge raspberries that bordered Grandpa's garden and went on walks with Grandpa, for once not afraid of the dogs that occasionally beset us because Grandpa had his stout stick with him. I do not remember that he ever used it, but its availability was protection enough to satisfy me. Every day, after lunch and dinner, Grandpa read to Granny and me while we knitted or crocheted. Granny made tablecloths worthy of a museum. Some had bouffant ruffled hems hardened and molded with sugar water. Grandpa read from the great nineteenth-century novels. Much later, in a college class, I read one of the books Grandpa read to us—*Tess of the D'Urbervilles*—and was astonished to discover that Grandpa had carefully edited out any suggestion of sex or violence as he read.

Here, even more than at home, I felt uneasily that I didn't belong. Once, during afternoon rest time, some neighborhood children came to the front door to ask if they could retrieve their ball from Grandpa's yard. I peeked at them from my bedroom window, and one boy turned and saw me in my slip. I was paralyzed with embarrassment; I felt that I had betrayed my grandparents. Moreover, I wanted to play with those children, be one of them, but I knew that I must not entertain that possibility. I must be firmly on Grandpa and Granny's "side." Once again, I must be "us," not "them."

My visits to Vancouver ended mysteriously (to me) when Granny, after a slight illness, retired to her bed for the rest of her life. Grandpa did all the housework and maintained his thriving garden from then on. Many years later, I asked Mother, "What was wrong with Granny that made her stay in bed for about a decade until she died?" "Nothing," Mother said.

April 8, 1994. Today, sitting quietly before a concert, I had a wonderful thought. I thought that, carrying my deceased parents within me as I do, I might be able to heal parts of them that were never resolved. I thought of fears and longings they had that I have already redeemed. For example, I have learned, as my father never did, to "take" criticism, to look it over and see if I can learn something from it. To evaluate whether it is about my work, my blind spots, rather than about the person giving it. The harshest criticism makes me cry and go to bed for awhile or a day. But then I get up and go on. In the *New York Times Book Review*, a woman author describes how she deals with criticism:

> I deal with it as a woman of no character at all and no moral fiber. . . . I go to pieces. If it's a bad review, I plan several letters rebutting it, which I never send. Then I tear down the critic's sensibility and ability to understand. Then I plot a hideous revenge. Then I get over it.

I have also redeemed Mother's frustration at not feeling that she could work outside the home. The idea that I could get over things on my parents' behalf made me feel very happy.

We, myself, my sisters and brother—our parents' children—have had difficulty learning how to care for ourselves. Mother always cared for us. Had Mother been less "perfect" we would have learned, little by little, to do for ourselves what she did for us. When my brother was an infant, one of his sisters had to rock him to sleep every night. We sat on the floor and gently and rhythmically shook his crib until he seemed to be asleep. Then we'd creep out of the room, often interrupted in our retreat by a shrill cry that meant that we would have to start all over again. I read once that at a certain time in its development, an infant needs to learn to put himself to sleep, usually crying a bit until he does. Since there was zero tolerance for noise in our home, my brother, and perhaps all of us, suffer from insomnia and, since the developmental stage is long past, we will probably never learn to put ourselves to sleep.

Several of us have had to learn how to stop ourselves. Mother always stopped us. On one occasion I have remembered and laughed about for many years, my brother, who was four or five was playing outside. Mother said to me, "Go out and see what Wendell is doing, and tell him to stop." Our parents' unexamined and desperate love for us, together with the intransigence of *knowing* God's will, did not allow us to make the small mistakes that would have taught us important life lessons. We have had to learn "the hard way" from adult mistakes and misery.

It is easier to speak as a daughter than as a mother. As daughters we can identify the shortfall of love, show our wounds, and comfortably remain victims. As mothers we cannot collapse into complaint; we must take responsibility. There is moral beauty in taking responsibility, in redeeming and recovering *in ourselves* our parents' mistakes. However, in attempting to correct their mistakes as we raise our own children, we inevitably make our own mistakes. I will write as a mother in chapters to come. In this chapter, I am a daughter.

During the Second World War, when I was four, I fell passionately in love with a nineteen-year-old soldier. A friend of my parents, Kenny came to our house in uniform frequently. He would often take me on his lap, call me his sweetheart, and say that he was going to marry me when I grew up. One evening he came to dinner at our house with a young woman. After I was put to bed his friend came to kiss me goodnight. As she leaned over me, a locket swung from her neck. I asked her what was in it and she opened it and showed me a picture of Kenny. "We're going to get married," she said.

I couldn't believe it. A lifetime later, Mother remembered that I cried intermittently for days. I, so small a girl, and (already) so great a literalist! Playing by myself I would suddenly burst into tears. The betrayal hurt ferociously. People should not smile condescendingly at little children's loves. Children's loves are real, unprotected, full of naked yearning, beautiful and serious.

I have been married three times, but I have not loved any man in quite the same way again. Since that experience, there has always been an element of caution, of self-protection, of something withheld. When I was marrying and divorcing I didn't make the connection with my four-year-old love. I didn't know why I felt jealous, risk-aversive, wanting promises, contracts, turning off my love if my husbands showed any attraction to other women.

Perhaps we *should* not love human beings with the defenseless vulnerability of a four-year-old. Augustine said that it is crazy (*dementiam*) to love other human beings as if they were immortal. (Plato said, "Why should we be surprised when mortals die?") And it is stupid (*stultum*), Augustine said, to be violently impatient with the condition of human life, which is mortality. Describing his feelings after the death of his friend, he wrote: *I stormed and sighed and wept and worried. I could not rest. I could not think intelligently. I was carrying about with me my soul all broken and bleeding* (4.7). Augustine's solution? *Blessed is the one who loves you, who loves his friend in you.... He alone loses no one dear to him, for they are all dear to him in one who is not lost* (4.9).

Augustine's concept of loving the neighbor in God has caused his readers much consternation. But there is a kind of love that eats another up *as people do with their food,* love that is greedy, consuming, not allowing "the neighbor" to stand in her own light. In short, there is a kind of love that demands too much of human beings who see *through a glass darkly, not face to face.* Augustine would not grant that this kind of love can rightly be called "love." But surely there is some admixture of "selfish" love in all human loves. It's what we frail and faulty human beings *do*. "Loving the neighbor in God" tries to correct for the *concupiscentia*, the anxious grasping that threatens human loves.

The German poet Rainer Maria Rilke described "loving the neighbor in God" (not, of course, using that phrase) in this way:

> On Attic stêles, did not the circumspection
> of human gesture amaze you? Were not love and farewell
> so lightly laid upon shoulders, they seemed to be made
> of other stuff than with us? Remember the hands,
> how they rest without pressure, though power is there in the torsos.
> The wisdom of those self-masters was this: we have got so far;
> ours is to touch one another like this; the gods
> may press more strongly upon us. But that is the gods' affair.[26]

Augustine thought that in order to understand soul's state and process, body, the site and symbol of subjectivity, must be closely observed. Bodily movements are the infant's first language, *a kind of universal language, expressed by the face, the direction of the eye, gestures of the limbs and tones of the voice, all indicating the state of feeling in the mind as it seeks, enjoys, rejects, or avoids various objects* (1.8). And body language is not abandoned as a child develops vocabulary and grammar, but continues to reveal the soul's affect. Feeling, expressed most directly by body, is the product and evidence of the intimate and necessary connection of soul and body. From the metaphorical fevers, wounds, swellings, and scabs of his youthful lust, to God's insistent turning of his head (*fovisti caput*), Augustine's body provided him with an observable and accurate key to his soul.[27] He did not imagine that clear thinking depends on the dissociation of body and feelings from mind.

Twenty-first-century intellectuals like myself have inherited philosophical dualism from Descartes' identification of the person as an entity that thinks: "I think, therefore I am" (*cogito ergo sum*). Having decided that this was the only fact that could not be doubted, Descartes found it difficult to explain how body was attached to this thinking being. He was forced to hypothesize an odd entity he called the

---

26. Rilke, *Duino Elegies*.

27. Recently neurophysiologists have described in detail the myriad changes in nerves and chemicals that create the feelings that inform consciousness. See Damasio, *Feeling of What Happens*, 288.

"pineal glad" that exists solely to perform the function of linking body and mind. Descartes' "body" has four characteristics: "it is a visual entity; it is a mechanical thing; it is a possession; and it is . . . a corpse."[28] Descartes' "body" is not Augustine's body. Augustine's body is exquisitely sensitive, accurately matching a feeling to every motion of the soul/mind and displaying that feeling on his face, by his posture, and through his gestures.[29] For Augustine, as for his mentor, Plotinus, body reflects and reveals mind. Plotinus wrote:

> We can come to conclusions about someone's character and also about the dangers that beset him, and the precautions to be taken, by looking at his eyes or some other part of his body. Yes, they are parts, and so are we; so we can learn about one from the other.[30]

Augustine believed that mind/soul should govern body, stabilizing the untrustworthy fluctuations and changes inherent in body, but he insisted, "I am a whole person and I want to be healed wholly."[31]

Body was "big" in the fundamentalist household of my childhood, not, however, as a site of pleasure and learning. No, bodies constantly threatened insubordination; they were needy and embarrassing; they had to be regularly fed, and they needed the bathroom at awkward times. They had accidents and they got hurt. They threw up, and they got dirty and smelly. But worst of all, they distracted from the only important thing, an interior relationship with God. They should be cared for in a perfunctory way and, as quickly as possible, ignored. But, the funny thing was that the more they were ignored, the louder and more insistent their demands became. Of which, more later.

Augustine was critical of his society and his own socialization. Whether describing the addictive power of gladiatorial contests or the sexual expectations of a man of his class, he condemned the *hellish river of*

---

28. Sheets-Johnstone, *Roots of Power*, 260.

29. But Augustine's "body" is not Damasio's "body," determining what mind will notice and understand by producing feelings that are "simply a reflection of body-state changes."

30. Plotinus *Ennead* 2.3.7.

31. Augustine, *Serm.* 30.4; see also *Serm.* 30.6.

human custom. His image of a river carries the force of a rushing current, impossible to swim against (without divine help), and eventually *dashing its victims against rocks* (1.16).

Augustine's autobiography lets us see more of society, his social location, and his socialization than any other writing of his time. Yet because he appears to invite his readers into an unvarnished account of his life, it also leaves us with frustrations and questions. We try to explain to ourselves why he did not name either the friend of his youth who died and left him utterly bereft—unable to enjoy anything but his tears (4.7)—or his partner of fifteen years and mother of his son, the woman *torn from his side* (6.15).

Augustine, acute observer and interpreter of human behavior that he was, noticed the continuity of behavior from the possessive infant at the breast through childhood acquisitiveness, to adults, desirous of gold, social positions of honor, and possessions. His alternative to anxious grasping, to consumption, was attentiveness and thoughtfulness—seeing what one looks at, and thinking about what one sees. These are not automatic skills; nor are they necessarily learned either from experience or a good education. They must, rather, be intentionally developed and exercised. In an Augustinian moment, Iris Murdoch wrote:

> Should we not . . . endeavor to see and attend to what surrounds and concerns us, because it is there and is interesting, beautiful, strange, worth experiencing, and because it demands (and needs) our attention, rather than living in a vague haze of private anxiety and fantasy?[32]

Egoistic anxiety prevents our accurately seeing the world, and "inner chat"—the tape we play repetitively in our heads—precludes thought. Egoistic anxiety and inner chat are *the way fear operates* in daily life. Getting over oneself, releasing the clinging *habit* of fear, shifting motivation from fear to love, can take a lifetime. Perhaps Augustine was stating a goal rather than describing something already achieved when he said at the end of the *Confessions*, *My weight is my love.*

Prayer is a practice of getting over oneself. Marilynne Robinson wrote: "Prayer, you know, you open up your thoughts, and then you can get a clear look at them. No point trying to hide anything."[33] Book 1 of

---

32. Murdoch, *Metaphysics as a Guide to Morals*, 318.
33. Robinson, *Home*, 132.

Augustine's *Confessions* is preoccupied with prayer. I too have struggled to find a style of prayer that strengthens and calms me. Just as Augustine's first fervent prayers were about being spared a beating, I began with the me-me-me prayers of childhood and youth in which I bargained with God: "If I get roller skates I'll never ask for anything ever again in my whole life." Augustine described the continuity of desire from the *footballs, nuts, and pet sparrows* of childhood to the *gold magistrates, and slaves* of adulthood; the persistence of me-me-me prayers is evident from the roller skates of childhood to my petitions for health and professional success of adulthood. Then came the middle-of-the-night desperate prayers for people I love.

Finally, in middle age, I learned a method of prayer from Plotinus. Plotinus taught that "the life of the universe does not serve the purposes of one individual but of the whole."[34] *Providence is of the whole.*[35] Plotinian prayer came as an enormous relief from my long effort to wrest the universe to my own purposes (by being good, by doing good, even by exercise and diet).

I am still learning. I don't pray *to* anyone. I don't ask for things. I don't imagine that the universe is interested in me. I pray by *imagining the real*, the large whirling universal circulation of life in which I am an infinitesimally small part. I pray in order to lift myself out of anxious fears, ego projects, and the exhausting maintenance of myself as my own favorite character in fiction. I seek to bring myself to acceptance of what Albert Camus called the "benign indifference" of a universe in which gifts and suffering circulate without design or target. I consider that it is up to me to "get with" the universe; it is not my part—nor is it possible—to attempt to make the universe further my agenda.

What I mean by "getting with" the universe is this: Both Plotinus and Augustine taught that the primary characteristic of the universe is beauty, and beauty is enough—richly, abundantly enough. So it is my responsibility to train my eye to see the great beauty that forms and informs all living beings. When I focus on beauty, I find that generosity, love, and aliveness are spontaneous by-products. I find my place of gratitude and rest there in silence. Perhaps this mode of prayer is more accurately called meditation or contemplation.

---

34. Plotinus *Ennead* 4.4.39.
35. Ibid., 4.4.45.

2 *Learning How to Live*

Spend your whole life learning how to live.
—SENECA

The world is so full of a number of things
That I think we should all be as happy as kings.
—ROBERT LEWIS STEVENSON,
A CHILD'S GARDEN OF VERSES

Memory offers up its gifts only when jogged by something in the present. It isn't a storehouse of fixed images and words, but a dynamic associative network that is never quiet and is subject to revision each time we retrieve an old picture or old words.
—SIRI HUSTVEDT[1]

"SELF" IS DIFFERENTLY DEFINED IN different times/places. In the fourth century Roman Empire, "self" was defined by social location; women and slaves weren't "selves." Medieval "selves" were defined by participation in the religious community; "heretics" weren't selves, but as threats to the community, must be exterminated. Early modern (reformation) "selves" were gradually coming to be defined by the individual's

---

1. Hustvedt, *Sorrows of an American*, 80.

religious commitment/beliefs. Since Freud, the "self" is largely defined by "sexuality" and sexual preference.

Augustine continued to be exquisitely aware of the missing self. The confident moments in which he plants the self firmly in God are usually preceded by palpable anxiety, rife with images of viscous liquids:

> Entrust to truth whatever truth has given you and you will lose nothing. What is withered in you will flower again, and all your illness will be made well, and all that was flowing and wasting from you will regain shape and substance and will form part of you again (4.11).

Augustine had no scruples about mixing metaphors, for each image contributes to the complex picture he seeks to communicate: a dying flower; a sick person oozing putrid liquid. Or do these images refer to male sexuality, which Augustine has described, in his experience, as waste and loss? In any case, solidity—shape and substance—can only be regained in the God who *does not pass away*.

For Augustine, the integrated self was a project. It could only be reliably formed by being planted firmly in God, who alone guaranteed its reality. His youthful experience was of a broken and scattered self, lying in fragments, dissipated, and lost in many distractions (2.1). Augustine's missing self was vivid and tortured; highly eroticized, it clutched at everything that crossed its path in the fear that something would be missed. This is not a mixed metaphor; fragments clutch! Augustine called this mode of feeling and action *concupiscentia*. The less satisfying the pursuit of sex, power, or possessions, the more insistently and strenuously does the person fascinated by them grasp at these objects.

Augustine was careful to say that it was not that anything he attempted to clutch was unworthy in itself; it was the anxious grasping itself that was the problem.

> Certainly the eye is pleased by beautiful bodies, by gold, and silver and all such things. . . . Worldly honor also has its own grace. . . . The life too, which we live here, has its own enchantment because of a certain measure in its own grace and a correspondence with all these beautiful things of this world. And human friendship, knotted in affection, is a sweet thing. (2.5)

Augustine, the "bad" child, stole some pears because he wanted to have some fun with his companions. Later, the theft fascinated him, not because this sin was so heinous, but because of its sheer gratuity.

There was no reason for it, no desire for those particular pears; it was not even big fun. So why do it? To be "one of the boys," to experience an *enjoyment of what is forbidden for no other reason except that it was forbidden*. In fact, the act of choosing and doing imitates God's activity in creating; it is *a darkened image of omnipotence* (2.6). Later, Augustine related to friends with the same eroticized grasping. He evoked very vividly the *foggy exhalations which proceed from the muddy cravings of the flesh and the bubblings of first manhood* (2.2). He was, he recalled, *ashamed not to be shameless* (2.9). Not ready for *true peace and life imperturbable*, he became *to myself a wasteland* (2.10).

A snapshot of me when I was two shows me sitting on a feeding trough among chickens on my grandfather Miles's farm in eastern Ontario. I appear relaxed, leaning chubby arms on my spread knees, offering the viewer a (later horribly embarrassing) glimpse of white panties. The picture tells a story: my grandfather had a large fenced chicken yard, with dozens of chickens pecking in the dust. On other days when Grandpa had brought me into their pen, I had been terrified because the chickens, disturbed by our arrival, rose into the air to about my height, frantically squawking and raising clouds of dust in my face. On the day the snapshot was taken, Grandpa instructed me that if I would just remain still and wait for a minute, the chickens would settle back down and resume their pecking in the dust. I did it, and the feeling of triumph over my terror was tremendous.

That episode became a model for me of how to act when overwhelmed by noise and dust in whatever form. When I gave my interview lecture at Harvard, for example, I feared most of all the moments after my lecture when I anticipated that all those intelligent and learned people would attack, disprove, and demolish my thesis. But I remembered the chickens, and I invited several questions and observations before responding to those that intrigued me. Sure enough, the noise and dust settled quickly—the questions were not unfriendly—and there was a lively and helpful exchange. Thanks to the chickens!

∽

I came to awareness of myself as *a piece of difficult ground, not to be worked over without much sweat* (10.16) in Three Hills, Alberta, Canada, named for the three tiny hills that barely interrupted the rolling prairie. My father taught at the fundamentalist Prairie Bible Institute. I recall bleakness. A train passed noisily at the bottom of our yard; when it rained, moisture seeped through the walls; indoor "plumbing" consisted of a port-a-potty in the basement that was emptied once a week by students while we sat at Saturday evening dinner. We bathed in a galvanized tub in the kitchen once a week, whether we needed it or not! In memory it was always cold. Mother had a miscarriage, and since Three Hills had only a nurse, a doctor was called from a neighboring town to give her a dilation and curette, which he did without anesthetic. I was seven, and supposed to be asleep in the next room. I was instead listening in terror to Mother's screams until they remembered me and took me to a neighbor's house.

∽

We were Canadians. Every Christmas morning we gathered around the radio and listened to King George VI give his annual state-of-the-union address. He stammered badly, and mother tearfully suffered for him as he struggled to speak.

∽

I wrote my first autobiography in Three Hills at the age of seven. Writing was a lonely eldest child's attempt to construct and stabilize a self. I yearned to be a good girl, but I often found that I was a bad girl in others' eyes. And others' eyes were decisive; a child has no eyes of her own through which to see herself. It didn't take much to be considered bad in a fundamentalist household and community, and there was no distinction between "bad acts" and "a bad person." An example: I was one of the younger children in my one-room schoolhouse so my desk was near the front. The door was behind me, and I was not supposed to turn to look when it opened and someone entered. But I did, not once but several times, and my knuckles were rapped hard with a wooden ruler for doing so.

Throughout elementary school I was never in the same school for more than two years. My intransigent fundamentalist father had a difficult time finding churches that agreed with him in every theological detail; hence the frequent moves. The issue was usually around "dispensationalism," a theological position whose meaning eludes me now as it eluded me then. We moved several times across Canada—Brantford, Ontario, to Three Hills, Alberta, to Calgary, Alberta—and, when I was eleven, to the United States. Alongside his work as the minister at the First Baptist Church of Wenatchee, Washington, my father entered a community college, eventually obtaining an MA at the University of Washington, and a by-mail doctorate. For the rest of his career, he alternated between two professions, sometimes a college teacher, sometimes a minister, switching back and forth when his sensitive "nerves" got troublesome. He was unable to tolerate criticism; any disagreement or criticism could prompt another resignation. Once an office worker told him that he had not been exhibiting much of the joy of the Lord recently, inspiring him to tell her that her work hadn't been very good lately either.

My parents created for me a world with clear rules for behavior, a world in which everything had religious significance. Nothing simply happened; nothing was coincidental. When I disobeyed or was otherwise "bad," I was punished by being assigned to memorize a chapter in the Bible. The theory behind this was based on Psalm 119:11, "Thy

Word have I hid in my heart that I might not sin against Thee." If I sinned, it was because I did not have enough of the Word "by heart." The solution: memorize more Scripture!

I was a pretty little girl, thus arousing my parents' fears that I could easily go astray, enticed by "worldly things." Since I was very likely to do wrong, I was always suspect, so they were always vigilant. My grade school teacher and parents thought me a sloppy child, especially in comparison with the little girl who lived next door and who had excellent, neat penmanship. Once I accused a small boy of pushing me from the narrow path into mud; I don't remember if he really did or not, but I was blamed for falsely accusing someone who had recently been "saved" and had mended his ways.

The shorthand term by which my parents described what they feared most in me was "pride." They took every opportunity to undermine any pride I might reveal. If someone remarked that I was pretty, Mother replied, "You should see her at home!" This happened many times. I suppose she was referring to how I looked with my hair in curlers (even though my hair was naturally curly). The problem was that they did not distinguish between "pride" and self-confidence or self-esteem, and thus I grew up with none of the above. Instead I developed a deadly impasse between desperately wanting to please in order to get love, and wanting to do things, have fun, and grow up.

I was given my first "store-bought" dress when I was thirteen. Until then, hand-me-down dresses, most of them ugly, from families in the church had clothed me. As a teenager, I liked to take the bus to downtown Seattle occasionally to window shop after school. One day I was looking through a rack of dresses when a woman from my father's congregation saw me and offered to buy me a dress. She did, and I still remember that dress.

I was considered vain because I cared what I wore. As an adult, I have a revised version of "vanity." Vanity occurs not when one feels pretty, but when one feels ugly. Preoccupation with how we look is very common among women who have grown up with media images of what female beauty looks like. But eating disorders, cosmetic surgery, and the more flagrant results of negative "vanity" were not common when I was a child. Eight-year-olds did not worry about their weight, as is presently common. My family did not have television until after I married and left the home. I was not allowed to go to movies and I could not afford magazines, thus billboards were usually my only information about how I "should" look. So I was probably spared the worst effects of unrealistic standards.

The fundamentalists of my childhood were painfully ambivalent about female beauty. They had little of Augustine's sense of natural beauty as revelatory of the beauty of its creator, but mainly worried that beauty, especially female beauty, was seductive, potentially harmful not only to its possessor, but also to others, especially men. Mothers are expected to be the liaison between patriarchal culture and daughters' frightening potential to grow up "wild." Among other things, it is the mother's job to train her daughter to place her attention on how she *looks* rather than on how she *feels*. My mother did a good job. She trained me so well that still, some sixty years later, I know—or think I know—what the person I'm with feels long before I laboriously figure out what *I* feel.

"What will people think?" My parents thought that a minister's family ought to model perfection for "clouds of witnesses." And I tried to please. More than anything I wanted Mother to say as she tucked me in bed, "You've been a good girl *all day*." However, there was a downside to my need for love and approval. Wanting love and approval so badly was what prompted me to lie.

I learned to lie for self-protection or advantage. I believed myself the perfect example of what it was to be a sinner, my "real self coming out." Augustine wrote, *I, so small a boy, and so great a sinner!* (1.12). I began to learn the spicy by-taste of furtive pleasures; "secret" and "pleasure" seemed to me to be synonymous. This learning deepened in my teenage years. I have had to work at overcoming this penchant for secret pleasures all my life.

Learning How to Live

We emigrated to the United States when I was in the fifth grade. To my parents, the "States" was an alien and wicked place, characterized pervasively by "Hollywood." Doubly alienated by nationality and religion from the values of American culture, an "us" and "them" mentality dominated. Nothing was "us" but home and church, and even then Dad felt that the church members needed frequent reproofs. Some of the women wore lipstick, and he detected increments of "worldliness" in many of the members. My school was an especially troublesome arena. Notes were sent to the teacher on days that we were to have folk dancing, to the effect that dancing was "against my religion." I longed to dance but instead sat against the wall while my schoolmates danced. If I questioned why an activity was wrong, my question proved beyond the shadow of a doubt that I was in imminent danger of being "them": "If you have to ask . . ." my parents replied.

I was not allowed to go to movies. So when a film titled *The Missing Christian* was shown at my church I anticipated it with great excitement. Unfortunately it also gave me bad dreams and night sweats for several years. Based on the New Testament book of Revelation, its protagonist was a young girl who was not a Christian. The "rapture" occurred, taking all Christians to heaven and leaving only evil people to launch and endure a reign of terror on earth. Mercifully, I forget the details, but the combination of reinforcing my anxiety about whether I was really "saved" with the visual depiction of evil people doing harm to one another was very frightening.

The damages—emotional and physical—of being a child brought up in a fundamentalist's household were—are—profound. My siblings and I each bear lifelong scars from the constrictions and expectations of our childhood home. However, tempting as it is to maintain a helpless victim position, to focus on my feelings of neediness and resentment, it is not accurate, and not enough, to simply trace the scars and their origin. There was also passion and anguished love. Life was not boring.

Attending an Al-Anon meeting, I saw a film about children of alcoholics. It described the problems they have and how these problems tend to shape their personalities. At the end of the film, the narrator commented that children of strict religious upbringing tend to experience the same damages as those from alcoholic homes. This made perfect sense to me. The commonality has to do with the constant orientation to maintaining the peace of the home, not causing parents' anger, always thinking first of pleasing the parents, and a compulsive alertness to the atmosphere of the home. With such attentiveness to parents, the child has no opportunity to craft a chosen identity.

I think that Dad would now be diagnosed as suffering from depression; we thought of him as "moody." My sisters and I became expert in reading his moods and acting accordingly. Sometimes, in a good mood, he joked and played with us; he lay on the living room floor and we would run by him while he tried to grab our ankles. Big fun. Mother would call from the kitchen (always, in my memory), "Someone is going to get hurt." And frequently, someone did, but it was worth it for the rare fun. Sometimes, however, Dad was in a black funk, irritable and angry at everyone and everything, especially those closest to him. On those occasions it was wise to keep a low profile.

Dad was not an ogre; rather, he suffered. He tried to contain his moods by working in his beautiful garden, in which vegetables and flowers were mingled in no apparent order. His other great passion was the violin. He could not remember why, in 1925 at age fourteen, he ordered a T. Eaton mail order fiddle and took lessons from a local Scottish fiddler. He played hymns on the violin all his adult life; in senior years he played with a few amateur musician friends in convalescent hospitals and retirement homes. He loved the old hymns best: "Rock of Ages," "My Faith Looks Up to Thee," "The Old Rugged Cross," "Blessed Assurance," and many others. He also enjoyed newer hymns, such as "In the Garden" and "How Great Thou Art." He assumed that people old enough to be in assisted living situations had had Christian childhoods and could be expected to recognize and love the "old favorites." He was not always right about that. Sometimes his efforts met with hostility. Not everybody remembered those hymns with affection!

What *is* difficult to tell accurately is Dad's bewildering mix of judgment and sweetness. His judgments were often very harsh. Behavior that other parents would have dismissed as unremarkable childish naughtiness reminded Dad that children are sinners from birth. The fundamentalist parent's task is to squelch children's sinful willfulness and construct from scratch in them habits of good behavior. Dad punished minor infractions with a wince that each of his children dreaded; all of us can still see that wince in our mind's eye. But most of Dad's punishments after we reached the "age of accountability"—seven years old—were verbal, vivid scoldings that reduced us to feeling ourselves the painful disappointments we were in Dad's (and God's) eyes, reduced us to nothing, to dirt. Yet we much preferred an angry father to a sorrowful Dad. Dad's sweetness made his harshness and/or his sadness over our behavior unbearable.

After his retirement from full-time ministry, Dad taught English as a Second Language at the University of Washington. He loved his international students, recording and enjoying their humorous mistakes in English. I'm afraid they were also helpless victims of his missionizing efforts. Proudly he told us that these students would return home to become leaders in their countries. He did not inquire about their political leanings! Whether they became dictators, tyrants, or humanitarian leaders, he was determined that they would speak grammatically correct English.

Mother baked all the family's bread. On the rare occasions that she was unable to do so, we ate white Wonder Bread. I am ashamed to recall that my sisters and I were excited on these occasions, exclaiming "Wow! Store-bought bread!" Proving that "the grass is always greener..."

⁂

Why not make life as wonderfully, terrifyingly, indigestibly rich as possible? Why not raise the stakes of human life to time beyond time—eternity—and space beyond space—heaven and hell? This is what my parents' fundamentalism did. Yes, of course we're all here now, treating each other variously, oblivious to some cruelties and acutely sensitive to others. But just beyond the stage on which we play our parts there's *real* life, *real* good, *real* evil. Our intentions and actions only imitate this real life in approximate and clumsy ways. Our best good falls far short of real good; our worst moments of blindness and nastiness, mercifully, also fail to qualify as real evil.

The presence of that other world was always palpable. It was a strange world, a world so strange that we won't even know how to breathe its air when we get there. But it was also a world so intimate that we will instantly recognize everyone. It will feel *ours*, fitting us perfectly. We learned about that other world, the world that leaned so heavily on the one we occupied, in Sunday School. Earnest teachers instructed us each Sunday morning in the hour before church about God's methods of dealing with human beings as recorded in the Scriptures. It was a spotty record, as far as I could see. God was inconsistent, often using overkill punishments for minor misdeeds like "pissing against the wall," while he blinked at, or even put people up to, major atrocities like wiping out whole populations. Our teachers' valiant efforts to wrestle a simple moral for fifth-graders from these stern Scriptures showed through their brave presentations. Our questions were not welcomed unless they provided an occasion for the reinforcement of a moral lesson.

Sometimes we had "sword drills" in Sunday school. The leader called out a verse location—"Ezekiel 2:4"—and we searched for it frantically, hoping to be the first to jump to our feet and read it aloud breathlessly. This exercise was intended to enhance our familiarity with Scripture, not so much because we listened when the verse was read—we didn't—but because it helped us "learn our way around" in holy writ. The more competitive of us memorized the order of books in the two testaments in order to compete successfully in these sword drills. Though certainly unintended, sword drills were counterproductive. There could have been no more effective way to turn our attention from the content and meaning of Scripture verses to the competition to find them first.

Sunday school papers reiterated and reinforced the lessons we learned in Sunday school. They also provided my first experience of religious images. In the iconoclastic fundamentalism of my childhood, the only religious images we saw were on calendars and Sunday School papers. These were invariably crudely representational in style and featured men in brightly colored bathrobes, sometimes following sheep, sometimes conversing earnestly; once, memorably, they were throwing stones at a woman in a bathrobe. I must have been about eight when a calendar featured a girl of about my age leaning chubby arms on a windowsill, staring out into the star-studded night. Beneath, the caption read: "There is no God beside me." The archaic meaning of "beside"—except—was lost on me, and I was perplexed by this apparent reversal of what I thought was the *main thing* my parents wanted me to understand, namely that there *is*, there *always* is, a God beside me.

The summer I was ten, our Sunday School papers featured a series on the Ten Commandments. Each week on the front page there was a full-color illustration of the breaking of one of the commandments. We waited for the seventh week with poorly disguised eagerness. When it arrived, it showed, in living color, a milkman pouring pitchers of water into vats of milk. Under the picture the text read: "Thou shalt not commit adultery."

Beliefs were important, but they were not the most important thing. The fundamentalist culture was the most important thing, being "us." "Them" was always out there, threatening; there had to be clarity and precision about our difference from them. The ritual moment that marked this difference was baptism. "Believer's baptism" was the rule in our Baptist church. The person being baptized must *choose* to "follow Christ" and state that choice before the congregation by undergoing immersion in the large tank behind the curtain on the church platform.

On the wall behind the tank, a pastel scene representing the Jordan River was crudely painted.

Everyone was baptized in a white robe made from a sheet. In the tank, the minister asked each one if she or he believed in the Father. They always said yes. The minister then held their nose and bent them backward into the waist-deep water until it covered their heads. This was repeated for acknowledgment of belief in "the Son" and "the Spirit." Then the newly baptized moved awkwardly up the font's stairs, dripping, the thin robe clinging revealingly.

When I was nine I asked for baptism. I had been under some pressure. Subtle but pointed hints that since I had made it to the "age of accountability" it was time to "make a decision." I sensed my parents' fear that a beloved child might neglect or resist, and thus become "them" instead of "us." If that were to happen, mother assured my sisters and me, the "circle would be broken," and she would never have another happy moment.

How could I be responsible for such a thing, I asked myself, when it was really so relatively painless to get baptized? Yes, painless, part of me responded, but certainly embarrassing. Yet the longer I waited, the more embarrassing it would be. If I expected to do it at all, I should do it while I had a straight up-and-down body to be revealed by the clinging white sheet. Besides, I wanted my parents and the church members to rejoice over me, as they promised they would when I was baptized. For a few dazzling minutes, the whole congregation would love me. That thought was delirious; it tipped the balance. I told mother I wanted to be baptized. She cried for joy.

My friend, the late Harvard Ethics professor James Luther Adams, had a somewhat different experience of baptism. His father, like mine, was a Baptist minister. His father's church baptized converts in the punishingly cold ocean—an ordeal for both baptizer and baptized. On the day of the boy Jim's baptism, the congregation gathered on the beach to witness this cosmically significant event. When his turn came, Jim panicked and fled up the beach, running for dear life. His father pursued him, caught him, and brought him back to where the congregation waited. Then he baptized him forcibly, dunking him in the ocean three times, without further ceremony.

Do such baptisms, whether subtly or overtly coerced, have the desired effect? Augustine thought of baptism as nearly magical. He tells of

Learning How to Live

a friend whose family had him baptized while he was lying in a coma, close to death. His friend awoke changed, unresponsive to the unconverted Augustine's teasing. Even if one doesn't credit such a magical interpretation of baptism, coercion was not all there was. An increment of chosen self, a sense of acceptance in the church community, a rite of passage: these were the evident benefits of baptism.

"Have I imagined them richly enough?" Toni Morrison asked, referring to the characters in her novel *Jazz*. The narrative of my family should try to explain how each generation came to terms with the harshness and beauty of life. In my grandfather's generation the harshness was largely held at bay. He occasionally retreated to his study for whole days. My father suffered more obviously from "nerves" that eventually forced him to retire early from both ministry and teaching. In my generation, the harshness began to overwhelm and outweigh the beauty, constricting or crippling the lives of my siblings and producing in me an ulcer at age twenty-two. In my children's generation, several collapsed into addiction. How do we explain to ourselves these effects, these slipping-down lives, if we reject, as I do, the scriptural statement that the "sins of the fathers" are visited on their children? (By the way, that is not a Scripture that fundamentalist parents were fond of quoting!) At present we imagine that the strong undertow of genes, mingled with cultural designations about what constitutes pleasure, direct us to act as we do. But, "have I imagined them richly enough?" Surely twenty-first-century language surrounding addiction and self-help do not make room for richly imagined people.

Around the age of ten I frequently lay awake in a cold sweat, fearing that I would die in the night and go to hell. The strong sense of sinfulness communicated by Calvinist religion was not alleviated or balanced by (nonexistent) assurances either of my goodness or of God's mercy. The doctrine of original sin, at its best, might be expected to relieve feelings of personal sin, but it certainly didn't do that for me.

As a child I was invaded and occupied. No secret place in my psyche, no self, belonged to me. The all-seeing eye of God—and his representatives, my parents—demanded *me*, not something I could give or do. I will probably never get over a fear of being engulfed, appropriated, and overwhelmed by someone. As a young woman in psychotherapy, Carl Rogers' "client-centered therapy" worked well because my therapist offered few interpretations. He listened and he *backed off* in order to give me room to *come out*. And I came out! Given the slightest invitation, I came out. Lusty, full of desires, coveting life, bursting with energy. The "me" that came out was a surprise.

> The true self is aggressive, rude, dirty, disorderly, sexual; the false self, which mothers and society instruct us to assume is neat, clean, tidy, polite, content to cut a chaste rosebud with silver-plated scissors.[2]

A memorable cartoon, heavily (if unconsciously) inspired by the Calvinist view of human nature, features a man saying, "You'll have to excuse me. I'm myself today."

---

2. Malcolm, "Annals of Biography."

3 *Laziness and Inertia*

Life is too short to devote much of it to activities that are not at the heart of what it is to be human.
   —MARTHA C. NUSSBAUM[1]

Should we not attempt to turn most of our time from dead (inattentive, obsessed) time into live time?
   —IRIS MURDOCH[2]

AND SO THE YOUNG AUGUSTINE came to Carthage, a city he called a *hissing cauldron of unholy loves* (3.1). Characterizing those youthful years as unambiguously painful, he piles image on image. Augustine, the hunger artist, *was starved . . . yet this starvation did not make me hungry for incorruptible food.*[3] His soul, he writes, was in poor health; it *burst out in feverish spots . . . longing to be scratched by sensory objects.* Generations of scholars have puzzled over these confessions, intrigued and titillated: *I muddied the clear spring of friendship with the dirt of physical desire and clouded over its brightness with the dark hell of lust.* What *exactly* did he mean? He's not telling, so we'll never know, and our guesses will say more about us than about Augustine. Our labels

   1. Nussbaum, *Therapy of Desire*, 347.
   2. Murdoch, *Metaphysics as a Guide to Morals*, 268.
   3. See also Kafka, "A Hunger Artist," 188.

do not fit him, for "sexuality" as an orientation had not been invented in his time. He described being with a lover as *being fettered enjoyably* [fruendi] *in bonds of misery so that I might be beaten with rods of red-hot iron—the rods of jealousy and suspicions, and fears and angers and quarrels* (3.1). This is a curiously ambivalent sentence. The adverb *fruendi*—that one word—undermines the rest of the sentence's insistence that Augustine's condition was one of torture. It is Augustine's minimalist acknowledgment that there *was* pleasure, but it is immediately overpowered by disapproval.

∽

In his biography of Augustine, Peter Brown states: "The *Confessions* are, quite succinctly, the story of Augustine's 'heart', or of his 'feelings'—his *affectus*."[4] As a Christian, he did not seek to extinguish the violent passions of his childhood and youth, nor did he try to tame them. Rather, he sought to direct them toward richer and more satisfying goals. Emotions comprised a highly valuable resource and energy. He analyzed in detail his feelings for a friend whose death brought such unbearable sorrow that Augustine was forced to move to a different city, one whose streets were not flooded with memories of his friend (4.6). Even in describing his youthful reading of Cicero's *Hortensius*, he did not say that it changed his ideas, but *it changed my way of feeling*.[5] In order accurately to name feelings, Augustine watched faces and bodies, his own and others. From the jealous infant in Book 1 whose face turned red with fury, to his own face at the time of his conversion in the garden at Ostia. After his tears and jerking body came resolution and, he wrote, *my face changed.*

Valuing strong feelings as he did, Augustine deplored entertainment that generates false feelings. *Why is it, I wonder*, he asked,

> that people want to feel sad at miserable and tragic happenings which they certainly would not like to suffer themselves? Yet as spectators they do want to suffer the sadness and indeed their whole pleasure is just in this. What a wretched sort of madness. (3.2)

---

4. Brown, *Augustine of Hippo*, 163.
5. *Confessions* 3. 4; discussed by Brown, *Augustine*, 163.

A person who suffers in actuality the tragedies displayed on the stage feels misery, and if we see others suffer, we feel compassion, but *there can be no real compassion for fictions on the stage*. Entertainment manipulates, producing feelings that are wasted in that they have no real object. Augustine went on and on about this, repetitiously blaming himself for enjoying especially performances that brought tears to his eyes. He concludes that he loved

> *imaginary sorrows the hearing of which had, as it were, the effect of scratching the surface of my skin. And, as happens after the scratching of poisoned nails, what came next were feverish swellings, abscesses, and running sores.* (3.2)

Although he mentions that the sorrows and joys of lovers were frequent subjects of Roman dramas, curiously it was not the content of plays that prompted his rant, but the creation of false feelings. He calls the enjoyment of sympathetic feelings that are directed neither toward oneself or others *a foul disease*, strong language for plays others undoubtedly considered innocent entertainment.

Entertainment was minimal in my childhood and youth, and for this I am grateful, for I was spared much cultural baggage! Roland Barthes said that while being entertained a person unconsciously "swallows" the cultural message, *coated by the pleasure*. As the song goes, "Just a spoonful of sugar makes the medicine go down." Sometimes my sisters and I put on bathrobes and acted out Bible stories, but we had no television and were not allowed to go to movies. There were only Christian magazines in our home, and few newspapers. I was allowed to read the "funnies" from the Sunday paper, but not on Sunday. Only spiritually edifying reading was allowed on Sundays.

1949; I was twelve. One day, walking home from school with several friends, one of them said that my violin teacher told her mother that I am lazy. I was terribly hurt and ashamed, but I also recognized the truth of the statement. I disliked playing the violin; my arm hurt holding it up for long practice periods during which I watched the barely moving clock. I instantly *saw myself* as a lazy person. Since that day I have struggled not to *act like* a lazy person. To others I seem to appear highly motivated, but the energy for that motivation comes from the self-knowledge that I "am" lazy. I learned in that moment that whatever I do must be snatched from the teeth of inertia, self-indulgence, and a preference for leisure.

I have nothing similar to Augustine's sexual fantasies and escapades to report. I was not allowed to date until I was sixteen, and then only to go to a Youth for Christ service or something similar. I had to be in by ten o'clock on weekends and couldn't go out at all during the week. Once the married leader of my youth group came to pick me up for a meeting; he saw a picture of me on the piano and remarked to my father that it was a sexy picture. Big mistake! My father was outraged.

When a boy called to ask me for a date, I asked Mother if I could go. If she were annoyed or angry at me for something, she would say the dreaded words, "Ask your father." Rather than endure that, I usually returned to the telephone and said that I couldn't go. Subsequently I have come to think that Dad suffered a form of sexual jealousy of me when I was a teenager. This was masked, of course, in the language of trying to protect me from the devil's seduction. But it was too intense, too erotically charged, to pass as simply doing his duty.

From the eighth grade through my junior year in high school I went to a large public high school in Seattle. I had no academic interests and I was not allowed to participate in school activities on the grounds that they were "worldly." School plays and football games were worldly. In fact, everything that was not church or home was worldly. I was supposed to carry my Bible everywhere I went, including school, so I carefully placed it under the other books I was carrying; when I sat at my desk I spread my full skirt over it. I wanted to please, to be loved, but I could not claim my parents' religious views as my own. I became cynical. In the eighth grade I wrote a precocious little essay disparaging conversion. I argued that in conversion nothing happened *really*. If intensive work was not done to establish, inform, and maintain the conversion, the convert quickly reverted to his former condition.

Growing up was apparently also worldly because I wanted clothes. I wanted to wear a bra, whether I needed it or not, so I wouldn't feel so odd in the locker room. These were considered things I shouldn't want. When I babysat, cleaned houses, or washed dishes in a local restaurant, I spent the money I earned on clothes. It should have gone to "the missionaries." This was a time—the early fifties—when girls wore bright red lipstick. I was not allowed to wear make-up of any sort, so when I walked down the school halls I felt that I had no face. I had to content myself with plucking my eyebrows (which didn't need it) and curling my eyelashes—both things that didn't show.

It is remarkable to me now that as a young girl I had no academic interests. Did I have poor teachers? I don't think so, though none stand out in my memory. I think I was apathetic because almost everything that interested or attracted me displeased my parents. I was afraid to invest in liking anything for which I would be criticized and that I would have to give up. Historically, fundamentalists have been suspicious of education, concerned that education created inequality within congregations. But my father the farmboy valued education highly, as long as it led to greater understanding of, and commitment to, the Bible. My refusal to develop academic interests was partly rebellion against my father's agenda for me.

∽

Augustine studied rhetoric industriously, he writes, because *I longed to make a name for myself.* Whatever his motives, it was in pursuing these studies that he encountered Cicero's *Hortensius* at the age of nineteen. The book both argued for, and inspired, the pursuit of wisdom. This was Augustine's first conversion, an intellectual conversion: *I was on fire, then, my God, I was on fire to leave earthly things and fly back to you . . . for with you is wisdom* (3.4). But Augustine drank in *with my mother's milk,* and *deeply treasured* the name of Christ, so Cicero was not fully satisfying to him.

He turned to the study of the Scriptures, disappointed that they do not exhibit Cicero's *grand style.* Swollen with pride (his images repeatedly return to tumescence), he was not childlike enough to hear the simple words of Scripture. *Too fond of the flesh and too fond of talking,* he chewed on *dishes* of alleged wisdom that left him undernourished and with a bad taste in his mouth (3.6).

∽

My intellectual nourishment as a teenager was similarly distasteful. By now an accomplished sneak, I smuggled *True Love* magazines to my bedroom. These boasted such articles as "I Was Beaten, Raped and Left for Dead by a Motorcycle Gang." Romance indeed! At least Augustine read the classics. I did not look for, nor did I encounter, literature that could inspire me to a wider range of ideas and feelings. Fleeing the constraints imposed by my parents, I avidly embraced my society's reiterated assumption that (some version of) romantic love was the way to find life, love, and excitement.

∽

Augustine thought of curiosity as a poor excuse for seeking knowledge (2.6; 3.3). Evidently he was troubled with it himself, as he confessed in later books. He did not recognize how important curiosity is to a child.

Laziness and Inertia

To stifle a child's curiosity is to block her energy for exploring the world in order to identify where her strong interests lie. Not being allowed to pursue the objects of my curiosity made me listless, underachieving, and rebellious.

> Should we not . . . endeavor to *see* and attend to what is interesting, beautiful, strange, worth experiencing, and because it demands (and *needs*) our attention, rather than living in a vague haze of private anxiety and fantasy?[6]

Augustine blamed *sacrilegious curiosity* for leading him to *the depths of infidelity*. He cites an example: *Once when your solemnities were being celebrated within the walls of your church, I actually dared to desire and then to bring to a conclusion a business which deserved death for its reward* (3.3). Needless to say, this minimal description permits the unlimited speculation that Augustine's interpreters have enjoyed. He will have more to say about the evil of curiosity in later books of the *Confessions*.

Augustine did not mention his siblings in his *Confessions*. I was the eldest of four children, all of us four or five years apart. My brother, the youngest of my siblings, was born when I was thirteen. Mother was, by then, forty-three. She tired of the constant care of an infant and toddler, so he would be handed out the door to me when I arrived home from my two-mile walk from school. I was to *take him away* and keep him entertained until it was time for dinner. I took him on walks in his stroller, often crossing the Fremont drawbridge to go to the public library on the other side of the canal. When passersby stopped to admire "my" baby, I did not correct them. I liked to pretend he was mine, though I often got impatient with having to care for him so frequently. After an afternoon when he was unusually fussy, I told Mother that I would have liked to throw him in Lake Union that afternoon. After that I was not allowed to take him over the bridge!

I will not presume to tell my siblings' stories, not entirely out of fear of presumptuousness, but also because in talking with them in adulthood I have learned that each of us, partly because of our age differences, grew up in a different household.

---

6. Murdoch, *Metaphysics*, 218.

Looking back on his youth, Augustine was very judgmental of himself. He sorted the good from the bad, firmly locating all sin and evil in his young self, and all goodness in God. On the one hand, his images of running sores, itching swellings, abscesses, and fever suggest a painful disease rather than willful evil. Yet sympathy for the *poor wretch he was*, is not evident (3.2). He presents himself as *swelling with arrogance*, proud, ignorant, and blind (3.3). His chaotic metaphors pile up relentlessly, mirroring his unfocused struggle. Solomon's *bold woman* deceived him—if in doubt, blame a woman!—*She it was who seduced me, for she found my soul dwelling out of doors, in the eye of my flesh, and chewing over in myself the cud of what I had eaten through that eye* (3.6). Only in hindsight did Augustine realize that he was, all the while, seeking God.

Can I be more charitable to my teenaged self than Augustine was to himself as a youth? Instead of reviewing harshly my bad judgments, my inattentiveness, my lies, can I remember the past more honestly and profoundly as a desperate struggle in which, at each point, I did the best I could with what I had to work with? Rejecting the perspective of a stern and condemning parent, I try to find compassion for the young woman I was—inexperienced, bewildered, frightened, and seduced by the promise of *more life* than I was presently experiencing.

In retrospect, Augustine recognized that his mother's anxiety about him was the *voice of God* to him. At the time, however, her lamentations, tears, and importuning were a major annoyance. According to his account, she fixated on him, ignoring her other children and her husband in order to foil his every attempt to get away from her. Weeping, weeping, weeping, her tears *fell streaming and watered the ground beneath her eyes in every place where she prayed*. A dream persuaded her that Augustine would come to believe as she did, but she *never slackened in her weeping and her lamentations, never ceased in all hours of her prayer to weep about me*. (3.11). She entreated an unnamed bishop to intervene with Augustine *to unteach me what was bad, and to teach me what was good* but he, annoyed with her persistence, had some good commonsense advice: *let him alone for awhile*, let him learn from his mistakes. But she continued her entreaties to God, to Augustine, and to the bishop. Finally, annoyed, the bishop told her, *Go away and leave me .... it is impossible that the son of these tears should perish* (3.12).

Was the bishop, in these words, reassuring Monnica that God would hear her so-fervent prayers? Or was he sufficiently astute to predict that her heavy psychological pressure would not—could not—be lost on her son? Like Augustine's mother, my parents missed no opportunity to pressure their children into conformity of belief and practice. With uneven results. I conformed outwardly, but rebelled inwardly, leading to the ulcer that erupted in early adulthood. Others of my siblings either conformed or suffered emotional and physical damage for their rebellion. None of us was unaffected by the emotional duress brought to bear on us so that "the circle would be unbroken." Mother's grief and Dad's anger combined to manipulate each of us to define *ourselves* in relation to their religious commitments, either by resistance or acceptance. The damages were—and continue to be—profound.

Even in old age, my parents did not attribute their children's mental and physical addictions and sufferings to religious coercion. My father had a pseudo-scriptural and, incidentally, self-serving reason for his children's problems, namely, that because he was doing "the Lord's work," the devil attacked him in the most insidious way—through his children.

Augustine worried over the question of why *good men* of the Hebrew Bible were permitted to do things that good men were presently not permitted to do. He can only surmise that God's commands change from time to time. The challenge is to determine *what is fitting for each particular member and time and part and person* (3.7). Recognizing *diversity of customs* and laws, he recommended that the customs and laws of one's time and place should not be frivolously violated. Nevertheless, whatever God commands must be done. Avoiding awkward questions about the multiple marriages of Hebrew Bible heroes, he preferred to stick with the obvious: *Can it at any time or in any place be wrong to 'love God with all one's heart, with all one's soul, and with all one's mind; and one's neighbor as oneself?'* (3.8).

As a high school kid I did have two interests of which my parents approved. When I was fourteen and fifteen I was on a Youth for Christ quiz team. The four team members studied a Scripture book or several designated chapters of Scripture very thoroughly. At Youth for Christ meetings, teams from different high schools competed to answer the master of ceremonies' questions; the first person to leap to her feet and answer the question accurately got the point. I was the star. I nearly memorized whole books of the Bible. My team won the local and state contests and we went to compete in the national contest at Winona Lake, Indiana. We fared poorly there, I recall, but the trip itself was exciting for a girl who had never been on a vacation or gone anywhere for fun. More importantly, I got a sense that my mind worked well and that, with hard work, I could achieve something with it. But again, the "quiz kid" format effectively obliterated any meaning those Scripture passages might have had.

Another activity also allowed me to show some talent. I was in a violin trio that performed at many church gatherings. We played hymns in harmony, then switched to singing (in harmony) the next verse. We were fairly popular, though I don't remember that we were ever paid for our efforts. At least it redeemed, to some extent, all those awful hours of practicing the violin.

At the age of seventeen I got a job in the fancy lunchroom of a large department store in Seattle. There I met and became friends with a girl who had no religion. Teresa fascinated me. I was amazed at the ordinary teenage things she was allowed to do. She liked popular music, movies, and dancing—all forbidden to me. I had never seen a Hollywood movie and wanted desperately to do so. One night I stayed overnight at Teresa's home and we went to see *The Glenn Miller Story*. It was a double feature and I've forgotten the name of the other movie, but images from both movies are still in my mind. I think the next time I saw a movie was when I was nineteen, on the first anniversary of my wedding. That movie was *Around the World in Eighty Days*.

For my senior year in high school I went to a Christian school, King's Gardens, north of Seattle. I wanted to go there because I thought I would not feel so out of everything if I was among others whose parents imposed approximately the same boundaries. There I became a bad girl. My friends and I made fun of our teachers and of the students who were earnest and obedient. My friend Cheryl told me about masturbation. I signed my father's signature on my report card. I lied about the clothes I bought, saying that a girl gave them to me. I leaned out of my bedroom window and smoked a cigarette. I had boyfriends and kissed them—not much more. I felt alive, and I had fun. I still had no academic interests; I was a mediocre student.

After my senior year, my parents allowed me to live for the summer with my friend Pat and her family in a small town in eastern Washington. Pat and I packed cherries in a factory. Her family was also remarkable to me. Her father was a somewhat dour fundamentalist minister, but he didn't have the moods and angers my father did. Here too I had fun. We swam in the (forbidden) irrigation ditches; we sunbathed on the parsonage lawn in our swimsuits until a young retarded man was caught spying on us. I remember laughing a lot with Pat, her two sisters, and her mother.

Much later Pat told me that she always thought my parents didn't like her. I replied that they must have liked her since they let me live with her for a summer. But then I realized that I didn't think they liked me either. I knew that they loved me, but "like" is different than love, and may be even more important to a child. My first memory of feeling liked by an adult was the summer I lived with Pat, and had the amazing experience of feeling liked by her mother.

> . . . I set about finding an occasion to fall in love, so much in love was I with the idea of loving. (3.1)

There was no question about where I would go to college. We lived a block from the Free Methodist college where my father taught. I desperately wanted to live in the dorm, but this seemed completely silly to my parents. They decided that not only would the dorm be an unnecessary expense, but I was also seventeen, a year younger than my classmates (having skipped a grade in elementary school in Canada), and they argued that I needed the additional supervision of living at home. Clearly, this was not going to be my way to get away from home. Again I was a mediocre student. Nonetheless, it was an eventful year. I was homecoming queen that year, and I met my future husband, the boy with the beautiful smile. I remember little about that year, except my father's fits over my relationship with Gene. On more than one occasion when Gene and I were studying in the library, I looked up to see my father hastily retreating around a corner. I'd hear about it later at home.

Dad seemed to understand that my newly designated savior, romantic love, usurped the space formerly held by my parents. Both of them were jealous. While other parents might simply resent their child's imminent adulthood and emotional, if not yet physical, abandonment of the family home, my parents' jealousy was fully rationalized by their religion. They believed that in replacing them as objects of my longing and love, I deserted God.

> I am leaving out much, since I am hurrying on to those things which I want especially to confess to you, and also there is much that I have forgotten. (3.12)

4 Beyond the Pleasure Principle

Here are the years that walk between, bearing
Away the fiddles and the flutes, restoring

One who moves in the time between sleep and waking wearing
White light folded, sheathed about her, folded.
—T. S. ELIOT[1]

We must bend easily lest we break.
—AUGUSTINE[2]

What am I, even at my best, except suckling the milk you give and feeding upon you, the food that is imperishable?
—AUGUSTINE (4.1)

IN BOOK 4 AUGUSTINE DESCRIBED his fifteen-year-long committed relationship.

> In those years I lived with a woman who was not bound to me by lawful marriage; she was one who had come my way because of my wandering desires and my lack of considered judgment; nevertheless, I had only this one woman and I was faithful to her. And

---

1. Eliot, "Ash Wednesday," 109.
2. Augustine *Epistula* 104.3.11, 180.

> with her I learned by my own experience how great a difference there is between the self-restraint of the marriage covenant which is entered into for the sake of having children, and the mere pact made between two people whose love is lustful and who do not want to have children—even though, if children are born, they compel us to love them. (4.2)

It is difficult to picture Augustine as he characterizes himself: *seduced and seducing, deceived and deceiving* (4.1), when he writes immediately after, that he was faithful in relationship and honest in his profession of teaching rhetoric. Yet even as he acknowledged the power of sex in his life, Augustine denied that sex is good for learning about one's capacity for pleasure and joy, or that sex is good for thought.

Advised by a respected older friend that one of his interests, astrology, was a false science, he was reluctant to relinquish this convenient explanation for why people do as they do. Claiming the influence of the stars relieved personal responsibility for one's deeds.

I had not been made aware of a large world in which many opportunities were available to me, among which I could choose. My effort to get away from home by living in the college dorm did not work, so I moved to the next possibility available to a girl of my time and social location. I fell in love, became pregnant, and got married, in that order. At the time, this seemed to happen "naturally," without the cynicism of retrospect.

> [B]ecause the subject is not a unity, it cannot be present to itself, know itself. I do not always know what I mean, need, want, desire, because these do not arise from some ego as origin. Often I express my desire in gesture, in tone of voice, without meaning to do so. . . . Subjects all have multiple desires that do not cohere.[3]

I lost my virginity to the boy I married after my first year in college and shortly after my eighteenth birthday, a skinny boy who was studying to become a Presbyterian minister. My father had once expressed

---

3. Young, "Ideal of Community," 11.

approval of Gene, saying that his former girlfriend was a lucky girl. On the evening that Gene asked my father's permission to marry me, they argued at length about infant baptism and Dad gave his approval with great reluctance. I was too young, he thought, and he was right. Within seven months I gave birth to my daughter.

Lying is an essential skill for a fundamentalist's daughter. A couple of years before Susan was born, an unmarried girl in the neighborhood, daughter of a friend of my father's, had a baby. My father commented that if that ever happened "to him" he would never preach again. How, knowing the stakes, could I let that happen "to him?" We lied. We said that the baby was premature; we even persuaded my doctor to put the wrong birth weight on her bracelet. I do not, to this day, regret that lie. It spared my parents endless anguish, and it was amply proven later that we had done the best thing, not only for them but also for me.

My unmarried sister became pregnant several years later. She did not lie, and my parents placed her in a "home for unwed mothers," giving her no other options than to relinquish the baby for adoption. The experience harmed her irreparably; her spirit was broken. She was a pretty, lively, and smart girl who could have done anything she chose to do with her life. But she eventually married an abusive, alcoholic, and unfaithful man, became herself an alcoholic for a decade and, soon after she stopped drinking, got multiple sclerosis.

Had I not lied, I would no doubt have been treated similarly and I probably would have reacted as she did. I could very easily have had her life. And she could have had mine, except that she did not lie. Another crucial difference in our stories was that my baby's father and I were in love and wanted to get married, while she did not marry her baby's father.

My daughter was born when I was still eighteen, and my son soon after my twenty-first birthday. I was wife and mother. I had accomplished the life to which I was socialized. When our daughter was a year-and-a-half old, we moved to northern California so that my husband could begin seminary. I cooked, cleaned, took care of my daughter, and typed his papers. My son was born at the beginning of my husband's second year in seminary. I tried to make a life out of caring for my children and my husband. Occasionally I went to a movie with another seminary student's wife. Or I went shopping—largely window-shopping—with a friend. We did not talk about our husbands or our discontents. That would have been considered disloyal. I attended the seminary wives' group—Parsonettes—in which we were groomed to be good ministers' wives. I had no interests of my own. I was *overcome with drowsiness, barely roused from sleep and in constant danger of sinking back into lethargy, half asleep* (8.5).

Some of the deadest moments of my life were spent sitting on the edge of a sandbox in a playground. I was consumed with boredom. The other mothers might have been friendly and interesting people, but I didn't make friends with any of them. I watched that their children did not hurt my children. And I had nothing to think, no poems, no ideas. I could have been learning languages. I regret those moments and hours of deadness. I would like to see, really *see* my little children again. I miss their little bodies. But *things pass away so that other things may take their places* (4.11). My adult children have taken the place of those sweet babies.

At the age of twenty-two I developed a duodenal ulcer, unhappiness chewing my stomach lining, painful and urgent enough to make me seek medical and psychiatric help. We had no money, but we had good insurance, so I received seven years of excellent psychotherapy. My therapist offered no ready-made interpretations. His largely Rogerian method was perfect for me. His method was, in essence, to step back in order to let me come forward. He listened; he made some observations, but mainly I experienced psychotherapy as a cleared space into which I could enter.

> There is no clear border between remembering and imagining. When I listen to a patient I am not reconstructing the "facts" of a case history but listening for patterns, strains of feeling, and associations that may move us out of painful repetitions and into articulated understanding.[4]

As a child I was completely invaded; no secret place in my psyche remained private, my own. The all-seeing eye of God and his representatives, my parents, invaded and demanded me, tireless, ubiquitous, imperious. My "self" was not something I could choose to give or do.

---

4. Hustvedt, *Sorrows of an American*, 80.

That's what my psychotherapy was about. Dr. Neale gave me room to *come out*. And I did come out, so eagerly. But the me that came out was a surprise: lusty, full of desires, bursting with energy. Very different from the passive, diffident, listless "me." I was "headstrong," as it were. Full of passion. Not at all the indifferent, disaffected, bored young woman I had been to date.

In addition to recalling childhood experiences with greater depth and accuracy, psychotherapy involved some important relearning. At one point my therapist remarked, "You are so hard on yourself!" I needed to understand that I had done the best I could, with the resources available to me, at all times. But I also had to accept that my best was seldom "good enough," as is often the case for human beings with limited perspectives—or as Augustine described, not enough knowledge, and not enough delight in the best choice. My self-talk, the tape that ran in my head, was often accusing and abusive. In therapy I *heard* those voices in my head call myself lazy, stupid, and ugly. I needed to change to more gently encouraging tapes. I needed to become the soothing and respectful mother I never quite had. I needed to forgive myself and go on.

The second issue I worked on in psychotherapy was changing the lying and sneaking habits I had learned so well in childhood. These mental habits were well ensconced and difficult to jettison. What I learned in psychotherapy did not eradicate either my negative self-talk or the urge—by now an instinct—to lie if it made things even slightly easier for me or (I imagined) for others. I did, however, learn to recognize those impulses as they arose, to acknowledge them, and then to *choose* differently.

Psychotherapy was exciting. Almost immediately the energy that had been consuming my stomach lining moved to my head and I began to read—primarily psychology—voraciously and promiscuously. I began to take courses at the nearest community college, feeling tremendous excitement. The ulcer disappeared and has not reappeared in the intervening fifty years. Fundamentally, this change was a "conversion" from passive sufferer to active seeker. Lacking any context or conversation partners, I read all of Freud's and Jung's translated works and found them immensely exciting. The energy formerly spent devouring my stomach lining now rushed to my head.

Beyond the Pleasure Principle

How is it that the weights and impulses toward all these different kinds of love are kindled in one soul? (4.14)

On Susan's second birthday, she got a new pail and shovel to play with in the communal sandbox at the seminary apartments where we lived. Within three minutes of appearing at the sandbox with her new toy, she was back in our apartment, crying. Kenny, who lived next door and was slightly older than Susan, bit her on the shoulder and took her pail and shovel. I was blindly furious, a mother animal whose offspring had been harmed. I had never experienced quite this feeling. I complained to Kenny's mother, something I would usually have been too timid to do. Susan had a tetanus shot and the pediatrician told me that human bites were more dangerous—"dirtier"—than animal bites.

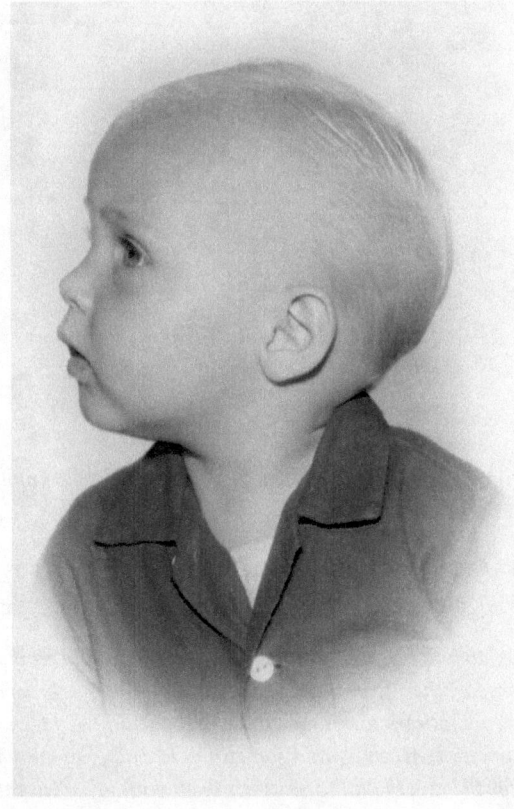

One evening when Ric was a baby, his pacifier could not be found. He screamed until he was purple, and I hurried to the drugstore to get a new one. In retrospect I can see that I was always afraid of his rage.

When Ric was four we went to Seattle to visit my parents. Checking to see whether, as he suspected, I was not bringing the children up properly, Dad asked Ric whether he loved Jesus. Ric, looking bewildered, looked at me, and said, "I love Mommy." A perfect Augustinian answer! Augustine said, quoting 1 John 4:16, that "God is love," and so anyone who loves, participates in God-who-is-love. But, unfortunately, not the right answer for my father!

> *I could not be happy, even in the way I then understood happiness, without friends. (6.15).*

Relationships with friends is a dominant theme of Book 4 of Augustine's *Confessions*. He gives a charming picture of friendship in late antiquity.

> *[T]o talk, to laugh and do kindnesses to each other; to read pleasant books together; to make jokes together and then talk seriously together; sometimes to disagree, but without any ill feeling; . . . to be sometimes teaching and sometimes learning, to long impatiently for the absent and to welcome them with joy when they re-*

turned to us. These and other similar expressions of feeling, which proceed from the hearts of those who love and are loved in return, and are revealed in the face, the voice, the eyes, and in a thousand charming ways, were like a kindling fire to melt our souls together and out of many to make us one. (4.8)

Yet, for Augustine, friendship was dangerous in several ways. First, no friendship, he writes, was free from *the high tides of foul lust* (3.2). *I muddied the clear spring of friendship with the dirt of physical desire and clouded over its brightness with the dark hell of lust* (3.1). No one can guess what Augustine meant by these dark confessions. No friendship? Augustine gives no indication in any of his writings that he could consider women friends. The second danger inherent in friendship, Augustine writes, is that it is crazy to love a mortal as if he is immortal. *Blessed is the man who loves [God], who loves his friend in [God] . . . . He alone loses no one dear to him for they are all dear to him in one who is not lost* (4.9).

Augustine described the influence several friends had on him. One well-respected old man, discovering Augustine's avid interest in astrology, helped him begin to understand that astrology is a false science, relying on chance coincidences for verification (4.3). Another friend with whom Augustine had grown up and who had accompanied him in his studies, died. Augustine said that this friendship *was sweeter to me than all sweetnesses that in this life I had ever known* (4.4). As his friend lay unconscious on his deathbed, his family had him baptized. Augustine assumed that the baptism would have no effect since his friend knew nothing about it. But when he briefly recovered consciousness, the friend was unreceptive to Augustine's joking about the baptism, saying that if Augustine wanted to be his friend, he must not talk to him in this way.

When the fever returned and he died a few days later, Augustine's heart *was darkened over with sorrow. All those things which we had done and said together became, now that he was gone, sheer torture to me . . . . Only tears were sweet to me and tears had taken the place of my friend in my heart's love* (4.4). In his anguish Augustine reflected on death: *The more I loved my friend, the more I hated and feared death . . . . I was at the same time thoroughly tired of living and extremely frightened of dying* (4.6). With a *broken and bleeding* soul, Augustine actually left his native town of Tagaste, *for my eyes did not search for him so much in places where they were not accustomed to see him* (4.7). In short, the death of his friend intensely affected the young Augustine.

∽

I too was greatly affected by the death of a friend. I was twenty-six and she was thirty; we both had two small children. Jeannie woke up one morning, had convulsions for thirty seconds, and died. I did not experience the debilitating sorrow over her death that Augustine had on the death of his friend, but I cared for her four-month-old son for a short time after her death. Five months later her husband remarried. *That* was the wake-up call for me. I realized that if I died, something similar would happen; my husband would soon remarry and someone else would raise my children. I resolved to take responsibility for my own life, rather than live through my husband and children, as I had been doing.

Within a year, another incident reinforced the effect on me of Jeannie's death. An acquaintance attempted to commit suicide. This woman was beautiful and a lounge singer, but on her fortieth birthday she realized that her looks and voice were fading. She wanted to die. I realized that I did not want to be thinking of my looks at all when I reached the age of forty. I wanted to be so engaged in work that I loved by then that the threat of fading looks would not affect me. Together these two incidents catapulted me to action. I began going to the nearest community college, highly motivated.

My marriage was good for about a decade, but it was not sufficiently flexible to permit change and growth. When we moved to my husband's first parish I tried to be active in the church, in nursery school, and in PTA, but my by-now desperate inertia worsened. It was in the early years of Gene's second parish that I met several people whose ideas excited me and who seemed to see some potential in me for which there was little or no evidence at the time.

∽

A journal entry from July 1964:

> I would like to say what I am, who I am, but I don't really know.
> I am a woman, twenty-six years old, married, and with two chil-

dren. Yet I am a girl, a gypsy. My husband is a Presbyterian minister, and it's not enough that the people have to like him; they have to like me too. In a way, I desperately want them to like me, but I "won't make the effort," as Mother would say. This can be seen two ways, and I seem continuously to vacillate between the two perspectives. It could be said that I do not have an attitude of Christian love for "the brethren." But it can also be said that I refuse to pattern my life after the expectations of others. That sounds better, so that's how I prefer to understand it. Is my nonconformity weakness or strength? At different times it seems to be both. I am not good at pretending, but I have a lot of practice at it, and when it is important to me I can do a great job. Also I can do it so well that I deceive myself; the best way to deceive others is to deceive oneself. It is only afterwards, when I come home and relax that I feel the tremendous tension I have been under, not only to play the role of the young minister's wife, but more, to convince myself that I *am* it.

I must know myself because I am determined to live as fully as I can and if this must sometimes inconvenience or hurt someone, I am overwhelmed with a massive and crippling guilt and feel that I have no right to be myself. I have read that if someone is bothered when I am me, it is their problem, not mine. This sinks in to my intellect, but it doesn't get down to where I *live*. I would like to be fearless and strong, with a sure sense of myself. I *am* that way sometimes, but only momentarily, only for long enough to say or do something daring, and then my other self takes over, the guilty, cringing one. I have spirit, but only enough to get me through a moment or two, not enough to sustain me through the inevitable aftermath of guilt and depression. I wish I had *either* more spirit, or no spirit. This way I am doomed to struggle, but in spite of this, I want very badly to live, and am willing to struggle.

About this time, I cut out an advertisement with a picture of a druggist smiling ambiguously, both encouragingly and warningly: It read, "If you have a winning number and don't enter, someone else will get your prize." For a long time I didn't enter. Didn't enter the job market. Didn't enter college. Didn't care to compete. And I didn't give a damn if someone else got my prize. They were welcome to it, in fact. That long phase of my life, lasting from sometime in my teens until my early twenties, was over, and I was avid to learn, to do, to be.

I wanted to study psychology, but the classes available to me focused on developmental psychology—rats instead of humans—so I changed my major to philosophy. With two children in school and an employed husband I could not consider a move, so I had to go to the nearest college. I began at a two-year community college, and I transferred to San Francisco State University for upper-division work. At San Francisco State I took an independent study with the chairman of the Humanities Department, Matthew Evans. We started with Aristotle and somehow migrated to Augustine, whose *Confessions, Enchiridion,* and parts of the *City of God* I devoured feverishly. Still in psychotherapy, I understood Augustine to be using a fully articulated and highly nuanced language of the psyche, a sophisticated forerunner of Freudian language. I was tremendously excited by my studies. I was also very aware that my husband did not recognize the "me" that was forming in psychotherapy and school. I was no longer the woman he had married.

Two required courses in symbolic logic prompted me to change majors from philosophy to Humanities. At that time—the mid-1960s—San Francisco State University had one of only two Humanities departments in the country. I took courses such as Baroque Culture, Renaissance Culture, Greek Culture, in which music, art, literature, and social and political history were combined in order to construct the ethos of a time/place. I loved this. Although I did not understand this at the time, this was interdisciplinary work, work that transgressed the boundaries of a single field in order to reconstruct a picture that could not be seen from within a single field.

Words carried tremendous energy for me. They articulated possibilities of thinking and feeling to which I otherwise had no direct access. I attempted to reject Christianity, but soon found that I had somehow to come to terms with religious words if I was to retain the energy they still carried for me. The fundamentalist language of my childhood had formed my psyche and bonded with my earliest experience. I began with single words: sin, temptation, pride, faith, trust, grace. I developed a method of "fastening" the word to the front of my mind, keeping it there, not consciously puzzling over it, but considering through its lens everything I read, everything I experienced, everything I saw or heard. I brought all this to the word and watched to see if the word was illuminated at all. Bit by bit, by this method, I began to understand the psychological referents of theological words. I had not before understood religious language as useful descriptions of experience, but as narrow cages, judgments on my attitudes and behavior.[5]

Safety and risk: Virginia Woolf's *Mrs. Dalloway* explores characters that need the right amount of safety before they can take risks. Too much safety is deadening, while too much risk is dangerous. From a combination of the right amount of safety and the right amount of risk comes the "sharp quick sense of life" described by Saul Bellow in *Henderson the Rain King*.

Wittgenstein's feeling of "perfect safety in the universe" is the statement of a religious person. But in the secular world of most Americans, a sense of safety must be constructed around loving and being loved by other people. Safety built on the presence and provision of other people is fragile, vulnerable, and precarious, as Augustine saw when his friend died. People, by definition, are mortal, in addition having their own needs, agenda, and volatility. They do not exist to reassure me but for their own complex projects and purposes. If we need others for our safety, we tend to *eat them up, as people do with their food*, in Augustine's words (9.2)

Christianity personalizes the universe with a God interested in my welfare in order to make it a safe place, a place in which death doesn't really matter because it is just a preamble to eternal life. In the Christian narrative, God watches out for me, will not allow anything to try me beyond my endurance, waits to welcome me "home" at the end of my life. This, I think sadly, endeavors to make the best of painful circumstances, but wanting as I do to believe it, I can't. I can only understand myself as in the orbit of a generous and terrifying universe in which gifts and pains circulate without design, casually, randomly. I cannot take the universe personally; I must accept and enjoy its gifts and its griefs,

---

5. Wittgenstein would say that I learned a different language game.

relinquishing them gratefully and gracefully when necessary. This is the appropriate attitude toward the universe of the One whose providence is of the whole, not of individuals.

~

There is more than a little Pelagianism in my psyche, a part of me that believes that "since perfection is possible, perfection is mandatory." It might be argued that there is a flaw in this reasoning in that, in fact, perfection is not possible. But even that can be rationalized by a psyche that learned in childhood that nothing short of perfection is acceptable. If/since perfection is not possible, I may expect always to feel that I have fallen short—and to try harder. In the early years of my first marriage I wanted to be the perfect wife, the perfect mother, daughter, and hostess.

Longing for perfection, in belief, in behavior, is endemic to fundamentalism. Along with literalness, it has proved—is proving—very difficult to overcome. It has little to do with conscious beliefs, so it can pop up in any area of life. There is no complete recovery from a fundamentalist childhood. There is only, with work, increasing ability to spot the predilections acquired in childhood before they have a firm grip on the psyche, so that one can gently peel off their clutching fingers. For many years I had the following quotation above my desk to remind me to be alert. (Yet, I have not failed to note that alertness also has its roots in fundamentalism, even though my alertness is not now to sin, but to less than fruitful habits of mind and behavior.)

> Things don't have to be perfect; in fact, it is better if they are not.[6]

I thought that I should be able to go to school if I could do so, not only without inconveniencing my husband or children, but without them noticing. I sneaked studying, baked all the family's bread, and of course, did all the housework and cooking. I thought I had to be superwoman, an old story. I had a good deal of energy so, mostly, it worked. I was still, and for many years to come, working with energy that had been freed from chewing my stomach lining and emigrated to my head. Looking back at this and several other things I've done, I think with a sigh, you had to be young.

6. Benjamin, *Bonds of Love*, 47.

Beyond the Pleasure Principle

∽

Virginia Woolf's *Orlando* "argues" that our lives are too short to have the experiences, and reflection on those experiences, that would allow us to see ourselves and others accurately. Woolf's protagonist migrates from a male body to a female body and back several times in the course of a four-hundred-year life. Alert as we try to be in our short lives, we just can't figure it out fast enough. Although we bring every intelligence we possess, every "learning experience," to attempting to imagine how it feels to be that other body, that other life, we get it wrong. It just goes by too fast. And it is exhausting to be as attentive every second as one needs to be—and even then it's not enough. Life is like a day: it goes fast at the beginning and again at the end, but in the long expanse in between, it seems that it will go on forever. Because life is routine, comfortable, even tedious, we become inattentive. Then, suddenly, it speeds up and is over.

∽

In addition to husbands that supported me financially while I went to school, two other men played important roles in helping me. One of them, a member of my husband's church, seemed to recognize something in me that was not yet there. He encouraged me and gave me opportunities to think and write. After my separation from my first husband, the other man, a professor, found me a small scholarship that allowed me to continue my education at the nearest four-year college, San Francisco State University.

Both men wanted payback. Ah, but this is so complicated. It isn't that they did me favors and then wanted sex. It was, in both cases, that they wanted to help me because they felt themselves in love with me. And then, having helped me, they wanted to pursue that attraction further. I resisted, not because they were both married, but because I was not attracted to them sexually. I desperately wanted to talk with them about ideas, about the new things I was learning. I tried to insist on that relationship with each of them. But both thought me "cold," because I was uninterested in sex (with them).

These were not, however, easy refusals for me; they were complicated and anguished since I felt great gratitude to them. I still feel gratitude today, knowing that each played a vital role in getting me to the next step in my education. Moreover, I recognize my complicity. I needed their help; I just didn't want to pay for it in the way that they hoped. Such an old story; nothing but wall-to-wall socialization, his and hers, different but interconnected. Augustine also condemned the *hellish river of custom. Who can stand firm against it? When will it ever dry up?* (1.16)

"Erotic" in our society means erotic for men. The shrinking, frightened, ashamed, desperate-to-cover-up Susannah (in Artemesia Gentileschi's painting *Susannah and the Elders*) is the erotic woman. It is not primarily her body that is erotic (for men) but the power asymmetry between the "object," Susannah, and the spectators—the Elders and viewers of the painting. I read that in pornography the faces of the women who are being sexually overpowered look frightened. I thought this was an oversight, because their faces don't matter, only their bodies do. But no, their frightened faces are an important part of the turn-on.

When I had been married for several years and had two children, Mother felt the need to give me an update on the rudimentary sex education she had provided when I was an adolescent. She had just learned, she said, that women could have sex with women. She said that I was not safe from sexual assault even in "ladies rooms." The last refuge for women unsafe at school, at church, at home, and on the street, was no longer safe. I should now fear women too.

Queer theory and the gay rights movement of the latter part of the twentieth century made major contributions to exposing the extent to which sexual orientation and sexual desire is socially constructed. Judith Butler's description of gender as "performance" opened my mind to the fragility and instability of gender and sexuality. Why should American culture *work so hard* to establish the "naturalness" of heterosexuality—billboards, movies and television shows, advertising—if it is so natural? Heterosexuality is massively supported in popular culture, while homosexual desire is still slenderly represented and supported.

Luce Irigaray wrote:

> Nothing of the special nature of love *between women* has been unveiled or stated, that a woman might desire a woman "like" herself, someone of the "same" sex . . . . Yet what exhilarating pleasure it is to be partnered with someone like oneself . . . . What need, attraction, passion one feels for someone, for some woman, like oneself.[7]

My friend described her lesbian experience: "It's about pace, not rushing; it's about beauty, beauty you feel on your skin and to the bone." She said, "For me, love between a man and a woman was all about someone else's urgency. Not mine. Now, there is urgency, but it's mine, and I get to it slowly, the only way I can get to it at all." "The beauty there is overwhelming."[8]

Augustine was an early proponent of Michel Foucault's maxim: "Everything is dangerous"; everything is susceptible to abuse. From the danger of allowing oneself to be derailed by the loss of a friend, he proceeds

---

7. Irigaray, *Speculum of the Other Woman*, 101, 103.
8. Plotinus *Ennead* 2.9.17.

directly to discussion of how one should enjoy *things of beauty*. Here also, however, dangers lurk. Here it is again: the problem of the missing self that attempts to solidify by attaching to a friend, or to sensory beauty: On the one hand, things of beauty reveal important information about their Creator, the great beauty. On the other hand, they too, like the neighbor, must be loved *in God*.

> *In these things let my soul praise you, God, creator of all things, yet let it not be stuck and glued too close to them in love through the senses of the body. For these things go along their path toward nonexistence, and they tear and wound the soul with terrible longings, since the soul itself desires to be and to find rest in what it loves. But in those things there is no place to rest, since they do not stay. They pass away and no one can follow them with his bodily senses. Nor can anyone grasp them tight even when they are present and in front of him.* (4.10)

༄

At College of Marin and San Francisco State University I learned how to learn. Learning is first of all recognizing that *I don't know* what I think I know. What prevents learning is what Plato called the "double ignorance," namely, not knowing, and not knowing that one does not know. Freud described the antidote to the double ignorance as restraining speculative tendencies and "looking at the same things again and again until they themselves begin to speak."[9] Foucault's description is more detailed: "If we want to know whatever we know, we must give up what we suppose about our individuality, our self, and our subject position."[10] We think and say so much with great assurance that we don't know at all; for example, we shamelessly label others' motivations. Why do we always seem to think we can read others accurately, when we are even opaque to ourselves?

༄

Augustine, in his mid-twenties, found it difficult to picture an incorporeal God. He imagined God as a sort of *vast luminous body*, and himself

---

9. Freud, *On the History of the Psychoanalytic Movement*.
10. Quoted by Davidson, *Emergence of Sexuality*, 215.

as *a piece broken off from this body. What an extraordinary perversity I showed!* He comments, *I had my back to the light and my face to the things on which the light shone; so my face saw things that were lighted, but on my face itself, no light fell* (4.16). Seduced by beautiful created things *on which the light shone*, he simply could not imagine a God who created them but himself had no body. He suffered from a kind of fundamentalist literalism. It will be some time before Augustine can picture a God who has substance, but no body.

The God of my childhood had a body! In Alice Walker's *The Color Purple*, Celie describes him to perfection:

> "Tell me what your God look like, Celie."
> "Aw naw," I say. I'm too shame. Nobody ever ast me this before, so I'm sort of took by surprise. Besides, when I think about it, it don't seem quite right. But it all I got. I decide to stick up for him, just to see what Shug say.
> "Okay," I say. "He big and old and tall and graybearded and white. He wear white robes and go barefooted."
> "Blue eyes?" she ast.
> "Sort of bluish-gray. Cool. Big though. White lashes," I say. She laugh.[11]

Sometimes I am a child and I long for the friendly Christian God, the Jesus who calls, "softly and tenderly, . . . Come home, come ho-o-o-me." But when I temporarily manage adulthood, I recognize the childishness of my longings and require myself to live with, to *make love with*, the One who is the source of Life, my life, and the life of the All, the life that will move on to other forms when my fragile body can no longer hold it.

Novalis wrote, "We are always going home." Book 4 is full of poignant images of return:

---

11. Walker, *Color Purple*, 201.

> *You will bear us up, yes, from our infancy until out gray hairs you will bear us up. Let us return now to you, Lord, so that we may not be overturned . . . [for] you yourself are our good. And we need not be afraid of having no place to which we may return. We of our own accord fell from that place. And our home, which is your eternity, does not fall down when we are away from it.* (4.16; also 4.11; 4.12)

Return, Augustine repeats, return to the source of life: *The Word itself calls you to come back . . . . Return to your own heart . . . . He withdrew from our eyes so that we might return to our heart and find him.* But to return is to go forward, to go toward.

Perhaps happiness is much overrated. Both Augustine and Freud understood the importance of unhappiness. *How unhappy my soul was then,* Augustine said, in relating the turmoil that led to his conversion, *unhappy, and you made me really see my unhappiness.* I too have often felt grateful that I was not even a little bit happier in my first marriage. Had I been happier, I would have stayed, but my unhappiness prodded me to the restlessness that forced me to change. Had my ulcer hurt less, I would not have been willing to undergo the massive psychic change involved in psychotherapy. In my experience only unhappiness and pain produce change; no one volunteers to change fundamentally. Freud described the pleasure principle as governing most lives at most moments. The habit of snatching the nearest, quickest, most easily accessible pleasure creates the kind of fatigue and inertia Augustine described. Freud urged resisting and going "beyond the pleasure principle" to a more complex and satisfying integration with bigger and better pleasures. Happiness is the goal, certainly, but unhappiness—and *awareness of unhappiness*—is the energy that can produce change.

5   *Staying Is Nowhere*

To see is to see others. We cannot, in fact, readily escape seeing others; we can only readily escape acknowledging them.
    —MAXINE SHEETS-JOHNSTONE[1]

BELIEVERS IN ORIGINAL SIN *LOVE* order. T. E. Hulme draws the connection well:

> [Man] is endowed with original sin. While he can occasionally accomplish acts which partake of perfection, he can never himself *be* perfect.... As man is essentially bad, he can only accomplish anything of value by discipline—ethical and political. Order is thus not merely negative, but creative and liberating. Institutions are necessary.[2]

Augustine left Carthage and went to Rome because of disorderly students. He *heard that in Rome the young men followed their studies in a more orderly manner and were controlled by a stricter discipline.... [In Carthage they were] disgracefully out of control. They come breaking into a class in the most unmannerly way and, behaving almost like madmen, disturbing the order which the master has established for the good of his pupils.* Augustine thinks that there ought to be a law! Their *disorderly*

---

1. Sheets-Johnstone, *Roots of Power*, 31.
2. Quoted by Murdoch, "T. S. Eliot as a Moralist," 163–64.

acts were, however, *protected by custom*, even though *by your eternal law such things can never be permitted* (5.8).

Augustine, master of language, equates his voyage from Carthage to Rome, the waters of baptism, and his mother's tears.

> *You saved me, full as I was with the most execrable uncleanness, from the waters of the sea and brought me to the water of your grace, so that, when I was washed in this water, the rivers that flowed from my mother's eyes, tears daily shed for me that watered the ground below her downcast eyes, should be dried up.* (5.8)

I continued to attend San Francisco State University. Gene didn't like my independent life, and threatened that if I did not quit school, he would leave me. I do not know, looking back, how I had the strength and courage to continue. I do remember thinking that since I was a happier person going to school, I was also able to be a more loving person. I didn't understand why that was not good for everybody, myself, him, our children. A deeper level of honesty, however, forces me to acknowledge that I was no longer the "parsonette" he had married and expected to live with for the rest of his life. I had changed. I understood why he felt betrayed. But I loved school and couldn't stop going. Psychotherapy had been a primary agent of change for me, so I urged it on Gene. But he would not accept it until finally, after our divorce, he did.

The following journal entries barely suggest the reams and reams of writing I did at the time of my divorce, trying to understand, trying to wrestle some good—some "growth," I called it then—from the pain I was experiencing.

> May 1966. We have some myths that come to us from long ago about one or two people who could love. Our society safeguards the teachings of these about love. And so it appears to us that we must know all there is to know about love and what is essential to it: promise, sacrifice, renounce. But, curiously, we are still helpless at this task of loving after we have done all these with all our will. And where now are the great teachers we supposed would save us? There is more to be done than we have yet dreamed; it is astonishing, but no one has done any of the work for us at all.

Oh, there is freedom, and we are forced to be free, to bear the responsibility of being born, and living, and moving, and loving, and dying. When will we take responsibility for our own unfreedom and stop blaming others for it, others who, in turn, are blaming us for their unfreedom: parents living for children, and children for parents; husbands living for wives, and wives for husbands, and *who is living?*

How is it that we have allowed goodness to be reduced to not hurting others? When will our love be a freeing and not a binding? Haven't we been taught about love exactly backwards, so that we think ourselves engaged in "self-giving love," when we have, as yet, no self to give, when we are still carrying our needs about looking for someone who will take responsibility for one or two of them? Now and then we actually find someone who will agree to take a couple of ours if we will take a couple of his. And so it is arranged, and for a while everything does seem more bearable; the other's needs don't scrape and bruise us because they have a slightly different shape than ours. But soon they too begin to chafe, and we try to shift the burden a bit, stealthily to slip back bits here and there, and we find that the other is doing the same.

Then what?

We refer each other back to the promises. But we were different people then, and besides, we were tricked, defrauded, because we had *no idea* of the burdensomeness of the other's needs.

> Ought not these oldest sufferings of ours to be yielding more fruit by now? Is it not time that, in loving, we freed ourselves from the loved one and, quivering, endured, as the arrow endures the string, to become, in the gathering out-leap, something more than itself? For staying is nowhere.[3]

May 1967. Next week I will be thirty. My friends give me effusive sympathy, so I began to think about what it is to be thirty. At first I felt bad thinking, "Here I am, thirty, and I've only been alive a couple of years in all." But then I started to think about why that is, about the anxiety and lack of pleasure I have lived with from my parents' home forward. So

3. Rilke, *Duino Elegies*, 1.

then I thought, Wow! I have no right to be alive at all. I thought, here I am thirty, and *already* I'm alive!

∽

November 2009: Reading my 1967 journal is painful; I am forced to see that I have compromised my young vision of the world, human relationships, and what constitutes integrity. Yet I could not have lived for long with the fierce intransigence I had then. I wrote in my journal primarily to articulate and hold my own perspective, to see the world differently than my middle-class world of church, neighborhood swimming pool culture, and fragile relationships.

> We are not isolated free choosers, monarchs of all we survey, but benighted creatures sunk in a reality whose nature we are constantly and overwhelmingly tempted to deform by fantasy.[4]

Did I deceive myself then? Do I now? "The easiest person to deceive is oneself."[5] It is easy to deceive oneself because one is so eager, desperate even, to maintain one's self image, one's own favorite character in fiction. But until we have a sense of how self-deception actually *works*, we are helpless. We can't detect it while it is happening, and perhaps only in distant retrospect do we even suspect that we have deceived ourselves about something important. And self-deception has long-term effects that are themselves so subtle that they seem "natural." It is often only when we have changed attitudes and behavior that we can look back and see the effects of self-deception.

The story I tell myself about my life differs from Augustine's self-story. Yet an underlying theme emerges in both our stories. We both endeavored to find a center *within*, rather than being tossed and jerked about by the expectations of our social worlds. When Augustine returned to himself, he found God there. He wrote:

> Let the restless turn and see, you are there, you are in their hearts, in the hearts of those who confess to you and who throw themselves upon your mercy and weep upon your breast after the difficult ways they have trod.... And where was I when I was seeking

---

4. Murdoch, "Against Dryness," 293.
5. Bulwer-Lytton, quoted by Fingarette, *Self-Deception*, 2.

for you? You were there, in front of me; but I had gone away even from myself. I could not even find myself, much less find you (5.2).

When I was able to develop an inner "place" (for want of a better word), it was fortified and strengthened gradually, not by reference to a personal God, but by fragments of poetry, axioms, friends, and experiences that felt trustworthy.

～

Augustine and I both identified with ideas, read philosophy, and discovered that acquiring knowledge was dependent on one's attitude: *The proud cannot find you, however deep and curious their knowledge.* He criticized the Manichaeans, with whom he had been associated for nine years, for their lack of a *religious spirit* of truth-seeking. Rather than looking attentively at the world, and learning from it about its creator, he alleged, Manichaean teachers drew *on a rich vein of pure fantasy* (5.3). The *kind* of knowledge one has is crucial. It is not important to be able to *measure the heaven and count the stars and weigh the elements* (5.4); what was important to Augustine was not to confuse (quasi-scientific) knowledge with Christian faith.

Having eagerly awaited the visit of a famous Manichaean teacher, Augustine was deeply disappointed by Faustus's answers to his questions. He found the teacher poorly educated and—understandably—not willing to get into a discussion with the intrepid Augustine.

Augustine was a snob. This young man from the provinces thought he was able accurately to evaluate the world-traveled Manichaean teacher. Faustus had some important gaps in his knowledge, Augustine said, and his knowledge was *very conventional* (5.6). I have some sympathy for Faustus! Like him I received a very conventional doctoral training. Over the years that I taught at Harvard I was asked several times how in the world I managed to get a job at Harvard when my doctorate was from a little known graduate school on the West Coast. In fact, I scrambled to catch up to Harvard's more sophisticated learning. But in 1967 that was far in the future.

In my M.A. work at San Francisco State, I had good teachers and poor teachers. I learned to expect nothing from a course except a syllabus and a bibliography, which I could then explore on my own. Part of learning how to learn, however, related to identifying what I could learn from a particular teacher. I discovered that it is not necessary to *like* a teacher in order to learn from him (my graduate school teachers were all men). One teacher in particular stands out in my mind as exemplary of this life lesson. I did not like him at all. I thought him arrogant, contemptuous of students, and unwilling to make an effort to teach. Yet he had a brilliant mind, and once I relaxed my dislike, I learned tremendously from him. Clearly, not everyone in the class did, but I realized when I became a teacher myself that every teacher teaches only a few students in any classroom. Certain teachers will have great ability to teach the slowest students while others will teach the brightest, and still others will ably teach the students who are hardworking, but neither especially intelligent nor especially resistant. From teachers I considered poor—perhaps at least partly because they taught a different kind of student than myself—I learned to avoid certain habits of thought and styles of communicating.

I didn't want the divorce and it gave me great pain. For a long time, perhaps a year, I experienced what I thought of as a "pain high." I felt the pain acutely, but it also made everything clearer, colors sharper and thoughts more visceral and vivid. I was equal parts scared and excited, no drugs needed. I felt alive. A character in Arthur Miller's play *The Misfits* says, "If I'm going to be alone, I want to be by myself." Since I was alone, there was a certain relief in being by myself.

What I was experiencing and feeling had intimately to do with the time and place: the 1960s, in Marin County, California. There was encouragement and support for being "myself"—whatever that was—for seeking pleasure, for challenging conventional expectations. There was the music, the nearby beach, friends, nature, and occasionally there was marijuana. There were also the slogans: "Be here now!" Rilke too, and the Carlos Castenada books. Even Aristotle advised, in *Nicomachean Ethics* (1.8), that pleasures should not adorn life like a necklace, but that life itself should be pleasurable. Of course we didn't notice that he went on to say that the highest pleasure is contemplation! It was a good time to be young, or young enough. I was limited only by the necessity of acting in such a way that custody of my children was not threatened.

Drug experience: In order to be profitable, as opposed to recreational, the mind must first be thoroughly stocked through long and committed study of great thinkers (not entertainment). The drug will spin all the mind's contents into a dizzying (literally, nauseous) swirl, chaotic, but if one can manage to *stay with it*, it will reconfigure (like a kaleidoscope). The beauty was barely bearable, "nothing but beginning of terror we're still just able to bear."[6] The "richness of the mixture" is almost too much, but that doesn't matter at all. Because now you see, you *see*.

This was the era of protests at San Francisco State, the Hayakawa era. I took no part in the demonstrations; indeed, my adviser told me to go home and study there until peace was resumed. I was, however, at San Francisco State on a memorable day. Several hundred faculty members joined arms and walked steadily up the campus, while police with clubs marched down the campus from 19th Street. They were close to encountering each other when someone hauled large speakers to an upstairs window of one of the buildings and blasted the Beattles' "All You Need is Love." A few people started dancing, and others joined. The confrontation was avoided. It was a beautiful moment.

After my first divorce, when I was poor and alone, I learned to console myself by thinking of people who were rich and happy in love. Remembering this condition, recognizing its actual existence somewhere in the world, made me happy too. To imagine those feelings was to participate in them. That learning, over forty years ago, still helps me when I feel anguish over my inability to help my son, and suffer from the irony that I have spent my life teaching other people's children. But I *can* help others' children, and so I do. And I hope that, in the broader generosity of the universe, there will be someone who can help my son. I endeavor to rest in the knowledge of this "enough," enough to go around, enough for all, if we will only cease trying to stipulate from whom/where it must come, but simply wait with confidence and accept with gratitude.

---

6. Rilke, *Duino Elegies*, 1.

Plotinus said it most directly and winsomely:

> But if someone is able to turn around [from the sensible world] . . . he will see God and himself and the All; at first he will not see as the All, but then, when he has nowhere to set himself and determine how far he himself goes, he will stop marking himself off from all being and will come to the All without going out anywhere, but remaining there where the All is set firm.[7]

Or, as a line from *The Odyssey* expresses it, "The heart within me is not of iron but pitiful, even as thine."

Journal entry, November 23, 1967. It was one of those times when pressures seemed too much, my French exam was coming up, for which I was neglecting other studies, and Ricky was being horrid. I was experiencing the "mortal cold of the universe" (Camus). When I was putting Susan (eleven years old) to bed, she said, "Why don't you sleep with me tonight, or lie with me a while now and I'll put my arms around you and love you?" I couldn't. I came upstairs and started to study, but felt incredibly and painfully cold and alone, focused on the fact that I didn't have a man. Suddenly I realized how ridiculously stubborn I was acting. There was a warm little girl downstairs offering to hold me. I almost laughed at the absurdity of preferring to be alone and unhappy because I insisted on dictating the *sort* of person who could love me. I switched off the light and went right down and got in bed with Susan. I cried and she held me, warm and gentle.

There is enough if one is willing to accept it, not in the expected form, but in strange and surprising forms. The novels of Annie Tyler, Toni Morrison, Marilynne Robinson (and others), revolve around their characters' discovery that there is enough, and that they *can* work out a way to participate in it, that they may finally abandon the effort to wrest what they need from their lovers, friends, and families. This is what Augustine meant when he said, *I relaxed a little from myself* (cessavi de

---

7. Plotinus, *Ennead* 6.5.7.

me paululum; 7.14). The world contains enough, and the perception of this comes with a stunning awareness of beauty and a strong feeling of gratitude. There is plenty of love in the world. Sun loves me; there is music that *loves* me. Breezes and green things love me. I lack love only when I presume to set up the conditions under which I will accept it.

I struggled financially. I did not want the divorce, but I could not live with the alternative, which would mean continuing to live as I had lived, *trying to please*. I chose to have nothing to do with the divorce. I did not get a lawyer or go to court; I did not even know when the case was going to court; I simply signed the papers when they appeared. I received $250 a month for both children's support, and I worked in a yardage store, coming home every evening with my eyes watering from the dyes. The evening the divorce was granted Gene called me to tell me. The children were in bed and I was alone. He was in a bar and there were party noises behind him. I felt excluded from all the world's pleasure and fun. It was a low moment.

Nevertheless, I was happy. I felt free, and soon I was in love again. It was 1967, a volatile time in the San Francisco Bay Area. The hippie movement was still in its happy phase, with free concerts in Golden Gate Park on Sunday afternoons at which Susan and I danced in the sun. I had friends, and I was able to finish my BA Despite difficulties, life was good.

My son was terribly disturbed by our divorce. Although divorce was common among his friends' parents, Ric experienced our divorce as the end of his world, the world in which he felt safe. He was bitter and hostile. I was financially unable to maintain the house Gene and I had bought, so Gene lived there. Ric chose to live with him so he could continue in the same school and with his basketball team. Although I had custody of our children, I accepted this. I had become frightened that I would soon be unable to manage Ric. He did not obey, and at the age of ten he was already physically stronger than I. I was frightened of his anger, and I failed to interpret it accurately as a signal that he needed help. Instead I regressed into my parents' diagnosis: I thought he was simply naughty. I hoped that he would "snap out of it"—also their language. Did I do the best I could under the circumstances? Probably, but "the best I could" was not enough.

Over the intervening years I have sorted—alone or with a therapist—the false guilt and the true guilt from this period of my life. False guilt comes from not recognizing that there were circumstances over which I had no control and in which I could not have done differently, and from ignoring the fact that I was not the only influence or person responsible for Ric. True guilt relates to distraction, inattentiveness, and poor judgment. There was some of both. I have tried to release the false guilt, while taking responsibility for the true guilt. I had the intellectual tools to interpret Ric's bad behavior as a cry for help, but in my emotional and financial distress, I weakly reverted to old ways of thinking. Only much later did I realize that *strength is a choice*. It is not that one simply *is* strong or weak in particular circumstances: one can *choose* to be strong. I didn't know that then. Or I felt too much fear. In any case, I did not get him professional help. I was distracted by working, going to school, and my second marriage. This is grounds for real guilt.

> How does one apologize for being a failure? When it's so pointless, so redundant. When might a human being reasonably be allowed to forego "I'm sorry," and say only to another human being, leaping past apology like an arrow, "Forgive me. I loved you."[8]

The fundamentalist's daughter had not recovered from repression sufficiently to identify sex as part of my self. It always seemed to threaten the fragile self I was slowly building. Sex was the last part of my life to become part of my self. Augustine, however, came to think of his desires, both for professional success and for sex, as God's method for shaping his life.

> You . . . were urging me to change countries for the salvation of my soul. In Carthage you prepared goads for me so that I should be driven from the place, and at Rome you provided attractions which would draw me there. . . . You were dragging me by the force of my own desires. (5.8)

---

8. Dressler, *Deadwood Beetle*, 68.

Staying Is Nowhere

After completing my BA at San Francisco State University, I married my second husband, a poet who became a community college teacher. He was eight-and-a-half years younger than I. My daughter, by now twelve years old, lived with us, while my son lived with his father. Susan and her friends were wild little girls, drinking, smoking marijuana, and occasionally taking LSD. Her friends' parents did not know what their daughters were doing, but I thought it better to know, and to provide a safe place for my daughter. Given the time—the 1960s—and the place—Marin County, California—I had no hope that I could stop her. Indeed, within a couple of years she had had enough and calmed down to a steady boyfriend and an interest in cooking.

I experienced nothing comparable to Augustine's struggles with Christian doctrine. He agonized over a long period about Christ's simultaneous divinity and humanity. Believing himself to be a broken-off fragment of divinity, Augustine thought of his flesh as alien cause of any evil in himself. *I was still of the opinion that it is not we ourselves who sin, but some other nature which is in us . . . something that was in me, but was not really I* (5.10). Interesting: Augustine thought that his sinful nature was alien to him; my mother thought that it was my "real self."

Because Augustine did not want to take responsibility for his actions, he told himself a false story about his own nature. The false story about his own nature caused his inability to understand the Christian doctrine of the Incarnation. Thus: *I was afraid to believe that he was born in the flesh lest I should be forced to believe that he was defiled by the flesh* (5.10). This is not the last Augustine's readers will hear about his problem with Christ's humanity. Nevertheless, disillusioned with Manichaeism, he decided to become a Catholic catechumen (5.14).

6 Mothers and Sons, Mothers and Daughters

It is difficult enough to breathe in and out, remain vertical, and remember one's temporary address.[1]
—KATE BRAVERMAN

AUGUSTINE LIED TO MONNICA AND slipped away from her in the night to sail from Carthage to Rome. He must have experienced great relief mingled with guilt when he left her, *frantic with grief,* weeping on the shore as his boat sailed. He blamed her for loving him *too much of the flesh* (5.8), and for her unwillingness to let him (and God) work out his future. Soon after arriving in Rome, Augustine was given a prestigious post in Milan. By now Monnica had joined him in Rome, and she followed him to Milan, still weeping and praying for him to become a Catholic Christian. With characteristic determination, she adjusted to the different religious practices she found there.

Visiting Bishop Ambrose whom they both, for different reasons, admired, Monnica and Augustine were astonished to find him reading silently, a practice unknown in Africa where the literate read aloud so that others who were not literate could hear. Augustine speculated as to why Ambrose read silently, concluding that he did so to save his voice.

---

1. Braverman, *Incantation of Frieda K.*, 98.

Mothers and Sons, Mothers and Daughters

He and Monnica sat in silence for *a long time, not venturing to interrupt him in his intense concentration on his task, and then* [they] *would go away again.* Augustine had no opportunity to question Ambrose about his intellectual quandaries. How, for example, could humans be created *in the image of God . . . who is everywhere in your entirety, yet limited by no particular space, yet you made man after your own image, and see, man is in space from head to foot* (6.3).

In Milan Augustine learned from Ambrose to read *in a different spirit,* [for] *the letter killeth, but the spirit giveth life.* Ambrose helped Augustine to get over his literalist reading of Scripture, which *appeared to be teaching what is wrong* (6.4). Still, reluctant to believe in case he believed wrongly, Augustine nevertheless *began to prefer the Catholic faith.* Realizing that he already believed many things that he had not seen, and of which he had no proof, he decided that he could commit to two beliefs: that God exists, and *that the government of human affairs is in your hands* (6.5).

> And now see, those things in the Scriptures which used to seem absurd are not absurd; they can be understood in a different and perfectly accurate way. I shall take my stand where my parents placed me as a child until I can see the truth plainly. But where shall I look for it? And when shall I look for it? . . . Where can I find the books? (6.11)

Learning *to read in a different spirit*: for me too, this was all-important. Augustine learned from Ambrose, who had learned from Origen, to read the spiritual meaning of Scripture, not its literal sense. Origen theorized that it is possible for the reader to enter fully into the same spirit that informed the author, and then he can interpret with great freedom. Similarly, I learned to read, not the *words*, but the *feeling* of the words. A part of the brain understands the words when it can define them. But this is the shallowest level of reading. I learned to *think with* the text, stopping to explore its range of meanings—the opposite of speed reading! Few texts are worth this kind of reading, however. This method, called *lectio divina*, was developed by medieval monks specifically for reading Scripture. Because as a child I was punished by being assigned to memorize portions of Scripture, Scripture has never attracted me. When I read it, a mechanical recitation voice emerges that cancels its deeper meaning. *The letter kills, but the spirit gives life*, Augustine quoted. The fundamentalist replies, "Ah, but a sin against the spirit always begins with a sin against the letter."

I was excited when I first read Augustine. I could *hear* him in a way I could not hear Scripture. That was partly because initially I read Augustine through the lens of my experience in psychotherapy, and I heard in Augustine a profound and nuanced language of the psyche.

> *I panted for honors, for money, for marriage, and you were laughing at me. I found bitterness and difficulty in following these desires, and your graciousness to me was shown in the way you would not allow me to find anything sweet that was not you.* (6.6)

Again Augustine's mixed metaphors shout his unhappiness: he was in *the gripping birdlime of death*, he says, and his *wounds were pricked on the quick*. Worrying about a coming event in which he would speak before the emperor, he noticed a drunk beggar who was *laughing and enjoying himself*. He envied the beggar for reaching a state that Augustine, with all his skill and efforts, had been unable to reach: *he was happy while I was worried; he was carefree while I was full of fears . . . . he was drenched in merriment while I was eaten up with anxieties*. He refuses to think that his learning makes him a better person than the beggar, and he knows that it does not make him a happier person: *I got no joy out of my learning* (6.6).

Unlike Augustine, I got intense joy out of my learning—out of learning itself. The size, moral quality, and feeling tone of the world increased exponentially with each book I read. I expressed my excitement in the metaphor of sight. I *saw* Aristotle's "golden mean," not as a watering down of two extremes to a diluted middle, but as a tensile holding together of both extremes in their full strength. I *saw* in the perfect body of the Artemesian Zeus the balanced poise possible to humans. I read such authors as Plato, Collingwood, Augustine, Wittgenstein, Camus, and Jonathan Edwards and *saw* the world as each of them saw it—or I thought I did. At least I brought as much intense excitement to reading as many authors do to writing. Unable to afford to buy books, I copied by longhand hundreds of pages of quotations and notes.

∾

My second husband, Edward, and I lived in beautiful places: a cabin on the beach, a cabin in the woods, (briefly) a house in the country with spacious lawns and a swimming pool, a house with tiny rooms and huge furniture built during the gold rush of the 1850s. These places gave me the calm and beauty that helped me complete my MA with minimal stress.

I had not attended church for about six years, since the separation and divorce from my minister husband. One Saturday I had a strange (and unwelcome) urge to go to church the next day. Since I scored low on impulsiveness on the Minnesota Multiphasic Personality Inventory, I have been trying to notice and honor my impulses. So the next day I went to a little red-spired Episcopal church in Sonoma. I enjoyed the quiet ritual of the liturgy, and we sang hymns (and said prayers) that my Granny could have sung (and said) in her English Anglican church. I liked the sense of being linked across generations, and I appreciated the anonymity of the clergy's robes—so different from my father in his navy blue suit. It was a powerful experience, so I continued to attend and eventually was confirmed and joined the Episcopal Church.

Most of the seven years of my second marriage were a time of enormous blossoming for me. I began to play a Renaissance lute. I had been struggling to play classical guitar, but my hand was too small to manage the difficult stretches required. I took lessons from a wonderful lutenist who specialized in lute song. Either singing or playing would have been difficult enough, but Donna Curry did both, and beautifully. I loved the gentle sound of the lute and practiced it faithfully. I never became fluent on the lute; it is, after all, a very difficult instrument. Closeted fundamentalists always choose the most difficult instrument to play (lute), the most difficult author to study (Augustine), and, eventually (but not yet in 1972), the most demanding place to teach (Harvard)!

I also painted with oils, mostly abstracts. I enjoyed *thinking* in colors and shapes. Painting is wonderful eye training. Painting a tree one suddenly notices that at least fourteen different shades of green are needed! I painted passionately, but again, I did not become very good at it. Nevertheless, there's nothing like attempting an art or skill to make one appreciate—notice and admire—those who do that art or skill well. Playing music and painting relieved my heavily verbal head, replacing words with notes and colors.

Ed and I traveled across Europe—my first trip to Europe. We went to Italy, Spain, Portugal, and spent a month on the Greek island of Cos. I am amazed at my travel journals; they say little about what we were seeing and experiencing; they are almost entirely about ideas, intricate philosophical ideas. It was a wonderful time, our only anxiety was shortage of money. But Europe was still fairly inexpensive in 1971, so we did well on the little money we had. Having to that point only seen European artworks in books, it was startling to me to see them "in the flesh," or in the bronze! Often art books fail to note the size of paintings and sculptures, so it surprised me sometimes to see paintings that I had thought were small were actually large, and sculptures I thought large, were small. Size matters! Artworks communicate differently according to their size.

Living in a whitewashed Greek house for the month of May 1971, I often sat in a little orchard next to our house to read. Occasionally a beekeeper came to tend his hives and I watched him. We did not speak but I learned a lot by watching and I began to want to keep bees. So when we returned to California, we did. The hive in the bedroom wall of our little house in Modesto swarmed, a huge sock of bees hanging from a low tree branch. Ed knocked them into a cardboard box and we ordered a hive from the Sears catalog. By the time it came, a week later, the bees had already sealed all the openings with their wax and were setting up their honey production.

We kept bees for the next five years or so, and I loved to lie naked by the hive in the sun, letting their constant OMMMM rest my mind. We took their honey from time to time, leaving them plenty for their own nourishment. I was usually stung once in the process—my dues. The bees were a source of pleasure and enchantment. There were many other pleasures too. In addition to writing poetry, Ed was a photographer, made wonderful beer, and taught film, so we saw many fine movies at home.

The community college district in which Ed taught had a rule that only one member of a family could hold a full-time teaching job in the district. There was no doubt as to who that would be. I was hired as an adjunct teacher and given courses that sometimes were cancelled for lack of enrollment after I had made extensive preparations for them. Because my master's degree was in Humanities, the Dean seemed to think that I could teach anything; I was given such courses as Semantics, World Religions, English Composition, and Science and the Humanities. Clearly, my coursework had not included all of these. I was scrambling, keeping one class ahead of the students. It was a very uncomfortable teaching situation.

There was some discrepancy between the reading list for my philosophy course and the "philosophy" the students wanted. However, I think that I seduced a few to prefer Plato to *Jonathan Livingston Seagull*. Disappointed in my part-time teaching, I decided to return to graduate study. I applied to the Graduate Theological Union, Berkeley, to study Augustine. I was accepted, and began the twice-weekly, three hundred mile roundtrip to Berkeley from Sonora, California, learning the requisite four languages as I drove. I held a card with vocabulary words and verb paradigms on the steering wheel, saying each word many times before I had to glance at the next, a practice I have never recommended to graduate students.

Much later, when I was teaching at Harvard, then-president Derick Bok was amused by the fact that I got my start teaching in California community colleges. He remarked on several occasions, "You can't get here from there!"

∽

Augustine believed that everything that happened to him was God's doing. Both his miseries and his joys were directly ordered by God. The closest I can come to seeing the hand of providence in the events of my life is to rejoice that I did not learn to type (without looking at the keys—still can't) in my youth. I am convinced that because I am not a high-risk person, had I learned to type I would still be somebody's secretary. Because I had no skills, I went to school.

∽

And lovemaking: There were what we called the "long times," three hours at a minimum. I had to be sure I would not be interrupted while I was "away," that I would not be unceremoniously jerked back suddenly into the ordinary. So doors had to be locked, telephones turned off, blinds drawn. There had to be enough time for me to go slowly into my body, to *get there*, and to come back gently afterwards into my head, where I live. Long enough to leave daily preoccupations, to gradually turn down, and then to turn off, the chatter in my head. To let go of all that busy head energy in order to gather it in my body. My demanding, insistent, aggressive mind must first be rocked to sleep. I knew it would take a long time, and I didn't try to hurry it. I knew that there would be time for staying with the strong pleasure. My image of those long times is from the *Epic of Gilgamesh:* when Humbaba slew the Bull of Heaven, the "blaze and the glory" that had been trapped in the Bull of Heaven was released. And it spread over the fields, the trees, and the streams. In the long times, the "blaze and the glory" in my head was released and spread over my body.

This happened in a very small room with a double mattress on the floor. In the bedroom wall a hive of bees made honey. Their OMMM and the smell of their rich strong honey made the room a secret and delicious place. And then, the slow touching. The great mutual generosity and kindness, the awareness that the other would some day die, and that this touching was a memorial to that day.

I had all that, those afternoons when we were not tired or hasty, when sheer white curtains turned slowly in a small breeze. Often I cried afterward because of mortality, nothing else; there is nothing else worth weeping over. Those afternoons spoiled me forever for the tired nights and hasty mornings that came later, spoiled me for lovemaking that was only about his body. From those afternoons I learned a standard I could never henceforth relinquish in order to match someone else's pace, someone else's urgency, someone else's desire. In Woody Allen's *Annie Hall*, Diane Keaton climbs out of her body while Woody is making love to her. Her astral body sits calmly on a chair, waiting until it's over, the sooner the better. A profoundly true filmic moment. All other sex than that of those long afternoons can be summed up in a line from Denis Arcand's film, *Jesus of Montreal*. Asked why she has sex with the priest, the woman replies, "Because it gives him so much pleasure, and me so little pain."

Again: "Staying is nowhere." Had I been happier teaching in community colleges—several of them, in order to put together a livable wage—I would have stayed. A full-time job, teaching subjects about which I knew something, would have made me happy *enough*. Instead, I learned Latin and returned to graduate school to study Augustine. Nobody I read or talked with liked Augustine or saw what I saw in his writings. He was the universal "bad guy," constantly and consistently caricatured as body-denying, world-rejecting, hierarchical, pleasure-rejecting—all the theological horrors of the 1970s. So, perversely, I tried to rehabilitate Augustine, demonstrating his profound and subtle mind, his commitment to love, and even his esteem for (what I then called) "the body."² The first seminar I taught in 1973, while still a doctoral student myself, was on Augustine, and so was the last seminar I taught before I retired in 2002.

I taught at Columbia Junior College in the Sierra foothills three days a week, commuting 141 miles each way twice a week to attend classes, gather the books I needed to prepare for the next week's classes, and return the same day to Columbia. On the way I learned French, Greek, Latin, and German vocabulary words. Or I "wrote" letters to my parents on the tape recorder, or, later, organized my dissertation on tape. No moments could be wasted, and most of the highway was very straight. I found that I arrived in Berkeley less fatigued from the long drive if I had accomplished something while I drove—a list of vocabulary words mastered, for example. The drive home was trickier because it was usually dark. But I had a friend, a professional harpsichordist, who lived approximately halfway between Berkeley and Columbia where I lived. Charlene frequently invited me to stop at her home for dinner and a private concert; those moments of beauty made all the difference in my ability to manage the drive.

One evening while I was at a class, Susan (twelve years old) was taking a shower and Ed took off his clothes and got into the shower with her. She ran to her bedroom, locked the door, and stayed there until I returned. For the next seven years, while I lived with Ed, there was hostility between Susan and Ed. It seemed that I was always trying to explain one to the other, but I had no idea about the cause of the hostility. She didn't tell me for seven years, until the night I left him. I asked her why she didn't tell, and she replied that at the time I was recently married, and that she didn't want to "burst my bubble." Sophocles' Antigone learned, as did I, that "from high good fortune in the blood blossoms the quenchless agony."

---

2. I try not to say "the body," a body no one has ever seen or touched, a generic, sexless entity. Our experience is of particular bodies, our own and others', always our own *among* others—animals, humans, and the earth's body.

Augustine's relationship with his mother is one of the major themes of Book 6. In other writings Augustine mentions briefly a brother and a sister, but in the *Confessions* it is as if Augustine were his mother's only preoccupation. His interpretation of her attention to him goes from considering her admonitions as the voice of God to him, to annoyance with her tears and persistence. She banned him from her home while he was a Manichaean, but was somewhat reassured by a priest who told her that the *son of these tears* would surely become a Catholic Christian. *I was washed in this water, the rivers of tears that flowed from my mother's eyes, tears daily shed for me that watered the ground below her downcast looks . . . . she labored with much greater pain to give me birth in the spirit than she had suffered when giving birth to me in the flesh* (5.8). A dream had assured her that *where she was, I was too* (3. 11). It was only a matter of time. But of course, no one knows that at the time.

As soon as he arrived in Rome, Augustine was struck with a mysterious illness. He nearly died, he wrote, from a fever that he was delivered from by his mother's tears and prayers, though she knew nothing of it. Sickness played a role in Augustine's life at several crucial junctures, as it did in mine. First, my ulcer forced me to get life-changing psychotherapy for the next seven years. During the period of my divorce I had another sickness in which I was semi-delirious for several days. As I lay on my bed I "saw" interactions between my parents, my siblings, and myself that helped me understand myself and my family of origin. During these scenes, I did not experience myself as thinking, but rather as being passively shown my parents' relationship with each other and with their children. I do not remember the content in detail, but these revelations came with strong feelings of vividness and accuracy. I recovered and retained the sense that my parents were no longer mysterious giants in my psyche, but flawed and frightened fellow pilgrims, suffering and struggling, and doing the best they could, even though, like my own best, it was often not good enough.

Augustine's society, like our own, featured entertainment in which bodies were publicly torn, mauled by wild beasts, sliced, stabbed, and killed. In Roman society, however, the sights, sounds, and smells of the coliseum were real, not simulated screen violence. No one in fourth-century Roman society could have been unaware of these so-called games, any more than a twenty-first-century person can be unaware of movies and television. Augustine's friend, Alypius, was obsessive in his fascination with these spectacles. Augustine gives a vivid account of Alypius's addiction: *He saw the blood and he gulped down savagery. Far from turning away, he fixed his eyes on it . . . . He drank in madness, he was delighted with the guilty contest, drunk with the lust of blood* (6.8).

The Roman Empire was the first entertainment culture, the first society to use entertainment to stimulate, reward, and pacify. The shows were free, and the Roman Coliseum, built in the first century CE, seated fifty thousand people, evidence that the gladiatorial and animal shows were indeed popular events. A mid-third-century calendar reserves 176 days of the year for spectacles, of which ten were specifically for gladiatorial and wild beast shows.[3]

---

3. Wiedemann, *Emperors and Gladiators*, 12.

Mothers and Sons, Mothers and Daughters

Emperors displayed power and gained popularity through lavish spending on shows featuring hundreds of gladiators, rare and exotic animals, and inventive stage sets.[4] In the morning of a commemoration of an emperor's birthday, for example, wild beast "hunts" occurred, involving the slaughter of animals brought from all parts of the empire at tremendous expense. At noon, most spectators took a lunch break while criminals and prisoners were unceremoniously executed. In the afternoon, gladiators fought, often to the death. Latin literature occasionally indicates that coliseum crowds empathized with wounded animals, but it is never mentioned that they experienced a similar sympathy with suffering humans.

Why did Roman crowds enjoy these bloody spectacles? Historians offer several possible reasons: the crowd context minimized individual feelings of responsibility for victims' suffering, and the class stratifications of Roman society identified "humanity" with the upper classes, while people of the lower classes were considered worthless, their bodies fair game for violent spectacle. But perhaps most importantly, the murderous games of the Coliseum were thought of as sports.[5] Their violence was not the point. The point was the gladiators' skill, style, and his mastery of himself and his body. According to historian J. P. Toner, a Coliseum crowd was "not a bloodthirsty mob but the most urbane sophisticates in the world."[6] They recognized, appreciated, and rewarded courage and skill, not merely brute strength.

American society exhibits some interesting parallels. Our society, like that of ancient Rome, depends on its entertainment media. Spectator sports are also a huge part of our entertainment. But the state no longer sponsors free events; citizens support them at the expense of billions of dollars annually. Sports heroes appear on our billboards, newspapers, and magazines; their faces are at least as familiar to us as Roman gladiators' faces were to Romans. For North Americans also, bodies are spectacle.

Fundamentalists are wary of entertainment, a trait I consciously retain, albeit with a different rationale than those I heard as a child. I

---

4. Futrell, *Blood in the Arena*, 10: "The amphitheater must be viewed in association with Roman Imperialism as a conscious means of persuasion of the legitimacy, supremacy, and potential for violence of the Roman State."

5. Hopkins, "Murderous Games," 27.

6. Toner, *Leisure and Ancient Rome*, 39.

am suspicious of entertainment's underlying agenda, which is much the same as that of ancient Rome; namely, it is a reward for performing the work needed to maintain the society. Unlike Romans, Americans pay dearly for entertainment, from pornography to sports events. Media's ability to train Americans to consumer values is stronger than in any society in the history of the world.

My tale is also that of a mother and a son. I was the mother, weeping not over my son's religious choices, but over his unwillingness or inability to grow up, take responsibility for himself, and support himself. The way *I* tell it is that I kept him alive for thirty of his adult years, until he was fifty. In the language and wisdom of our society, however, I "enabled" him to abuse alcohol and drugs. I repeatedly pled with him to use the help available in our society, and over the years, he agreed to three month-long detoxification and rehabilitation programs. These were my idea though, not his, so of course he/they didn't work. He merely took month-long vacations from the harshness of his alcoholic life. He also agreed to psychotherapy, but after more than a year, his therapist called to tell me that he thought I should know that 90 percent of what I was paying for was missed appointments. For thirty years I inhabited some point on the cycle of hope and despair, endeavoring not to allow myself to be overcome by these feelings since I also had important and interesting work to do.

How can we seek happiness, Augustine asked, unless we have had some experience of it? His proposed method was to gather memories of pleasure—any old pleasures will do—and put them together to build a feeling of the happiness we all, yes, every human being seeks. Even, said Pascal, the person who hangs himself. I have slowly learned that moments of pleasure, if I am attentive to them, provide uniquely valuable information about who I am, what I long for, what makes me happy. Pleasures testify to the range and depth of a person's desires, even furtive and guilty pleasures, pleasures that derail and destabilize "my own favorite character in fiction." Perhaps the "self" is not a simple entity, but a multiple, contradictory, polymorphously perverse, messy aggregate of longings and fears.

But far from defining myself by my pleasures, I sometimes act as if I believe that it is really my *suffering* that will save me. I *tell* my suffering; I don't tell my pleasures. What I want is recognition that I *suffer*. I identified the (fundamentalist) origin of the part of me that enjoys—and advertises—suffering when I was in graduate school. Browsing in a bookstore I noticed a sentence that said that people emphasize and dwell on whatever feature of our lives we think is redemptive. I realized with a start that a piece of my fundamentalist psyche, unexamined through years of psychotherapy, stubbornly believed that I would get to heaven through suffering. That, despite my sins, I would be welcomed into heaven because I had *suffered so much*. I recognized further that the selected arena for my suffering was relationships, especially with men, but also with my family. I resolved to stop suffering. But easier said than done.

Someone has said that pain is inevitable, but suffering is voluntary. Upon leaving a concert in which the program notes had opined that there is too much suffering in the world, John Cage remarked that, on the contrary, there is just the right amount. He was wrong. The "right amount" is suffering from which one can learn, and there's far more than that in the world. Only for (a few) enormously privileged people is there just the right amount of suffering.

While I was being reviewed for tenure at Harvard I returned to psychotherapy for several months. I did this primarily in order to spare my friends my repetitive rants. My therapist, reflecting on my pressures and anxieties, and my lack of pleasures—or time for pleasures—said, "Why, you're suffering from malnutrition!" Yes and no. I adapted. I learned to distribute my longings for nourishment, to get small bites from many people, to eat delicate, disciplined meals in many relationships rather than to banquet greedily at one table. I taught myself to take my pleasure through various senses, to see, hear, taste, and touch beauty. Oh, there was loss, of course. But there was also gain. I missed the long times and the beautiful quiet places I had lived, but having *had* them, they stay with me; they are mine to keep.

Terrified by my sins and the mass and weight of my misery, I had pondered in my heart a purpose of flight to the wilderness (10.43). But God gave him strength, Augustine says, for the strenuous work ahead.

He was not granted the luxury of flight, but shortly after ordination, he obtained permission for a leave in order to study Scripture. Those months, in which he stored up energy and knowledge, were of the greatest importance to him. My several years in Philo, California, were, for me, a similar time. Quiet reading, wandering in woods and meditating by a river, with frequent trips to the nearby Pacific Ocean, living on very little money: these set a standard of simplicity and beauty I have not forgotten and have endeavored to weave through the busy life in public spaces that followed.

Augustine thought that in order to fully accept Christian faith, he would have to give up his profession, his aspirations, and his hopes for marriage, all things he had passionately desired. He lets his reader eavesdrop on his thoughts.

> *But wait! These worldly things are too sweet; the pleasure they give is not inconsiderable; we must not be too hasty about rejecting them, because it would be a shame to go back to them again. Now think: it would not be difficult to get some high official appointment, and then what more could I want? . . . Then I should marry a wife with money . . . . And then I should have nothing more to desire. There have been many great men, well worth imitating, who have devoted themselves to the pursuit of wisdom and have also been married.* (6.11)

Augustine could not imagine himself celibate: *I believed that continency was something which depended on one's own strength, and I knew that I had not enough strength for it* (6.11). Awash in self-pity, Augustine and his friends, *sighing and complaining,* made no decisions. *My soul,* he wrote, *turned over and over, back and side and front, and always the bed was hard and you alone are rest* (6.15). Book 1 of the *Confessions* begins with the restlessness (*inquietum*) of the insomniac; Augustine returns to this image at the end of Book 6, adding more detail to the picture of the insomniac, turning this way and that, unable to find comfort and rest. His condition had worsened significantly by his thirtieth year.

California in the 1970s was the culture of "I want it all now." It was a bad time and place for marriage. It was a time of experimentation, with little encouragement for conventional marriage. One day Ed announced that he wanted an "open marriage." I did not. So we separated and I moved to Berkeley to continue and complete my doctoral program.

In writing this chapter I realized that the story I had been telling myself about my life was inaccurate—or only partially true. In my mind I had reduced my second marriage to two book-end incidents: close to the beginning, Ed's move on twelve-year-old Susan, and at the end, Ed wanting an "open marriage." But even more egregiously I had omitted the great blossoming of my life during this time: The painting, the lute playing, the European travel, keeping bees . . . I acknowledged the wonderful sex. But there was so much else. Those two incidents at the beginning and end of the marriage should not represent the whole. "It's the richness of the mixture," Saul Bellow's hero, *Henderson the Rain King*, mutters. It's not the pains and the problems alone that boggle the mind and defy description, but the *richness*, the life—the beauty *and* the pain that must somehow be told together because they are inextricably interwoven.

7 *Relaxing from Myself—a Little*[1]

I breathed in you a little.
—AUGUSTINE[2]

BOOK 7 OF AUGUSTINE'S *CONFESSIONS* is largely about his intellectual problems and his development toward Christian faith. His discussion illustrates the limits of intellectual understanding without emotional conviction. It also reveals that intellectual understanding is intimately connected to one's experience and how one interprets that experience. His main theological problem was his inability to understand how God could become human without entailing devastating compromise to his divinity. God's weakness in wearing our *coats of skin* required an acceptance of bodies that Augustine did not have when he was thirty years old. He recommended "humility" highly; later he said in a letter: "The way is firstly humility, secondly humility, and thirdly humility."[3] But he seems to have thought of humility solely as an intellectual virtue.

The young Augustine distinguished intellectual "humility" from the "humiliation" of embodiment. *I had not the faintest notion of the mystery contained in 'The Word was made flesh,'* he acknowledged (7.18). It was in struggling to understand the doctrine of Christ's incarnation

---

1. Augustine *Confessions* 7.14.
2. *Confessions* 13.14.
3. Augustine *Epistula* 118.

that he came to place a different value on bodies and their needs. "Take away death, the last enemy, and my own flesh shall be my dear friend throughout eternity."[4] Recognizing the humble Jesus who *ate, drank, slept, walked, was glad, was sad* [and] *preached,* helped him see that it was precisely in his human weakness that Jesus mediated between God and human.

> He built for himself a humble dwelling out of our clay, by means of which he might detach from themselves those who were to be subdued and bring them over to himself, healing the swelling of their pride and fostering their love, so that instead of going further in their own self-confidence they should put on weakness, seeing at their feet divinity in the weakness that it had put on by wearing our "coat of skin." (7.18)

"Humility" is a word that no longer has positive meanings. In contemporary usage it usually is understood to mean abjection, low self-esteem, or lack of self-confidence. Yet, as Augustine used it, the word had powerfully positive meanings. In this, and many other instances, language is a poor tool of communication; words—the same words—change their meanings dramatically across time.[5] A close reading of the contexts in which Augustine advocated humility indicates that by it he meant something like receptivity, an intellectual and emotional posture inviting learning, an attentiveness in which others' perspectives are generously entertained, listening not for what the author *said*, but for what she *meant*. Augustine's "humility" is about getting over oneself sufficiently to be free to be attentive to other people and the world.

Augustine sought Truth, and he thought that once he had arrived at it *in the flash of a trembling glance* (7.17). All he could articulate about this brief insight was that truth is unchangeable and infinitely to be preferred to anything changeable. This meant, of course, that because the very definition of human life and the earth is change, nothing in ordinary human experience can be considered truthful. Truth is always and necessarily abstract, a goal never to be fully achieved. Yet happiness, Augustine's highest priority, depended on living in *the Truth*. For him,

---

4. Augustine *Sermon* 155.15.

5. An example of a word's dramatic change of meaning across time: "gratitude" in Middle English meant "resentment."

a certain detachment from physical, emotional, and social investment was essential to the attempt to live *in Truth*.

> It shouldn't be surprising that in the manner of seeing permitted to us in this life, "through a glass, darkly," our struggle to see at all must be a hard one.[6]

In both professional (academic) life and personal life, a defining ingredient of humility is acknowledgment that all human beings necessarily make choices and act while lacking essential knowledge. "We are not isolated free choosers, monarchs of all we survey," Iris Murdock wrote, "but benighted creatures sunk in a reality whose nature we are constantly and overwhelmingly tempted to deform by fantasy."[7] Augustine noticed and felt sympathy with the inadequate condition in which humans must choose and act.

Augustine has often been both vilified and praised for his development of the doctrine of original sin so essential to fundamentalists. As discussed in chapter 1, he thought he saw sinfulness in the infant's first *intentional* act—recall the jealous infant at the breast. But later in his career he had a more subtle analysis. Approximately twenty years after he wrote the *Confessions* he figured out why people with the best intentions nevertheless cannot be "perfectly righteous." In *The Spirit and the Letter*, he described the factors that prevent right action.

> Perfect integrity . . . would come about if there were brought to bear the will sufficient for such an achievement, and that might be if all the requirements of integrity were known to us, and if they inspired in the soul such delight as to overcome the obstacle set by other pleasures and pains . . . . For we are well aware that the extent of a person's knowledge is not in his own power, and that he will not follow what he knows to be worth pursuing unless he delight in it no less than it deserves his love . . . . "For we see now through a glass darkly, but then face to face." . . . So, as it appears to me, . . . much progress in this life has been made by that one who knows by his progress how far he is from the perfection of integrity.[8]

---

6. Augustine *De trinitate* 15.16.
7. Murdock, "Against Dryness," 293.
8. *The Spirit and the Letter*, 64.

Relaxing from Myself—a Little

We do not have sufficient knowledge, nor can we choose which objects will attract and delight us.[9] Therefore, the humility that recognizes that we—and others—do the best we can, in the dark and cold, is necessary. Willingness to forgive is an important aspect of humility. We must repeatedly forgive ourselves, and we often must forgive others. Lest we forgive ourselves and others easily and automatically, however, self-criticism and criticism is also important—that is, self-criticism preceding criticism of others.

We ought always to inquire not only about the content of a belief, but also about its *effects*. Augustine's doctrine of original sin can have some interesting effects. If a person walks around with the belief that people are fundamentally sinful, what you tend to notice are unexpected and gratuitous acts of kindness and generosity. These acts startle because they are in conflict with your theory of human nature. If, however, you think that people are fundamentally good, you tend to be disagreeably jarred by bad acts because *these* are in conflict with your theory of human nature.

My own intellectual development as a young adult was not focused on a search for *the Truth*. Rather I began to realize that the ideas and assumptions I lived with (and by) should enable me to see the world and other people with the loving generosity Augustine called "humility." Humility, loving generosity, became my goal both in my professional life and in my personal relationships.

Taking a word or a concept that he very evidently thought important, I sought to understand it in relation to my own world. The following quotations illustrate how I began to understand what humility would look like in my professional life as a historian.

> Respect for fellow historians . . . requires a presumption that others are thinking, searching, and writing in good faith, a willingness to consider arguments [and evidence] on their own terms before offering alternative "frames of reference," and an obligation to paraphrase those arguments fully and fairly in the process of criticizing.[10]

9. Ibid.

10. Ribuffo, "Confessions of an Accidental (or Perhaps Overdetermined) Historian," 147.

A fundamental assumption underlies fair scholarship:

> Someone with whom we disagree may be drawing on very different cultural resources than our own. Although that person's disagreement may feel like a blow to our grandiosity or ideals, we can minimize the hurt and assimilate it more easily . . . if we realize that the opposing viewpoint expresses less a desire to upset us than a piece of a complex and interrelated view of the world and manifestations of the person's own past.[11]

The traditional scholarly strategy of demolishing others' interpretations in order to spotlight the greater veracity and beauty of one's own is inadequate and unkind.

> . . . the only thing that can displace an intellectual world is another intellectual world—a new alternative, rather than an argument against the old alternative . . . . I do not think that demonstrations of "internal incoherence" or of "presuppositional relationships" ever do much to disabuse us of bad old ideas or institutions. Disabusing gets done, instead, by offering us sparkling new ideas or utopian visions of glorious new institutions. The result of genuinely original thought, in my view, is not so much to refute or subvert our previous beliefs as to help us forget them by giving us a substitute for them.[12]

The discovery of the central importance of perspective created a sea change in scholarship in the last half-century. That *all* people see the world through lenses crafted by our social location, race, sex, education, and sensitivities had not, until recently, been recognized. Until women, people of color, and many others who had not formerly participated in scholarship came into institutions of higher learning and began to share in reality-defining discourse, it had been generally assumed that the perspectives of educated white men were normative. Although the formerly privileged often feel the change as "the end of civilization as we knew it," recognition of the centrality of perspective distributes the privilege of interpretation. To acknowledge the importance of perspective is, in brief, to understand Augustine's idea of humility.

In personal life, cultivating a positive humility essentially means *not knowing* about things I do not know. Augustine insisted that from

---

11. Dixon, *Scattered and Gathered Self*, 392.
12. Rorty, "Is Derrida a Transcendental Philosopher?" 208–9.

Relaxing from Myself—a Little

the appearance of an act, *we cannot be sure what the real motive was* (3.9). We surely do one another more harm out of the various fears that lead us to ascribe hurtful motives to others than we do out of evil intent. The fundamental commitment to the other, whether a stranger or someone we love dearly, is to *hear* what the other tells us.

∾

Augustine obsessed on the problem of evil. *Suffocated* by his irresolvable thoughts, he *struggled on* to understand the origin of evil: *What agonies I suffered, what groans, my God, came from my heart in its labor!* (7.3). The problem, as he understood it, had two distinguishable aspects. First, the right attitude and approach is essential. A sort of intellectual *hubris*, coupled with preoccupation with *inferior things, swarmed around me on all sides in clouds,* and *when I tried to think, these bodily images stood in my way and prevented me. . . . I was separated from you by the swelling of my pride. It was as though my cheeks had swollen up so that I could not see out of my eyes* (7.5).

Pride is the opposite of humility; it is the stubborn intransigence that prohibits attentiveness and learning. Here, as elsewhere, Augustine used images of physical swelling to describe pride. When he finally came to his famous conclusion that *there is no such thing as evil*, his image is not of straining every nerve, but of relaxation: *[Y]ou laid your kindly hand upon my head so that I should not see falsehood, and then I relaxed a little from myself* (7.14).

Second, Augustine sought to understand the cause of evil (7.3-5). Refusing to think of God as source of evil, he floundered, for he knew that nothing *exists* that was not created. Round and round he goes with the characteristic pinched reasoning that always fails to yield his objective. Still asking, *What is the origin of evil?* he feels his question physically, emotionally, and intellectually: *What agonies I suffered, what groans, my God, came from my heart in my labor!* Even his closest friends could not know the extent of his *roarings and groanings* (7.7).

Finally, he broke through to an understanding that things that exist can suffer corruption, but everything that exists, *so long as it exists, is good; all things that are, are good.* Evil *is not a substance, since, if it were a substance it would be good.*

> *So I saw plainly and clearly that you made all things good, nor are there any substances at all that you have not made. And because you did not make all things equal, therefore they each and all have their existence; because they are good individually, and at the same time they are altogether very good. . . . To you, then, there is no such thing at all as evil.*

Is *peccatum mundi* (as in *agnus dei qui tollis peccatum mundi*) the same as Augustine's original sin? *Peccatum mundi* doesn't carry the intensely personal guilt of original sin. *Peccatum mundi* isn't actually what we think of as sin, much less sins; it is mortality and the cumulative heaviness, the dark undertow, of human life. Some feel it more than others. Tertullian accurately called it *vitium originalis*—weakness, evisceration, a quasi-physical weight like very high humidity. It is Luther's "wrath of God," against which one must struggle in order to approach the merciful God; it is Calvin's torpor, lethargy, inertia. Augustine described it very powerfully as a combination of restless insomnia and lethargy. *Peccatum mundi* is the weight of the world. Augustine described it as informed by fear:

> *I was frightened . . . . The pack of this world was a kind of weight upon me, as happens in sleep . . . [I was] like someone who tries to get up but so overcome with drowsiness that he sinks back again into sleep . . . . I could find nothing at all to say except lazy words, spoken half-asleep . . . . For the law of sin is the strong force of habit.* (8.5)

Bodies participate in *peccatum mundi* in aching, in small pains, and eventually in disease and death.

∽

Maxine Sheets-Johnstone describes multiple efforts by philosophers and anthropologists to identify some "uniquely human" attribute. She shows that it cannot be walking upright, for chimpanzees are far better at walking upright than humans are at brachiating one hundred feet in the air in a rainforest. Chimps also use the opposable thumb that permits grasping and wielding tools. It cannot be intelligence, for apes' rationality, intelligence, and ability to think through to a solution of a problem have been well documented. Chimps also raise their young, disciplining them when they violate the rules of the community. In short, "any affirmation of human uniqueness spelled out in terms of behavioral, *morphological*, or genetic differences appears doomed."[13] "To describe the nature of human being-in-the-world is necessarily to situate it in the reality of animate being-in-the-world."[14] An existential-evolutionary perspective assumes that there are no breaks in evolution, that humans develop from our biological ancestors; unique features do not happen *ex nihilo* in human beings. I wonder if Augustine would say that the "endowment" of original sin is the only attribute unique to humans.

The existence of evil has never been puzzling to me or seemed to demand a theory of human nature. The categories of "good" and "evil" are too crude to articulate the complexities of human nature. Even if acts can sometimes be categorized as good or bad, *people* can't. All of us fail while earnestly doing our best, but we also have moments in which our inadequate best results in good that we could not have anticipated.

"When music was difficult to find, it was very powerful," wrote novelist Arthur Phillips.[15] The same could be said for books. *Where can I find the books?* Augustine moaned. Books, the right books, are perhaps perennially difficult to find. They were for me, but when I found them, they were very powerful. Most of them came to me as suggestions from friends. In *Reading for Life* I describe seven books from which I learned enormously. "I was on fire," Augustine wrote of his reading of Cicero's *Hortensius* when he was nineteen—not too strong a description of my own avid reading. Later I learned to be critical of books, to read suspiciously, asking how authors' perspectives directed their interests and knowledge. I learned to notice what is *not* in the text, as well as what is there. But beyond critical and sympathetic readings, I was solidly hooked by what can be learned *for life* from books.

Because of my experience of being cured of a painful ulcer by psychotherapy, I began reading psychology. I read all of Freud and Jung that had been translated into English, probably understanding very

---

13. Sheets-Johnstone, "Existential Fit and Evolutionary Continuities," 66.
14. Ibid., 67.
15. Phillips, *Prague*, 294.

little because I lacked any intellectual context. But I was fascinated by analysis of the workings of that vivid kaleidoscope, the human psyche. Gradually I began to see that neither clinical nor theoretical psychology addressed my search for orientation in the universe. So I read philosophy, beginning with Plato. The *Republic*'s allegory of the cave frightened me and called my attention to the high level of self-deception many (or most, or almost all) humans find not only tolerable and comfortable but necessary. Aristotle's *Nicomachean Ethics* called me powerfully to the well-lived life. His proposal of the "golden mean," I understood, was neither a shaving off, nor a dilution of two extremes to a watery middle, but a tensive *holding together* of extremes.

I read Augustine for the first time in the 1960s in a special study course at San Francisco State University with the Humanities Department Chair, Matthew Evans. This was not, for me, a literary experience. Augustine's passion, the violence of his no-holds-barred search for Truth, and—not least—his rich Latin prose fascinated and captivated me. By the time I read Peter Brown's powerful biography, *Augustine of Hippo*, I was teaching at a California community college in the Sierra foothills.

So now my passion was all for Augustine. He combined the ancient philosophers I had read with the scriptural and theological language that had shaped my childhood. I understood for the first time that twentieth-century philosophers and psychologists were not the first to create an articulate and nuanced language of the psyche. Augustine had already done so, combining philosophical and theological ideas with religious passion.

But modern authors who wrote about Augustine almost unilaterally blamed him for despising bodies and the natural world, for "dualism" and for hierarchical thinking. They accused "Neoplatonism," especially Plotinus, of conveying these ideas and attitudes to Augustine. I became curious about this seemingly invariable consensus. So I wrote my doctoral dissertation, *Augustine on the Body*, in order to figure out his puzzling statements about bodies. I found that he alone of all Christian authors of his culture and generation *worried* that Christian affirmations of body, so explicitly articulated by doctrines of creation, incarnation, and the resurrection of body, did not fit well with the classical model of human beings as stacked components, body on the bottom, irrational soul above, and rational soul on top. Although he did not have the philosophical tools to resolve the dilemma of an accurate and adequate model of the human medley, he brought the problem to the attention of Christian authors who subsequently struggled with it—to our own time. His reviewers are justified in seeing his resolution as inadequate in that he never managed to include bodies' most intimate and pleasurable activity—sex—in his esteem for body. Nevertheless, he should be acknowledged for identifying that there was a problem with classical understandings of body and working on it throughout his career.[16]

I read Plotinus in order to figure out whether multiple allegations that Augustine was influenced (and marred) by Neoplatonic dualism were accurate.[17] I found that Plotinus and Augustine shared the problem of the ambiguity of bodies, *both* "lowest rung" on the ladder of value and *starting place* for spiritual ascent. Both professed respect and admiration for bodies, but both could, on occasion, also insist that bodies are distracting and must be "overlooked," literally, looked over. Significantly, Plotinus's harshest statements about bodies occur in his latest (chronological) treatise, when he was nearing death and needed to persuade himself that bodies are nothing but an epiphenomenon of human being.

To make a very long story short, Christian authors usually resolved the question of the meaning and value of bodies ambivalently and confusingly. They disparage bodies when they are exhorting readers to look beyond bodies *at all*, and they praise bodies to the skies when they discuss creation, incarnation, and resurrection of body as the Christian's ultimate reward. This ambivalence means that prooftexts are not reliable; but *as a rhetorical strategy*, it is understandable. Nothing depends more for meaning on context than body.

Plotinus influenced Augustine in a much more central way, however. He understood the universe to be pervasively characterized by its

16. For more on Augustine's revaluation of body, see Miles, *Augustine on the Body*.

17. Gerson, *Aristotle and Other Platonists*, 61. Of course, Plotinus did not think of himself as a "Neoplatonist"—a seventeenth-century term. Rather, he thought of himself as a faithful interpreter of Plato, but also as needing to address the questions about Plato's philosophy that had been raised by Aristotle, himself a Platonist (as Gerson has demonstrated). After a lengthy discussion of various proposals of the components of the human person, Gerson concludes that while Plato and Aristotle shared the *problem* of describing the relationship of body and soul, both taught that "body is a tool or possession of the soul and that the soul is the true person."

source in the great beauty (*mega kalon*). For Plotinus, all living creatures emanate from the One, for whom he has various interchangeable names (among them God, the Father, as well as the great beauty). They are sustained in being by the One, who "does not give and pass, but gives on forever." Similarly, for Augustine, creation witnesses to God the Creator by its *beauty*.

> And what is this God? I asked the earth and it answered: "I am not he," and all things that are on the earth confessed the same. I asked the sea and the deeps and the creeping things with living souls, and they replied: "We are not your God. Look above us." . . . And I said to all these things that lie about the gates of our senses, "Tell me about my God. Tell me something about him." And they cried out in a loud voice: "He made us." My question was in my contemplation of them, and their answer was in their beauty. (10.6)

The ability to perceive beauty has little to do with appreciating art, sunsets, or brides. It is not born in humans, but as spiritual exercise it can be developed, trained, and exercised. Beauty is a gift of the universe, an ethical resource that sponsors and incites a response of loving generosity—humility. Plotinus said, "Beauty is reality."

What do we mean when we say that we "believe in God"? The question has two parts: First, what is the "God" we say we believe in? Second: what is the act of belief? I answer (for myself) the first question in this way: Augustine had three ways of describing God. First, he said that anyone who thinks of God as anything *other than* "life itself" has an absurd notion of God.[18] His second definition of God was: "God is love," and he added, that's *all* you need to know about God.[19] Third, he called God Beauty (*pulchritude tam antique et tam nova*; 10.27). For Augustine, God is life, love, and beauty.

What about belief? In what sense does one believe in life, love, and beauty? What we see, we don't need to believe, and don't we *see* each of these? Take each in turn: First, how does one "believe in" life? According to Augustine, a moment of belief *is* required. He said that we don't

---

18. Augustine *De doctrina Christiana* 1.8.

19. Augustine, *Homilies on the First Epistle of John*, 8th homily; see also *Sermon* 34.3.5.

actually *see* life; we experience our own life and from that experience, we *infer* that of others.[20] Similarly, we do not actually *see* love. We see people *acting* in ways we think of as loving, and we (rightly or wrongly) *infer* love. Augustine wrote: *She sees him, he sees her, no one sees love.*[21] Again, an act of belief is required to get from what we see to the existence of love.

And beauty? We certainly see beauty, but still, Augustine said, the beauty we see is not God.

> *But what do I love when I love you? Not the beauty of the body, nor the glory of time, not the brightness of light shining so friendly to the eye, not the sweet and various melodies of singing, not the fragrance of flowers and unguents and spices, not manna and honey, not limbs welcome to the embraces of the flesh; it is not these that I love when I love my God. And yet I do love a kind of light, melody, fragrance, food, embracement, when I love my God; for he is the light, the melody, the fragrance, the food, the embracement of my inner self—there where is a brilliance that space cannot contain, a sound that time cannot carry away, a perfume that no breeze disperses, a taste undiminished by eating, a clinging together that no satiety will sunder. This is what I love when I love my God.* (10.6)

Not until a person contemplates visible beauty *with the question,* "tell me about my God," does natural beauty become *evidence.* Until then, it just "is what it is." Here too then, an act of belief gets a person from natural beauty to created beauty and its creator.

So, there is sense in the statement that I "believe in" life, love, and beauty. And, of course, we are strongly assisted in belief by *seeing* indications that support our inferences. So belief consists of the act of inferring. Does it add something to call life, love, or beauty "God?" Perhaps inferring God from these seen factors simply acknowledges that they are gifts, unearned and with no guarantees, for which the appropriate response is gratitude.

---

20. Augustine *City of God* 22.29; cf. *De trinitate* 8.6. Similarly, centuries later the English philosopher George Berkeley said that we do not actually see life; we see movement and we *infer* life; *Concerning Human Knowledge* # 148.

21. *Serm.* 34.3.5; Przywara, *An Augustine Synthesis,* 354.

Augustine and the Fundamentalist's Daughter

What about the motivation of delight? Is there a way that delight can be, if not created, at least cultivated? I think it can. We can conspire to sit next to someone who *loves* the object we would like to find delightful. Delight is contagious; like a disease, one *catches* it from someone who has it! Whether in conversation, in a classroom, in a museum, or even in a book, delight is communicable. As a student and teacher I have found that warm bodies in a room circulate delight in learning among the participants. As an undergraduate I learned to find ancient Greek sculpture delightful from a teacher who, in his short rotund body and coffee- and cigarette-stained shirt and tie, took the pose of the Artemesian Zeus. The tension and power of the pose was perfectly communicated in this unlikely imitation, and the sense in which this sculpture *stood for* ancient Greek culture became palpable to me.

We must bend easily lest we break.[22]

Augustine, a small-town boy from the provinces, assumed that more cosmopolitan thinkers than he had the answers. He expected to be educated and enlightened by individuals like Faustus the Manichaean, but when Faustus came to town, Augustine was disappointed. Although Faustus knew his literature, he was no philosopher; thus, Augustine's burning questions remained unanswered. So he turned to books. He had been stymied in his effort to imagine a God who was not "diffused through space," and his voracious reading of *those books of the Platonists*, helped him imagine incorporeal substance. But he did not fully trust the Platonists because he did not detect humility in their writings. Until he discovered the mediator—Jesus Christ—between a changeless and incorporeal God and humanity, he had no method; he saw the goal *without seeing how to get there* (7.20). The crucial moment of insight was not defined by intellectual insight, but by a soul-searing moment of cataclysmic feeling. But, in Book 7, he was not yet there.

22. *Epistula* 104.3.

Relaxing from Myself—a Little

My second divorce occurred as I was living in rented rooms in Berkeley and finishing writing my dissertation. I kept a couple of pieces of fruit on my desk to nibble on as I wrote, and one morning the banana and apple that were there were both scooped out by an animal with large teeth. I saw it later, a cat-sized rat. I was evicted from this room in the basement of a large house because the owner, a single mother with an adolescent daughter, had hoped for more "energy exchange" from me. It's true, I kept to myself, but writing a dissertation is not usually a social activity. I needed to focus.

1977 was not a good year for recent graduates in history to find jobs. One day I saw a letter posted on the bulletin board at school inviting applications for a position in Historical Theology at the Harvard University Divinity School. I had not had a single job interview as yet, but I thought I'd apply in order to get some practice at interviewing. To my great surprise I was invited to come to the school for an interview lecture. I went on December 7, 1977; I had a good time talking with faculty and students, but I figured that would be the end of it. On January 18, 1978, I was offered the position. So I had a job, to begin Fall 1978. I was forty-one years old.

8 Conversion and Conversions

I am yours. Save me.
—MARTIN LUTHER

BOOK 8 IS THE EPICENTER of Augustine's *Confessions*, the pivot from the terrible struggles of his youth—intellectual, emotional, and sexual—to the stability, security, and productivity of his maturity. In book 8, Augustine dramatized the moment of conversion, ignoring the many mini-conversions he had described in the earlier books. The earlier conversions were primarily intellectual, though they had a particular feeling tone that Augustine always expressed in bodily images. They also required more than rationality; they could not have been achieved without humility, an intellectual and emotional stance that was difficult for the young and self-confident Augustine.

The earlier conversions, however, though highly important, did not touch what Augustine described as his central problem, his sexual compulsiveness. The overachieving Augustine could not be content with a conversion that allowed him to live as most Christians, married and occupied with a business or a profession. Yet Augustine's personality is not the full explanation of his insistence that, for him to be Christian he would need to be celibate and withdrawn from worldly pursuits. At the end of the fourth century, asceticism was a communal excitement among Christians. With avid interest Augustine and his friends read accounts of famous ascetics like St. Anthony, as well

Conversion and Conversions

as those of ordinary people who refused marriage in favor of living in celibate communities (8.6). Nothing less than following these examples would do for Augustine. But he was *still closely bound by [his] need of woman* (8.1).

Woman? They all look alike? We know that Augustine was committed to a particular woman who was his partner for fifteen years and the mother of his son.[1] Rather than thinking of his connection to his partner as a commitment, he interpreted his attachment to her in the following way: *I was not so much a lover of marriage as a slave to lust . . . the slave of an unbreakable habit* (6.15). *The law of sin is the strong force of habit, which drags the mind along and controls it even against its will* (8.5). When Augustine dismissed her in order to make a prestigious and economically beneficial marriage, she returned to North Africa vowing *that she would never go to bed with another man*. Yet, even though Augustine says that his heart, *which clung to her was broken and wounded and dripping blood*, he immediately goes on to say that he could not wait the necessary two years for the child bride he and his mother had selected, so he found someone else to sleep with in the interim. Habit trumps willpower, becoming addiction, partly physical and partly behavioral. Augustine, helpless to free himself from sexual desire, *feared like death to be restrained from a habit by which [I] was melting away into death* (8.7).

How does intentional change occur in an individual? How can a person *get closer to* happiness? Augustine said that only conversion could produce real change. What is the individual's role in conversion? Hindus have long argued about whether the redemptive operation of grace is best described as the "cat-carrying method" or the "monkey-carrying method." The kitten collapses and its mother seizes it by the scruff of its neck; it dangles limply from her mouth. The baby monkey, on the other hand, climbs onto the mother's back and holds on for dear life as she carries him. Augustine said that God led him to conversion *by the force of his own desires* (6.11). His own frenzy and fatigue brought him to the end of his agenda. Augustine's prescription most closely resembles the cat-carrying method; he repeatedly, throughout

---

1. For a full discussion of Augustine's partner, see Miles, "Not Nameless but Unnamed."

his writings, pictures himself as utterly helpless to effect his own conversion, entirely dependent on God's forcible "turning his head" *(fovisti caput)*.[2]

> *But you, Lord, were turning me around so that I could see myself; you took me from behind my own back, which was where I had put myself during the time when I did not want to be observed by myself, and you set me in front of my own face so that I could see how foul a sight I was—crooked, filthy, spotted, and ulcerous. I saw and I was horrified, and I had nowhere to go to escape from myself. . . . You were setting me in front of myself, so that I might see my sin and hate it. I did know it, but I pretended that I did not. I had been pushing the whole idea away from me and forgetting it.* (8.7)

Augustine's conversion, as he describes it, was not his prerogative. He, for his part, had been actively avoiding the honest and profound assessment of himself that might have led to change.

༄

Conversion was a strong interest in Augustine's community and society. He describes the "coming out" of several well-known and respected people as an immediate influence on his own conversion. Humility was mandatory. Victorinus, *an extremely learned old man, an expert scholar in all the liberal sciences . . . did not blush to become the child of your Christ, an infant at your font, bending his neck to the yoke of humility and submitting his forehead to the ignominy of the cross.* Invited to make his profession of Christian faith privately, Victorinus insisted on publicly stating his faith. As he rose to do so, the congregation recognized him, muttered his name, and then fell respectfully silent to hear him. *With a fine confidence he declared openly the true faith, and they all wished that they could draw him into their very hearts. And in their love and their rejoicing . . . they did take him into their hearts* (8.2).

This is what Augustine wanted, and what I wanted when I sought baptism: a community's love, *for when many people rejoice together, the joy of each individual is all the richer, since each one inflames the other and the warmth spreads throughout them all* (8.4). When Augustine's

---

2. O'Connell, *Augustine's Early Theory of Man*, 66.

friend, Simplicianus, told him about Victorinus, Augustine said, *I was on fire to be like him* (8.5).

As he came closer to a resolution, his anguish increased. He *wasted away with gnawing anxieties, compelled to put up with all sorts of things which I did not want simply because they were inseparable from that state of living with a wife to which I was utterly and entirely bound* (8.1). The tension escalates; he seeks counsel from a fatherly friend; he has no control over his feverish thoughts; he begs for cure: *Come, Lord, act upon us and rouse us up and call us back! Fire us, clutch, charm us with your sweetness. Let us love, let us run!* (8.4). Eager to follow the example of men who have publicly embraced Christian faith, he is *held back, not by fetters put upon me by someone else, but by the iron bondage of my own will* (8.5).

Two wills warred against each other, *self against self*, both very strong (8.11). Curiously, in Book 8, Augustine is no longer judgmental of himself. Rather, the extreme anxiety he experienced at the time elicits his sympathy for the young man he was: *I was sick and in torture* (8.11). *All I had to do was to will to go there, and I would not only go but would immediately arrive.* His *half maimed will, turning and twisting this way and that, struggling*, is mirrored in his body: *I tore my hair, beat my forehead, locked my fingers together, clasped my knee . . . . I gave free rein to my tears* (8.8; 8.12).

Nearing the climax of his struggle, Augustine says that God *redoubled the lashes of fear and shame*, weakening one will in order to encourage the other. This passage gives a somewhat different picture than his insistence throughout the *Confessions* that God brought him, limp as the kitten carried by its mother, to conversion. There is something of the monkey-carrying method in his struggle: *I tried again and I was very nearly there; I was almost touching it and grasping it, and then I was not there, I was not touching it, I was not grasping it* (8.11). In the midst of this frenzy, Augustine heard and obeyed a voice that gave him a simple direction. The rest, as they say, is history. His will united, he achieved peace and the lifelong domination of his preferred will, with only minor infractions that he will examine minutely in Book 10.

Another way to describe Augustine's dramatic conversion: he returned, physically (in his movements and gestures), psychologically, and emotionally, to the psychic "place" in which the infant gasped/grasped breath. Only at that point was he was able—with God's help—to replace the settled habit of grasping (*concupiscentia*) with a conscious decision to trust—to "await with confidence and accept with gratitude."[3]

∽

Let us resist, for a moment, Augustine's headlong rush to conversion and pause to reflect on the impasse in which he finds himself. His anxious head and urgent body have brought him to the brink of *madness and dying* (8.8); he is utterly convinced that his dilemma is unsolvable. But I am not convinced. Why didn't he *relax a little* from himself and reflect that God, who created him, endowed him with his sexual desires as surely as he endowed him with the desire to seek wisdom? Why did he not, as so many Christians before and after him, pursue *both*, even seeking wisdom from and in his sexual experience?

Augustine's conversion was to celibacy *as a sexual orientation* (my emphasis). I see intransigence and ingratitude in his insistence that he can only be Christian as an "overachiever" celibate ascetic.[4] His defenders usually rationalize that; based on his subsequent productivity, this choice was the right one for him. But we do not *know*, do we, that he would not have been similarly productive as a happily married Christian? Or, reading too literally Augustine's language of *slavery*, defenders of his option for celibacy claim that Augustine was a sexual addict, that his sexual compulsiveness defied integration. Yet, his alleged faithfulness to one woman for fifteen years—and why shouldn't we believe him?—does not support a charge of sexual addiction. Why did he disallow "carnal knowledge" as an important kind of wisdom for humans?[5] An adequate answer to these questions would require exploration not only of Augustine's psychological and intellectual assumptions but also those of his society and Christian community, and his friends.

   3. Dinesen, "Babette's Feast."
   4. Fox's word for Christian ascetics of late antiquity; *Pagans and Christians*, 370.
   5. In fact, there is a French verb, *denaiser*, that means "to lose one's silliness by gaining carnal knowledge"; Miles, *A Complex Delight*, 127.

Conversion and Conversions

Augustine's famous conversion, as he described it, was fully scripted, a drama with dialogue and stage directions. Reading Book 8 we tend to forget those other conversions that together comprised a long slow *process* of intellectual and emotional change, a search for *happiness*, to use Augustine's word. The high drama of tears, voices, and flailing limbs described in Book 8 effectively mask his earlier mention of dissatisfaction with the Platonist books that did not mention Christ, and his impatience with any faith that differed from the Catholic faith he had imbibed with his mother's milk.⁶ Later, but still before the conversion recounted in Book 8, he wrote:

> *The faith of your Christ, our Lord and Savior, professed in the Catholic Church, remained steadfastly fixed in my heart, even though it was on many points still unformed and swerving from the right rule of doctrine. But nevertheless, my mind did not abandon it, but rather drank more and more deeply of it every day.* (7.5)

Convinced of the existence of incorporeal truth, he *no longer had any reason at all to doubt. I would sooner doubt my own life than the existence of that truth* (7.10). But Augustine was not yet at the point of conversion.

My Grandfather Brown had a similarly passionate, religious experience. He described it in a letter dated August 3, 1947:

> Long ago, when I was only just passed sixteen I went on August 7, a Sunday, to a meeting held for boys only, at the seaside apartment occupied by a Christian lawyer from London, who was spending his summer vacation at Ilfracombe in north Devonshire, doing Christian work among children; there, after a brief talk, which I cannot remember a word of, we were asked to kneel in prayer and while kneeling were invited to accept the Lord Jesus Christ as a personal Savior. I remember that I had

---

6. Similarly, Martin Luther described his conversion as a single moment of startling insight. In fact, his realization that "the just shall live by faith," occurred after years of monastic practice, spiritual direction, and teaching. Moreover, the mantra given him years earlier by his spiritual director, Johann von Staupitz, vicar general of the Augustinian friars, was "I am yours; save me" (*"tuus sum ego; salvum me fac"*); Psalm 119:94.

a great inward struggle for I had often attempted to become a Christian and live an exemplary life and I felt it was just one more useless decision to make, but this time was different; I became conscious of a vision, I could not see the form or face, but I knew it was Jesus Christ who stood where two ways parted, and I was there at the parting of the ways! I was conscious of feeling at an utter end of myself and after a brief inward struggle I cried in great distress on the Lord to help me to take the way that led to life eternal; the answer was immediate and I have never for one instant since then doubted the reality of what took place; I was born again by the Holy Spirit and I rose from my knees a new creature in Christ Jesus.

Since then all down the years I have never wavered in my loyalty and sense of His complete ownership of my life and all that goes to make up life; I have put Jesus first in everything and have striven to know and do His will. I am not boasting of this; I have fallen far short of my own conception of what I ought to be and I am amazed that I have accomplished so little, especially when I think of what others have done. I have always had a very slow heartbeat and I suppose that is why I don't exhibit the ecstasy which some Christians feel and express, and I can only prove my love by a quiet, steady, unselfish devotion to what seem to me to be His interests and I try earnestly to keep before me the fact that He is my Lord; so when my brief life on earth is over I think he will welcome me as one of His faithful servants and say nothing about the many things I am ashamed of. And I hope I shall not live until the grasshopper becomes a burden but go to meet Him in the full possession of my faculties with the flags flying and the bands playing!

The fundamentalist Christianity of my childhood focused on conversion as the central moment of religious commitment. I recognized this as a very young child and, at the age of five, I "converted"—from what to what?—led by a visiting friend of my parents. Hindsight is cynical, but I cannot remember or imagine that I could have had any sense of identifying my "self" as a Christian at that age. I think, rather, that the incident should be understood as similar to one in which, after I saw my father conduct a marriage ceremony, I solemnly married my teddy bear. In fact, both of these "commitments" were performed with the

Conversion and Conversions

utter seriousness of a five year old. Later, my five-year-old conversion allowed me to claim that I was already "saved" when altar calls were given.

When I was a teenager, the evangelist Billy Graham attracted huge crowds to the Seattle Stadium. George Beverly Shea's rich bass voice set the emotional tone for the rally ("He's Got the Whole World in His Hands"). By the time the altar call was given, streams of people moved forward, to be met by Graham's team of workers who led them through a vividly emotional experience of "accepting Jesus Christ as [their] own personal Savior." Then what? Billy Graham moved on, and these new Christians were expected to join one of the approved area churches to continue and reinforce their decision to practice Christianity. I do not recall that I ever "went forward," so I suppose I didn't. I would have remembered such an experience. I did invite a friend to go to a rally with me, and was disappointed when she declined to go forward.

"Getting saved" was not the only opportunity for commitment offered by the fundamentalist churches. Once, in Baptist summer camp, at the end of a service in which a missionary was the preacher, an altar call was given for parents who would offer their children as missionaries to come forward. My parents went. Then the call came for the children of those parents to come forward, indicating their willingness to go to a mission field when they became adults. I did not go. Fortunately I have forgotten or repressed any memory of what happened next. My parents must have been angry—or worse, disappointed. I confess that I am still proud of this rare refusal to seize this occasion in order to win love and approval.

My parents loomed so large that I never got beyond them to feeling a connection with their God. Finally, as a teenager, I settled for trying to *appear to be* good. Still desperately seeking love, I replaced my longing with romantic love. Popular songs described this love to me as I listened to the radio I sneaked under my bed covers at night, as did the *True Love* magazines I hid under my mattress. Romantic love would save me!

∽

Like Augustine in his fundamentalist moments, my father imagined a universe in which God created everything, and continued minutely to manage even the tiniest things that happened to me and that I did. Augustine believed in a God who pursued him relentlessly, preparing circumstances and events in order to bring him to certain realizations, and whispering in his ear (sometimes using Monnica's voice). Augustine made the fundamentalist move of personalizing, and thus objectifying, God. No matter how much Augustine insisted that love knows God because it participates in God-is-love, by describing a God who directs his every thought and action he cannot dismantle God as object. The fundamentalist's "own personal savior" God is the final idolatry.

Plotinus's One doesn't love in any personal way, but *is* love in that it provides life, the essential loving act. "Providence is of the whole," Plotinus said. The One cannot be appealed to for special favors, special attention. Rather, humans are part of the great universal generosity; we attract both the gifts and the inevitable pains of a universe in which living beings are dangerous to one another in our struggle to retain life. We can learn to turn toward, rather than away from, the gifts, but we will also inevitably collect a mix of the pains circulating in the richly varied All.

For Plotinus, the beauty of the world is *primary evidence* that the All of the universe is generated by the One in a spontaneous, effortless generosity. Yet the One is not the Great Beauty, the All is. Failing to get this right is to succumb to Augustine's dualistic thinking, his insistence that God and the world are radically separate. Loving Augustine's God distracts from loving the All. Admittedly, loving the All is not an easy discipline. That is why Christians find Plotinian Platonism cold. But it isn't; it just has a kind of love with which we are not familiar, a surround-love, the wealth of the All, not love that is personalized and located in a single provider.

At this point the chasm between theology and religion becomes evident. Theology reasons, exploring relationships between the various claims within a theological system, identifying contradictions and endeavoring to resolve them. The religious person cares little for theology. It is not argument, but the "heart strangely warmed" (John Wesley), or

Augustine's heart, *set on fire, red hot* (13.9), that is compelling to the religious person. For this to occur, it helps to have a personal God.

∽

Throughout the history of Christianity many authors have recognized that the way to increase devotion is to strengthen the community's and the individual's personal relationship to God. Examples too many to cite come to mind. The fourteenth-century *Meditations on the Life of Christ* names scriptural characters who are unnamed in Scripture so they can be related to more intimately: the woman at the well is "Lucy," for example. Charles Wesley's hymns, permeating the repertoire of twentieth-century fundamentalism, repeatedly insist that it was *for me* that Christ died.

∽

Is it possible to forego the fundamentalist's need for a personalized universe and yet retain the passion my father had as he preached? I believe it is possible. And is it possible to be both passionate and generous? Yes. For me the key to a generous passion was conversion to beauty. At first, when I took my little children to the beach, the large rhythm of the ocean waves calmed my body and mind. All right! I said to myself, here is a large clue. If I can develop and refine my ability to *see the beauty* of the visible world, I will understand something fundamental and substantial about the universe. The gift, the provision, the providence is beauty. So how do I become a person who *sees* beauty, not at the level of intellectual or aesthetic judgment, but at the level of *perception*.

I began to notice that the practice of seeing beauty was accompanied inevitably by a certain emotional state that can be described most accurately as a tremendous feeling of gratitude.[7] Not *for* anything in particular, and not *to* anyone, just gratitude. If I were pressed to say what the gratitude is for, I would say, for life and beauty. Perhaps it is what Freud described as an "oceanic feeling," rooted in infantile omnipotence. Or, perhaps it is what such strange bedfellows as Plotinus,[8]

---

7. Meister Eckhart said, "If the only prayer you say in your life is thank you, that would suffice."

8. Plotinus *Ennead* 3.4.4 (151).

Calvin, and Wittgenstein described as a strong feeling of the "perfect safety of the universe." The acute sense that I belong to the whole but am not selected for either benefit or injury, can be triggered by many things, but also it can suddenly appear without a discernable trigger as a sudden feeling of relaxation and gratitude.

Among his many conversions, Augustine experienced gentle as well as violent conversions. One such gentle conversion was to the significance of the visible world. In *Confessions* 10.6, the passage quoted on page 126, Augustine asks the trees, the sea, and other features of the sensible world, Who is your God? and they reply *in their beauty, He made us*. Something can be known about the character of the Creator by attentiveness to the creation. That "something" is that created beauty mirrors and echoes the great beauty, the beauty that is reality.

My conversion to religious practice was slow and incremental rather than sudden and dramatic. It occurred after I had studied Augustine intensively for about six years. Increasingly I recognized Augustine's religious language as an alternative to psychological language, a complete and highly nuanced language of the psyche. This was fascinating to me, coinciding at it did with my years of psychotherapy. The religious language of my childhood, around which my psyche formed, was now recognizable and understandable to me through my experience in psychotherapy. The intellectual piece was now in place. Augustine wrote, *I now no longer desired to be more certain of you [God], only to stand more firmly in you* (8.1).

My adult religious conversion to church affiliation and religious practice, described in chapter 6, had little to do with belief in God. It had more to do with the reemergence of old longings and habits. I became a member of the church my dearly loved Granny had been in as a child in England. I understood my affiliation with a church as only a step in a long process of *becoming* Christian. My participation in the religion of the *Word made flesh* involved a changed life. Acting on Augustine's instruction that *you must be emptied of that of which you are full so that you may be filled with that of which you are empty*, I regularly fasted from food, and I fasted from media for years. I did not see any movies or watch television for more than ten years. I did not read newspapers or magazines for a long time. If I could have figured out how to avoid looking at billboards, I would have done so. I avoided entertainment of all kinds. These mild asceticisms would not have been tenable, I acknowledge, had I not had friends who were happy to tell me what I needed to know about what was going on in the world, not because of curiosity, but in order to participate in the responsibility of citizenship. The purpose of visual asceticisms was to strip from my eyes the socialization that directs me to see as beautiful only the very narrow range of objects considered beautiful by my culture. The disciplines helped. For example, I began to see with awe and great pleasure the unique particular beauty of every face.

Along with attention to the beauty of the sensible world came the difficult realization that I must give up the fundamentalist's personalized universe for the benign indifference of a universe to which I could relate only by imagining the real of which I am an infinitesimally small part. It took me a long time to recognize and accept that the grove of madrone trees in which I experienced peace and gratitude for being did not love me back. Finally, however, I am comforted by the realization that there is no plot—and nobody plotting—either for my good or my harm.

Fundamentalism is not confined to religion. There are many historians who display a fundamentalist intransigence, unwillingness to entertain others' proposals, and confidence that they have the right interpretation, as if God whispered in their ear. Fundamentalism in scholarship halts exploration and discussion, preferring dogmatic adherence to both methods and outcomes. "The truth was not found, not because it was not sought, but because the intention always was to find again instead some preconceived opinion or other, or at least not to wound some favorite idea."[9]

---

9. Schopenhauer, quoted by Murdoch, *Metaphysics as a Guide to Morals*, 184.

Augustine's community was excited about conversions to Christianity; a different kind of conversion draws the attention of twenty-first-century American families, communities, and the public sphere, that is, conversions from addiction to sobriety. Media excitement over celebrities who undergo well-publicized detoxification and rehabilitation programs is reminiscent of Augustine's fascination with Victorinus and other well-known converts to Christianity. Established beliefs concerning addictions go virtually unquestioned in American society.

But Philosopher Herbert Fingarette challenges these beliefs. His book, *Heavy Drinking: The Myth of Alcoholism as a Disease*, exposes the falsity of "almost everything the American public believes to be the scientific truth about alcoholism."[10] The "myth of alcoholism" states that heavy drinkers inevitably slide further into regular drinking, "hit bottom," and can only recover by embracing total abstinence. However, this myth lacks physiological or psychological validation. The National Council on Alcoholism has stated that "all attempts to identify and define 'alcoholism' have failed because the concept itself is fundamentally flawed. 'Alcoholism' exists in our language and our minds, but not in the objective world around us."[11]

In fact, Fingarette writes, "[M]any drinkers with numerous and severe problems 'mature out' of trouble. The descent to 'the bottom' is not inevitable, and a return from heavy drinking to moderation is common."[12] But a several-billion-dollar-a-year industry of recovery relies on the myth of alcoholism. Perhaps, Fingarette suggests, those who profit most evidently from this myth do so cynically, for the well-established belief that alcoholics exist, and that their only hope is abstinence, is statistically proven to *produce* recidivism—for which the only treatment is another recovery program.

Yet it must be acknowledged that millions of people have overcome life-threatening addictions by accepting Alcoholics Anonymous's assumptions and methods. They work. Fingarette's primary target is not Alcoholics Anonymous, an organization that does not charge anyone any money, but with the hugely remunerative rehabilitation business. In a decade, I spent $26,000 on three month-long recovery programs

---

10. Fingarette, *Heavy Drinking*, 1.
11. Ibid., 49.
12. Ibid., 21.

for my son before I recognized that the main tool of recovery featured by these programs is several Alcoholics Anonymous meetings each day, meetings that could be found free of charge and close to home rather than in a camp or hospital setting.[13]

Fingarette points out that the myth of alcoholism benefits not only the business of recovery programs; the liquor industry profits also from the identification of a relatively small group of drinkers as "alcoholics," while the vast general population is not thought to be at risk. The public—us—is also complicit: "We prefer not to hear that *heavy drinking* and *alcoholism* are merely labels that cover a variety of social and personal problems caused by the interplay of many poorly understood physiological, psychological, social, and cultural factors."[14]

Like the young Augustine, who preferred to think of his "sin" as caused by an alien force not under his control (5.10), Americans prefer to imagine that "the ingestion of alcohol biochemically triggers additional alcohol consumption." But it is "the drinker's mind-set, the drinker's beliefs and attitudes about alcohol, that influence the level of consumption."[15]

Both "the old simplistic moralism, which taught that a sincere resolve was enough, and the loss-of-control hypothesis, which viewed each failure of willpower as proof that the drinker's will had been incapacitated by disease" must be put aside. Rather, according to Fingarette, there must be "an acceptance of personal responsibility," followed by "actions intended to achieve a reshaping of [a] way of life that fosters change and precludes situations that frustrate the will to change."[16] Rather than the unrealistic goal of total abstinence, Fingarette advocates that the heavy drinker can be helped to set reachable goals, including "a substantial reduction in the number of drinking days a month, or a major reduction in the amount typically drunk at any one time."[17] The

---

13. Fingarette writes, "Despite the ubiquitous good opinion of Alcoholics Anonymous, there are no satisfactory data to justify the widespread confidence in it, in part because Alcoholics Anonymous has long been reluctant to gather or publish statistics." Ibid., 88.
14. Ibid., 27.
15. Ibid., 40
16. Ibid., 111.
17. Ibid., 121.

success of Fingarette's proposals depends upon a number of factors, different for each individual.

Clearly, it works for some people to imagine their problem as a disease—the A.A. model. But it is not for everyone. One night, on the long drive to Sonora from a graduate seminar in Berkeley, I listened to an evangelical radio program. A man testified that he had always been told that his alcoholism was a "sickness." He inferred from this diagnosis that he could do nothing about it. But when he came to the skid row mission, he said, he was told in no uncertain terms that it was sin—and they told him what to do about it! So he got "saved," and the alcoholism retreated.

My sister also experienced an unlikely conversion from heavy drinking. A drinker for years, she suddenly—I do not know the exact circumstances—stopped, never again, in the next thirty years, desiring alcohol. Before her conversion to sobriety she had participated in two month-long recovery programs that failed to help her. But she never attended an A.A. meeting after the day she decided not to drink anymore. The question is not, Which diagnosis is accurate—sin or disease? The question is rather, What language *works* for a particular person at a particular time and place? My sister, who grew up in a fundamentalist home, assumed that sin was the accurate diagnosis, and conversion—Augustine's *fovisti caput*—was the remedy.

Augustine's conversion, narrated in Book 8 of his *Confessions*, became a model of conversion throughout the history of Christianity. It is *this* model of conversion that has gripped the imagination of Western Europeans to our own time. According to this model, conversion is granted by God, with the convert playing no role (the cat-carrying method); conversion changes everything instantly, resolving all hesitancy and overcoming all barriers; and conversion is permanent.[18] But this is not what Augustine painstakingly *describes* in the *Confessions*. His *whole* discussion contradicts his—and his readers'—focus on his "conversion" in Book 8. In fact, the *Confessions* is all about the gradual and

---

18. This point has been contested, however, most directly at the 1614 Council of Dort in which Arminians and Calvinists argued over whether salvation, once given, could be lost.

cumulative shift in his intellectual, emotional, and erotic attractions. And the work of converting went on, as he narrates in detail, long after the climactic moments in the garden at Ostia.

The daily *work* of conversion, whether from addiction or from any kind of anxious and frustrated life, is not only more likely to achieve the desired results, but is also more realistic about human life. The instantaneous, permanent satisfaction we all seek is not forthcoming. Centuries later, Freud agreed with Augustine that "the goal towards which the pleasure-principle impels us—of becoming happy—is not attainable."[19] His discussion of happiness in *Civilization and Its Discontents* is interrupted by lengthy analyses of human unhappiness and common responses to it. One such response is the use of the various forms of intoxication that temporarily enhance pleasure and suppress pain. (Recall Augustine's drunken beggar.) According to Freud, religion is another common strategy for managing unhappiness. In *Beyond the Pleasure Principle,* Freud reiterated his belief that "we cannot do without palliative remedies .... Something of this kind is indispensable."[20]

Could we consider the personal and social problem of addiction as evidence of Augustine's idea of original sin? If we imagine that original sin lies at the root of addiction, we must also see its ugly head in the greedy multibillion dollar business of recovery. For in spite of G. K. Chesterton's remark that original sin is the only well-documented Christian doctrine, "original sin" is an abstraction that lacks specific explanatory value; "there is no one reason that motivates all our self-defeating conduct."[21]

---

19. Freud, *Civilization and Its Discontents* II, 775.
20. Ibid., 771.
21. Fingarette, *Heavy Drinking*, 103.

9 *Parents or Fellow Pilgrims?*

I've always thought of wholeness and integration as necessary myths. We're fragmented beings who cement ourselves together, but there are always cracks. Living with the cracks is part of being, well, reasonably healthy.
—SIRI HUSTVEDT[1]

IN EARLIER BOOKS, AUGUSTINE MENTIONED that he and his partner had a son who was left with Augustine when she returned to North Africa. In Book 9 Augustine speaks briefly as a father: *We had with us Adeodatus, the son of my flesh, begotten by me in my sin.* He reiterates: *I myself had no part in that boy except for the sin.* Augustine took no praise for raising Adeodatus *in your discipline; it was you and no one else who inspired us to do this* (7.6). An odd way to introduce a beloved child, but Augustine goes on to describe Adeodatus's *awe-inspiring intelligence.* Augustine wrote a dialogue, *De magistro*, with Adeodatus, who supplied his own ideas for his part of the dialogue. This promising boy died at the age of 16. Augustine writes, *as I think of him, I am perfectly at ease, for there was nothing in his boyhood or youth or indeed his whole personality to make one feel fear for him* (9.6).

After his conversion, Augustine withdrew from his professional life, prompted by *pains in the chest and the inability to breathe deeply*

---

1. Hustvedt, *Sorrows of an American*, 139.

(9.2).[2] This ailment seems to have disappeared mysteriously as soon as he *gave notice to the citizens of Milan that they would have to find someone else to sell words to their students* (9.5). He and his companions *were baptized and all anxiety for our past life vanished away* (9.6). That one sentence is all that Augustine says about his baptism.

Augustine and his friends sought *otium*, a leisurely and secluded life that would allow them to focus on thinking together. The owner of a country estate at Cassiciacum allowed them to use his estate, *far from the tumult of the world* (9.3). Here Augustine experienced the *inward goads and stings* by which God *tamed* him—the Latin word means literally "to plane" his rough edges. Augustine, baptized and a catechumen, rested there with his mother, son, and friends. Reading and conversation occupied them, and *that heavy sluggishness of ours that might have dragged us down again to the depths was utterly burned up and consumed* (9.2). Years later, the forty-year-old author of the *Confessions* remembered those days with longing. He read Scripture with excitement; images of *boiling* and *fire* describe his feelings as he read.

> My God, how I poured out my heart to you as I read the psalms of David, those faithful songs and sounding syllables of holiness, quite excluding the swelling boasting of the spirit! . . . How I cried aloud to you in those psalms! How they fired me toward you! How I burned to utter them aloud, if I could, to the whole world! (9.4)

Augustine may have invented a literary strategy that was later used extensively in early modern pornography: overheard conversation, eavesdropping. He described the greater force of allowing listeners to *overhear*, rather than directly addressing them. According to Augustine, for maximal effect, both narrator and listeners must be ignorant of the other's presence.

> *I should have liked* [the Manichaeans] *to have been standing somewhere near me (without my knowing that they were there) and to have seen my face and heard what I said when in this time of quietness I read the fourth Psalm, and to have seen what effect those words of the Psalm had on me. . . . I should have liked them to have heard me without my knowing whether they heard. Otherwise they might think that what I was saying when I read those verses was being said because of them. And in fact I should neither say the same things nor speak in the same way, if I realized*

---

2. Augustine referred to his illness in *De ordine* I.2.5 as a *dolor stomachi*.

> that they were watching me and listening to me. And even if I did say the same things, they would not have understood how I was speaking with myself and to myself in front of you [God], out of the natural feelings of my soul. (9.4)

In the so-called golden age of illustrated narrative pornography, from 1650 to 1800, sex acts were often described from the perspective of an eavesdropping "peeping Tom." Augustine recommended spying and eavesdropping as powerful ways to communicate religious passions, but pornographers found that these methods were effective in arousing other passions also![3]

I too "dropped out" for a couple of years in the late 1960s. Ed and I lived in the tiny town of Philo, California, inland from the Mendocino coast. We rented a little house in the woods, near the Navarra River. We thought it a beautiful house, but when Ed's mother saw it she accused us of lying about it. It was small and the floor was uneven and sloped; a dropped pencil would roll to the far wall. But there was an intricately carved door and a detached studio with an underground root cellar. We grew as much of our own food as we could, supplemented by food supplies given out weekly by the county. We tried to make the small money we had last as long as possible.

In that place I came upon the true ease of myself. I walked around thinking poetry; once I saw the trees moving to Bach's *Magnificat*. When we drove down the dirt road in our old VW a colorful pheasant that lived nearby ran along in the dust behind the car, flying up into the back window when he could no longer keep up. I washed clothes on the sagging porch with an old wringer washer and hung them on a line to dry in the sun. Susan went to Booneville High School, the only girl in the school who didn't shave her legs. She was trying to be a hippie, while all the farmgirls were trying to be the models they saw in magazines. One summer Susan and I made a blackberry pie every day with blackberries we picked along the road. There was a sheep ranch in the next field, and in the summer evenings the sheep could be heard "talking" to one another, some with high childlike voices, some with deep male voices.

3. Darnton, "Sex for Thought," 203; see also Darnton, *Forbidden Best-Sellers*, 97.

Nobody had a salaried job, and eventually it became imperative that we return to the city to seek work. It was a sad day when we drove down the dirt road for the last time, going to Modesto, both of us with part-time jobs at the community college. We hoped that living in a beautiful place was addictive and that we would soon find another such place. But the idyll was over. We became responsible citizens. The effects of living in quietness were lasting, however, if only as a longing to return.

Rosemary Hennessey describes the unacknowledged sacrifices that workers in capitalist societies tacitly agree to, in exchange for wages. Quoting Karl Marx she writes: "Workers at all levels of society are expected to forfeit 'certain needs—aspects of his human potential,' such as 'time for education, for intellectual development, for the fulfilling of social functions and for social intercourse, for the free play of his bodily and mental activity, even the rest time of Sunday.'"[4] Moreover, in American society, if a person wants to minimize frustration, she must be content with a life that can be interrupted at any moment. Of course, there are some very important activities that are not interruptible, such as praying, lovemaking, meditating, thinking, and writing, to name only a few. In order to do salaried work I gave up: baking bread,

4. Marx, *Capital*, vol I, 264, quoted by Hennessy, *Profit and Pleasure*, 216.

playing the lute, painting, dancing, lying in the sun, keeping bees, reading books outside my field, and long love-making; and my attentiveness to my children diminished.

In returning to the academy, I gradually relinquished the rich variety of my life for the necessary focus and concentration my job demanded. At first, while I was teaching in a California community college, I continued some of these activities. When I was hired at Harvard, however, I focused almost exclusively on work. I gave up living in the country, a nourishing relationship to nature, and leisure. For these I exchanged: deeply gratifying intellectual work, a salary, travel, respect of colleagues, and professional opportunities.

All my time and attention were required if I was to handle everything that was coming at me thick and fast—teaching and advising students in four degree programs, committee work, and publishing. That attention "paid off." In 1985 I was the first woman to be awarded tenure at the Harvard University Divinity School; shortly thereafter I was named to the Bussey Professorship. I don't regret the simultaneously privileged and stressful life at Harvard; I simply had a rich life of a different kind, but I do acknowledge the losses.

> *I shall never be able to recall and write down the whole story of those days of quiet. But I have not forgotten . . . (9.4)*

Parents or Fellow Pilgrims?

∽

Augustine described the origin of hymn-singing in the Christian liturgy. Justina, *mother of the boy emperor Valentinian,* threatened to appropriate the Catholic basilica for the use of an Arian congregation. The congregation staged a sit-in, lasting several days, during which they sang hymns *in the manner of the Eastern churches. The practice continued to this day, and was copied by almost all congregations in other parts of the world.* Augustine was very moved by congregational singing: *Those voices flowed into my ears and the truth was distilled into my heart, which overflowed with my passionate devotion. Tears ran from my eyes and happy I was in those tears* (9.7).

I am convinced that more people learn theology from hymns than from verbal instruction or reading. Words set to music enter the heart directly, as Augustine described. The hymns of my childhood remain with me, one or another erupts into my consciousness at random times whether I want it or not. The hymns favored by fundamentalist churches have two characteristics: they mention blood a lot ("... washed in the blood of the lamb"; "there is a fountain filled with blood ..."), and many of them have choruses that are repeated after every verse.

Singing does more than instruct and delight individuals. Congregational singing is a powerful bonding experience; people who sing together breathe together. Leaders of the Protestant reformations of the sixteenth century were very aware of this. Luther wrote hymns himself and encouraged others to do so. In the Roman Catholic reformation, the Council of Trent considered banning music from the liturgy. Just then Palestrina began to compose masses, one of which was performed at the Council, convincing the delegates that rather than distracting, music enhanced worship.

∽

The emotional Augustine, who wept freely hearing hymns, scolded himself for weeping at the death of his mother: *something childish in me was bringing me to the brink of tears.... And I was deeply vexed that these human feelings should have such power over me.* Only after her burial did he *find solace in weeping for her and for myself* (9.12).

However, he thinks he may have sinned in doing so. *I blamed myself for a too carnal affection* (9.13).

His mother's death at Ostia prompted Augustine to write a long eulogy about her life. Shortly before her death, his mother was with the group at Cassiciacum *in her woman's clothing but with her masculine faith, tranquil in her age, maternal in her love, Christian in her goodness.* But it is not these qualities that occupy Augustine in his eulogy, but stories that would certainly have embarrassed Monnica about her childhood, her *excess of high spirits* that prompted her to fall into *such a habit of drinking that she would greedily drink down cups* which were nearly full of wine. She stopped drinking when a servant called her a *drunkard.* Augustine gleefully told this story on his mother: *Where then was that wise old woman with her stern prohibitions?* What woman would want to be eulogized for posterity only by her son?

He praises Monnica for her adjustment to marriage. She served her unfaithful husband *as her master,* scolding other wives who failed to regard *the marriage contract as a legally binding document by which they were made servants.* She avoided the beatings and bruised faces other wives received by waiting until her husband *calmed down* before she *explained to him the reasons for what she had done.* Eventually, *she won her husband over to you.* She served the little group at Cassiciacum, giving her son, grandson, and their friends *the care that a mother gives to her son and to each one of us the service which a daughter gives to her father* (9.9).

Augustine and Monnica enjoyed a moment of ecstatic vision of *Wisdom* shortly before her death. *We did, with the whole strength of our hearts' impulse, just lightly come into touch with her, and we sighed, and we returned to the sounds made with our mouths, where a word has a beginning and an ending.* Having experienced that vision, *the world with all its delights seemed so worthless,* and Monnica declared herself ready to die. Five days later she *fell into a fever,* from which she died shortly after at the age of fifty-six. She asked only to be remembered *at the altar of the Lord* (9.10–11).

∽

My mother prayed on her knees at midday, at night, and first thing in the morning. Every day opened up to her to have God's will done in it. Every night she totted up what she'd done and said and thought, to see how it squared with Him. That kind of thing is dreary, people think, but they're missing the point. For one thing, such a life can never be boring. And nothing can happen to you that you can't make use of. Even if you're racked by troubles, and sick and poor and ugly, you've got your soul to carry through life like a treasure on a platter. Going upstairs to pray after the noon meal, my mother would be full of energy and expectation, seriously smiling.[5]

My mother's spirituality influenced me perhaps as much by my resistance to its quietism and unquestioning acceptance of what she perceived as the demands of her social world as by my attraction to her passionate commitment to God. She imagined her life as an entity to be shaped, exercised, and painstakingly developed over a lifetime. A talented woman, she accepted as absolute that she should not work outside the home. It had not been granted her to serve as a missionary—the highest calling of her religious orientation. So she served at home, right where she was, offering up her life to God. She saw the duties and events of her ordinary existence as spiritual discipline.

When she was not cooking or cleaning she read and wrote. She wrote gospel tracts for new mothers, which sold well. She wrote short stories for Sunday school papers in which the protagonists fell gently in love and, after facing numerous obstacles, went off together to some "mission field." When I was a teenager she wrote devotional manuals for children, with daily Scripture readings, thoughts, and hymn verses to ponder. She read avidly and furtively, her reading an unmistakable resistance to her daily work; she sneaked reading. During my childhood she read far into the night. Later, whenever I visited, no matter how early in the morning I got up, she was always hunched in bed, a blanket around her shoulders, reading her Bible. My mother was the most immediate and intimate representative of a fundamentalist Christianity whose particular beliefs I have largely replaced, but whose passion and intensification of ordinary life I continue to seek daily. All my life I've tried to find exciting without scary, but I have never managed it. I want a "large and real emotion," a "quick sharp sense of life."[6] I can't

5. Munro, *Progress of Love*, 4.
6. Bellow, *Henderson the Rain King*.

accept dullness—"immortality through my work." As Woody Allen said, "I want immortality by *not dying*"—at least while I'm alive.

As a young woman I wanted any life but my mother's. I was aware of her resentments and anxieties, the burden of a passivity so uncompromising that she refused—or did not know how—to extricate herself from an endless telephone monologue. Moreover, she required herself not to pursue, or even to respond to, people she especially liked, befriending instead the lonely and those in pain or trouble. She consented to suffering. As a young woman I found this deplorable; I still struggle to identify and change similar tendencies in myself. I work to revise my mother's spiritual legacy by unwinding confining socializations, and working for political and social change, and for more just relationships within the family, the academy, and the church. Yet it was my mother who taught me that the reason for developing a spiritual life is that it offers a life that is not at the mercy of "whatever happens," but a life that is examined, cultivated, intentional. People like my mother, whose lives were constricted both externally and internally, have sometimes enjoyed rich spiritual lives.[7]

I was called to my mother's death while I was teaching a class at Harvard. I flew from Boston to Seattle that afternoon, arriving in the early evening. My sister was caring for our mother in her home. When she was a little girl, Dorothy once said that when she (Dorothy) grew up, Mother would "grow down," and she (Dorothy) would take care of her. And that is exactly what happened. When I arrived, those who had been caring for her were very tired, so I stayed up all night with her. She was in a coma, and I didn't know if she heard me or not, but in case she did, I did not want her to feel abandoned in *the valley of the shadow of death*. I talked to her; I knew the words she would want to hear, and I repeated Psalm 23 many times. I held her hand, and from time to time she gave my hand a little squeeze—voluntary or involuntary? I don't know.

Her harsh breathing went on and on. It seemed that she was struggling to hold on to life, so the next morning I told her that she was safe in the universe. Then it occurred to me that, so characteristic of her, she may have been hanging on, not for herself but because she felt that her family needed her. So I told her that we will miss her terribly, but that

---

7. Based on Miles, "Resistance and Affirmation," 1197–98.

we would take care of one another and be all right. By this time she had been breathing harshly for more than a day. She died that afternoon.

As a child I could make myself cry by imagining Mother's death. I thought it the most terrible thing that could happen. But when it did occur, it felt right. She died of a brain tumor, gradually slipping into a coma and apparently feeling no pain. Since her four children had gathered, there was a shortage of beds that night, so I slept in the bed she had died in that afternoon. I do not consider my tears over her loss sinful. At the interment, my sister Marilyn saw a long white hair attached to the coffin, blowing in the slight breeze. That night I got out all her snapshot albums and watched her grow from a tiny child to an old woman. She is a completed moment of beauty.

> Send me out into another life
> lord because this one is growing faint
> I do not think it goes all the way[8]

Dad spent the last year of his life in my sister's home. I went to visit him as frequently as I could, and once took care of him for a week so that Dorothy could have a rest. He had had a number of small strokes that made him unable to swallow or talk. I ground his food to an unpalatable-looking pulp and he ate by himself in his bedroom, choking down tiny bits of food as the rest scattered in a wide arc around his plate. This man, speech teacher at the University of Washington, who had a plaque over his desk for many years reading "Thy speech maketh thee known," now talked like a drunk. For a while he could write, shakily but legibly. And that is how we communicated.

When Dad was old and vulnerable, I wanted to be kinder to him than he had been to me in my youthful vulnerability. When he could no longer talk or write, I felt a sudden surge of love for him. While he could write, I still got notes from him, ("Does Ric have a job?") that seemed to me calculated to make me sad. But when he could no longer turn away my love for him by judging me, my church ("veering toward Rome"),

---

8. Merwin, "Words from a Totem Animal," 150.

my school ("modernist"—not a compliment), my divorces, I could just let it all go and see him as a fellow pilgrim.

Dad enjoyed humor, and when we were children, Marilyn perfected the art of finding jokes that were just a little "off color," but not obscene enough to offend him. He laughed guiltily but helplessly at Marilyn's jokes: For example, one guy says to another, "I'm going fishing." Second guy says, "Do you have worms?" First guy replies, "Yeah, but I'm going anyway." About a month before his death, Dad, my husband Owen, and I were sitting on Dorothy's lawn on camp chairs, enjoying the evening cool after a blisteringly hot day. Dorothy's chicken was entertaining us, officiously hunting and pecking. Behind the lawn, across a fence, was a vast meadow where sheep grazed. Now, at the end of summer, the meadow was brown and dry as dust. We watched Chicken Little laboriously make her way through the fence to the dry meadow, leaving the green lawn. Observing this, Owen remarked, "This proves that 'the grass is always greener on the other side.'" Dad collapsed in helpless laughter—his last laugh.

Dad left the farm, but the farm did not leave him. On one of my visits, he insisted on taking me to see a new Sears store, amazed—this old farmboy—by its size, spaciousness, and long escalators. He was a wonderful gardener, with a luscious and messy flower and vegetable garden. After his last stroke, Dennis found him crouched over on the lawn. He at first assumed that Dad was picking a weed, as he had done so many thousands of times.

Through the long night, I listened to his breaths, talking and talking, so he wouldn't feel alone, not knowing if he heard. Calling him "Kenny," his childhood name, the only name he might recognize now. I recited Psalm 23 again and again, and finally, tired of talking, having no more words, but wanting to let him know I was there, I sang the old Baptist hymns he loved, many of which I haven't heard or sung for years, decades. I knew all the words of all the verses, my voice strong, not thinking of the pain of losing him, just wanting him to feel safe in his last moments.

His breaths became slower, irregular. I called my sister and together we listened as his breaths stopped, then started again, one breath, two breaths, three breaths. Dorothy said, "Don't come back, Daddy, there's nothing for you here." I said, "Almost home, almost there, Kenny." Then there was nothing, no sound, no breath.

He didn't seem to be really gone until, an hour later, I returned to the room, and touched him. He was getting cold. When the morticians came to take him away, Dorothy and I sat on her bed, holding hands, listening, but deciding we didn't have to watch him leave the house for the last time.

When Augustine began his career as priest and bishop, he was about ten years younger than I was when I began my teaching career. He wrote his *Confessions* at about age forty, several years after becoming a bishop. I went to teach at Harvard Divinity School in 1978 at the age of forty-one. I moved across the country alone, frightened and excited about my new job. As a graduate student Teaching Fellow I had usually given one lecture in a course, and I worked on that lecture for weeks. As a new Assistant Professor, I lectured on the History of Christianity three times a week and had a three-hour seminar on another day. Moreover, I was hired to teach the course on History of Christianity that had been taught by a well-known and superbly knowledgeable senior professor who had recently retired. That is the kind of person who *should* have taught the course, not a recent doctoral graduate who had worked intensively only on Augustine and the fourth century.

Nevertheless, the course had the distinct advantage that every time I taught it for the following eighteen years, I learned a great deal. Academics go into the profession because we love to learn, or because, as children, we loved to read. But frequently our disciplines encourage us to smaller and smaller foci. This was never either attractive or possible for me. I felt that it was a great privilege to be able to work in seventeen centuries of the history of Christianity—Ignatius of Antioch to Kant, where others took over. This course became my favorite because of its amazing and limitless riches. Each time I taught it I deepened my knowledge and appreciation of historical authors.[9]

---

9. After I retired I used the lectures from my History of Christian Thought course as the basis for my textbook, *The Word Made Flesh: A History of Christian Thought*.

Augustine and the Fundamentalist's Daughter

Book 9 ends quietly as Augustine asks that his readers remember his parents at the altars at which they pray. Augustine did not write about his father except to say that *though* [he was] *an extremely kind man by nature,* [he] *was also very hot-tempered.* He eventually became a Christian. He does not mention his father's death, and refers to Patricius only as Monnica's husband. His parents have been transformed from being the giants of his psyche to being *brethren, fellow citizens of Jerusalem, and fellow pilgrims.* He has appreciated, forgiven, and finally, loved them. Now he seeks only that *my mother may have her last request of me still more richly answered in the prayers of many others besides myself* (9.13).

The ability to see his parents as fellow pilgrims, for all its lack of Augustine's usual drama, is a marvelous achievement. To *get over* one's childish anger, resentment, and even passionate attachment to parents, to see them simply as suffering, struggling human beings who at every stage of their lives had not been there before, in those particular circumstances, and didn't know what to do. For which, perhaps, they overcompensated by pretending that they knew exactly what to do. Who converted their fear of failing as parents into anger at their child's misbehavior; who laughed—in Augustine's case—at the beatings their child received in school. Adulthood means no longer seeing one's parents either as ogres or angels, but simply as precious and fragile fellow pilgrims.

It took me years of psychotherapy to come to a similar understanding of my parents, even though, beyond the occasional spanking when I was a young child—a common thing sixty years ago—I was not physically disciplined. But I was not allowed, let alone encouraged, to construct, *ex nihilo*, a self by my choices, my interests, and my mistakes. I did not learn as a child to stop myself from self-damaging behavior, to consider consequences, and to direct my energy fruitfully. I belonged to my parents; they made the choices, prevented the mistakes, and savored my accomplishments. For me, it was all about making them happy, making them proud. Because everything I thought or did directly reflected on them. I was a fundamentalist's daughter.

10   *The Difficulty of Beautiful Things*

For me, Lord, certainly this is hard labor, hard labor inside myself, and I have become to myself a piece of difficult ground, not to be worked over without much sweat. (10.16)

IN BOOK 10 AUGUSTINE MADE the transition from writing about *what I once was*, to writing about *what I am now* (10.3). Books 10–13 are not as easily recognizable as autobiographical because they lack the personal narrative of a life story. For this reason, books 10–13 are often omitted from college reading assignments. They *are* autobiographical, however. They place a human life—Augustine's life—in a larger framework than his personal experience, namely, in the context of cosmos and history. Augustine was aware that personal experience was interesting to his audience, but personal experience was only part of a picture that was incomplete without the larger setting of time and eternity, creation and the universe.

    I do not know of any twentieth- or twenty-first-century autobiographers that set their experience in such a frame. Moreover, in Augustine's time, no one started a biography or autobiography with earliest infancy as he did. Cyprian's biography started with his conversion, his "true" life, ignoring his first forty years and focusing on the four years prior to his martyrdom.

Although the topics of memory, time, and creation occupied Augustine in the closing books of the *Confessions*, for him people would always be the greatest marvel. He was amazed that, within the vast universe, full of wonders,

> Men go to gape at mountain peaks, at the boundless tides of the sea, the broad sweep of rivers, the encircling ocean and the motions of the stars: and yet they leave themselves unnoticed; they do not marvel at themselves. (10.8)

Augustine marveled at himself. A disobedient reading of the *Confessions*, that is, one that notices features that Augustine did not plan to communicate, reveals that the aspect of himself most fascinating to Augustine was his sin. Sin *is* himself, because *confession to you [God] is the same thing as not attributing my goodness to myself . . . . if you hear any good from me, it was you who first told it to me . . . . I am ashamed of myself and renounce myself and choose you and, except in you, can please neither you nor myself* (10.2). Given his attribution of all goodness to God, the only way for Augustine to be "himself" is to be a sinner.

In Book 10, however, Augustine proposes another understanding of himself. He was amazed at the seemingly infinite storehouse of his own memory and its uses. *Great indeed is the power of memory! It is something terrifying, my God, a profound and infinite multiplicity; and this thing is the mind, and this thing is I myself* (10.17).

> By the act of thought we are, as it were, collecting together things which the memory contained, though in a disorganized and scattered way, and by giving them our close attention we are arranging for them to be, as it were, stored up ready to hand in that same memory where previously they lay hidden, neglected, and dispersed, so that now that will readily come forward to the mind that has become familiar with them. (10.11)

Exploring the information stored in memory and potentially accessible, Augustine recognized that the mind stores not only memories of events and experiences, but also memories of feelings. Mind remembers happiness, sadness, and even physical pain. Out of all these memories, he said, we can cobble together a sense of self. Memory is self, eroded here and there by forgetfulness: *without it I should not be able to call myself myself* (10.16).

Augustine vividly describes his field trip into his memory.

The Difficulty of Beautiful Things

> *And I come to the fields and spacious palaces of my memory where are the treasures of innumerable images, brought into it from things of all sorts perceived by the senses.... When I enter there, I require what I will to be brought forth, and something instantly comes; others must be longer sought after, which are fetched, as it were, out of some inner receptacle; others rush out in troops, and while one thing is desired and required, they start forth, as one who says, "Is it maybe me you want?" With the hand of my heart I brush them away from the face of my memory, until the thing that I want is discovered and brought out from its hidden place into my sight.* (10.8)

Some memories come effortlessly, pushing aside other memories. Others are elusive, and must be pursued to the shadows to which they have been banished. I suspect that, for Augustine as for me, it is often the pleasure that has been forgotten, and that it has been disavowed because it turned out badly, painfully, in the loss of a lover or the dissolution of a marriage.

Augustine repeats the image of incessantly buzzing flies—annoying, inescapable, and distracting from a chosen purpose—when, later in Book 10, he describes the temptations that pester him daily.

Captive to whatever flashed into his mind, Augustine seemed to have no idea that mind requires governance. He placed all his obsessive attention on governing his body, and though his sexual desire was miraculously alleviated, other sensory temptations still require minutely detailed scrutiny. He worries about *what temptations I can and what I cannot resist* (10.5). Does he enjoy music too much (10.33)? Does he grieve over his mother's death inappropriately (9.12)? Does he allow himself to be distracted from his work to watch a hound chasing a hare (10.35)? Why does he still have wet dreams (10.30)? He wonders if he enjoys eating too much: *I should have the same attitude toward taking food as I have toward taking medicine* (10.31). Even though he *is not much concerned* that he is tempted by smells, he nevertheless fears that *I may be deceiving myself* (10.32). And what about the *pleasure of the eyes . . . that love beautiful shapes of all kinds, glowing and delightful colors. These things must not take hold on my soul* (10.34). Even delight in *learning and knowledge* are dangerous, constantly migrating into mere curiosity. *In this enormous forest, so full of snares and dangers, temptations* abound; they *buzz around our daily life in all directions* (10.35). The passages in which he discusses the ubiquity of temptations are very similar in anxious tone to the anguished mental state he described in earlier books. *Plus ça change, plus la même chose.*

It is not only *the delight we take in all the pleasures of the senses* that Augustine finds dangerous, but *even more dangerous is a kind of empty longing and curiosity which aims, not at taking pleasure in the flesh but at acquiring experience through the flesh. This disease of curiosity* does not pursue sensual pleasures, but is prompted simply by *the lust to find out and to know.* Curiosity enjoys horrible sights (Augustine's example is *a mangled corpse*)—*things which it does no good to know and which we only want to know for the sake of knowing. . . . This curiosity of ours is tempted every day, and it is impossible to count the times when we slip. It is one thing to get up quickly*, he comments, *and another thing not to fall down* (10.35).

It is not surprising that Augustine felt himself greatly tempted by curiosity; curiosity is a mark of intelligence! But I use the word differently than he did. He seems not to have distinguished between distractions and curiosity. Indeed, the distinction is subtle and depends, not on the object, but on the subject's attitude toward the object. I define most entertainment as distraction, what Augustine called *pressing throngs of vanity,* but I value curiosity because I think of it as an urge to understand something, to find something out.[1] What would be a distraction for one person could be an object of curiosity for another.

I sympathize with Augustine's annoyance with distractions—if that is what he means by "curiosity." I am jealous of my "brain space." If it is stuffed with trivia, there's no room for thinking. I don't want to walk around with news pictures, advertising jingles, and popular music in my mind. I don't watch television. At breakfast I read Plotinus instead of the morning paper. If I do, on occasion, read the paper, I often cry about the misery I encounter, and can't do anything about. If

---

1. The title of Feynman's book, *The Pleasure of Finding Things Out.*

I can't help, I think, I need not know about it. Choosing what I want in my head is a fundamentalist trait, but it has also taken me far. I learned languages when I could have been watching television. Even today, working on a writing project, I carry it in my mind all day and night, undistracted, and often that is when I get insight about it, not when I am hunched over my desk.

Presently my mind is weak and lazy compared to the days when it never simply wandered. In graduate school I was always "on task," either memorizing vocabulary words of the language I was learning, or thinking my way through my dissertation—in the bathtub, washing dishes, or driving. Since then, I have *relaxed a little from myself*, but I needed that focus and passion when I was young (7.14).

Augustine claimed that he has been cured *of my lust for asserting myself against others*, but that he still sins in his *lust to be feared and loved by men*. Indeed, he considers this a particularly heinous sin in that pleasing others can easily become more important than pleasing God. These *temptations occur every day; without intermission we are tempted*. Augustine, the converted rhetorician, was especially concerned about the pleasure he took in pleasing people with his tongue. *You know how on this matter my heart groans to you and my eyes stream tears* (10.36).

I struggle to treat myself with the gentleness with which I want to treat others. Jesus' words, "love your neighbor as yourself," are, I think, less a command than a simple statement of fact: "You do love your neighbor as yourself. You love your neighbor with the same love with which you are able to love yourself." In fact, come to think of it, the love with which you love both your neighbor and yourself is God-is-love, God's love. In his treatise on the Trinity, Augustine even says that one needn't worry about how much to love God or the neighbor, because whenever one loves, one participates in God's love. Loving the neighbor *is* loving God.

Augustine states the principle of addiction: *I can see how far I have advanced . . . simply by observing myself when I am without these things,*

either from choice or when they are not available. For I can then ask myself how much or how little I mind not having them . . . . unless a thing is not there I cannot tell whether it is difficult or easy for me to be without it. Clearly, this practical test does not work with his love of praise—he cannot give up preaching—so he cannot tell how much he depends on it. *Show me myself,* he begs God (10.37).

I find Augustine's test for addiction helpful. If in doubt, remove the suspected object and see whether it is difficult to do without it. Some years ago I did this with coffee, and I suffered from headaches for a month, a sure sign of addiction! After I had adjusted to doing without, I then permitted myself one cup a week—for pleasure, not for need. But coffee is my writing drug; it opens the cupboards of my mind and lets the contents mingle, creating interesting insights. So, while writing my latest book, I began to have one (large) cup every day. Nor did I return to one cup a week when I completed the book. Augustine would worry about this, but I don't. "Habit" is a slightly gentler word than "addiction," in my vocabulary, but not in Augustine's! Notice how Augustine used the word. He says that he finds *sweet delight* in meditating, but that he cannot remain in that happy state. *My sad weight makes me fall back again. I am swallowed up by normality; I am held fast, and I weep heavily, but heavily I am held. So much are we weighed down by the burden of habit* (10.40).

Habits dull the sharp quick sense of life. They create an undertow, a *sad weight*. On the other hand, scrupulosity is also a waste of brain space, energy, and attentiveness. There is no formula. The fourth-century desert ascetics had a suggestion: they worried only when their prayer life was disturbed. Then they had to figure out why and design an asceticism that addressed the problem. So their solution would be to identify what you consider the single most important activity you have, and when it is disturbed, examine your habits.

"What will people think?" was Mother's mantra, heard daily in the fundamentalist minister's household. We were to consider ourselves "surrounded by crowds of witnesses." It was not that we had to please others, but that we had to be good examples. The vividly imagined scrutiny of others was the basis for self-scrutiny. There was little opportunity to experience *the vanity of those who are pleased with themselves.* We adopted Augustine's formula: Whatever is good in oneself is God's gift; whatever is sinful is myself, my self the sinner. *The fault is in taking pleasure in good things which come from you as though they came from oneself* (10.39).

∽

Fundamentalists focus on the individual and her relationship with God. They are concerned with individual sins, not corporate or social sins. The fundamentalist conscience is preoccupied with sexual temptations, with lying, with neglecting to read Scripture and pray on a daily basis, in short, with the kinds of temptations Augustine described. He did not worry about the sins of his society, such as slavery, poverty, military aggression; these were, according to Augustine, necessary social evils. It is only in the liberal churches I attended as an adult that I have heard preaching about the social evils that create suffering for countless people within American society and across the world.

At present, liberal Christians seldom protest the sins of our society based on their religious convictions. The name "Christian" has been appropriated and over-determined by the Christian Right. A teacher in a Roman Catholic college once told me that her students had told her, "We're not Christians, we're Catholics!" The Christian Right has been much more active in the public sphere than liberal Christians; they protest abortion, homosexuality, euthanasia, and genetic engineering, among other things, on the basis of their religious beliefs. Yet, in the name of the God-who-is-love, liberal Christians might contribute to the creation of a loving society.

Americans live in a culture of fear, but we do not fear the most dangerous things. News media cultivate such fears as killer bees and swine flu, but largely ignore such imminent dangers as the long-term high cost of inadequate education, poverty, and hunger. At least partly this is because we do not receive regular information about these ongoing conditions in American society.

Marc and Marque-Luisa Miringoff have demonstrated that while Americans receive constant information about economic health, reports on the nation's social health are few and episodic. Social health is measured by multiple factors, such as "the well-being of America's children and youth, the accessibility of health care, the quality of education, the adequacy of housing, the security and satisfaction of work, and the nation's sense of community, citizenship, and diversity."[2] The statistics the Miringoffs provide are alarming, and have become incrementally worse since they wrote at the end of the twentieth century. In the present economic crisis, American society is becoming meaner by the day as funding for social causes is cut and marginalized people are left without safety nets. The twenty-first-century ecological crisis also testifies to the sins of many generations of Westerners who have taken literally the permission given in the book of Genesis to appropriate the earth's resources for humans' pleasure and aggrandizement. Next to the overwhelming suffering caused by social sins, most individual sins are negligible, harming the sinner more than anyone else.

Augustine shares with contemporary fundamentalists a neurasthenic anxiety about besetting temptations. Yet his anxiety is balanced by ecstatic pleasure in Book 10. He has arrived at the goal of his suffering and struggles; he is confident that he has been brought to participate in God's love.

> *What do I love when I love you [God]? Not the beauty of the body nor the glory of time, not the brightness of light shining so friendly to the eye, not the sweet and various melodies of singing, not the fragrance of flowers and ointments and spices, not manna and honey, not limbs that welcome the embraces of the flesh; it is not these that I love when I love my God. And yet I do love a kind of light, melody, fragrance, food, embrace when I love my God; he is the light, the melody, the fragrance, the food, the embracement of my inner self—there where is a brilliance that space cannot contain, a sound that time cannot carry away, a perfume that no breeze disperses, a taste undiminished by eating, a cleaving together that no satiety will dilute.* (10.6)

Exploring the *spacious palaces* of God's provision and his own memory, Augustine undertakes an analysis of human nature. *I turned my attention on myself and said to myself: "And you, who are you?"* Where once he felt himself the slave of mysterious and nonnegotiable emotional and

---

2. Miringoff and Miringoff, *Social Health of the Nation*; see also Miringoff, Miringoff, and Opdycke, *Social Report*.

physical desires, he now recognizes *a body and a soul*, each of which has capacities and a purpose. *The interior part of me is better*, he decides, but the *outer man* is dependent on *reports from the body's messengers*. In spite of his hierarchical arrangement of body and soul, I read here a new (to Augustine) sense of the possibility of integration and compatibility. *The inner man knew these things through the ministry of the outer man, I, the soul, knew them through the senses of my body* (10.6). Now Augustine believes that he has it right: *And now, my soul, I say to you that you are my better part; you animate the whole bulk of the body, giving it life— a thing that no body can do for another body. But your God is for you too the life of your life* (10.6). Later, in *The City of God*, he called body the spouse (*sponsa*) of soul; he said that the separation of body and soul in death is not a good thing for anyone, but a "harsh and acerbic experience."[3]

The beauty of the universe should make the existence of a creator *evident to all whose senses are not deranged*, Augustine said. But it is essential that his question be asked of sensible things: *What is this God?* Only then will created things respond: *He made us.* Gazing at a flower or a beautiful landscape, my father often said scornfully, "And they say there is no God!"

Augustine's interest in the fruitful *question* is not characteristic of a fundamentalist mind-set. He insists that questions must be asked before they can be answered. And he has no problem with responding to a question, *I don't know* (10.10). The fundamentalists I knew had answers; they did not welcome questions. Even though created things provide valuable information in response to Augustine's question, there is a problem. By loving sensible things, Augustine says, we *become enslaved to them, and slaves cannot judge*. Slaves lose their ability to ask questions or to evaluate answers. Augustine does not comment here, as he does elsewhere, that slaves, whether of habits or substances, also lose their ability to *enjoy*.

Fundamentalists distrust pleasure, but trust suffering. The fundamentalist in me still needs to rationalize small pleasures such as watching DVDs, buying clothes, or eating popcorn as just rewards for working very hard. In spite of a vastly altered worldview, beliefs, and

---

3. Augustine *City of God* 13.6.

values, in less obvious ways—some chosen, some unconscious—I am still a fundamentalist.

Freud said, you must relinquish the pleasure principle. I know now what he meant. By "pleasure," he meant what's easiest, close at hand, not an effort. Relinquish (over)eating, drinking, and TV for more subtle, larger pleasures. Being trained to almost infinite delay of gratifications as a child, I'm not keen on delay. But I can distinguish between infinitely delayed (until heaven) and *a bit* delayed (until tomorrow). Recently, after two weeks of minimal food, no wine, a few dizzy spells, a fragile feeling, I saw quicker and sharper. My life, meaning *me, my* life.

I promised myself that I would not again experience the boredom and deadness of my mid-twenties. I found strategies for avoiding the boredom inherent in meetings, exercise, and daily tasks. One of these

The Difficulty of Beautiful Things

was to memorize poems. I found that my childhood Scripture memorization, though it had not endeared Scripture to me, had nevertheless taught me skills of memorization, skills that seem to be dying out in our entertainment culture. Not just any poems, but those I loved and with which I wanted to have a particular intimacy. The longer the better—up to a point. I did not memorize *The Iliad* or *The Odyssey*, but I did memorize Wallace Stevens' "Sunday Morning," T. S. Eliot's "Ash Wednesday," and numerous others. When boredom threatens I have only to say one of my poems silently to be transported to a world of vivid beauty. No one knows; I can look fully attentive and engaged in what's happening in the room; indeed, if something requires my attention, I notice and attend.

Moments of beauty and delight are treasured because they occur *in between* crises, pain, and terror; they are time-out. They bring a strength that balances those other times. Some music does this superbly. Who could fail to be happy while hearing Beethoven's Violin Concerto in D-major? The music carries a relaxed excitement, or an excited relaxation. These are moments of happiness, real, sensual, and concrete happiness. The feeling tone is gratitude: this beauty is what we are given, not freedom from pain and death. *This beauty*, in spite of . . . (fill in the blank).

In mid-life, exhausted and depleted, I needed new methods to counterbalance the misery of hot flashes, the anxiety of a breast biopsy, anguish over an alcoholic son, and the pressure of teaching responsibilities. Would religion work? Religion is complicated for me by the cynicism of clergy friends and the quite different cynicism of feminist friends. Even so, community and ritual are strong for me, the community that stands together to witness events that happen in eternity, unconscious time—the baptism of a child, marriage, funerals. In these moments I experience the great beauty that holds us in life and death, in the perfect safety of the universe. Tears and cleansing strong feeling mark the presence of the great beauty—Augustine's "beauty so ancient and so new." Carl Jung said that the task of the second half of life is to develop a religious perspective, a "hygienic" belief in immortality, so that one goes forward fearlessly, in happy anticipation. I remain (at best) agnostic about immortality; the beloved community is enough for me.

The task is not to perpetuate or renew activities that in another time of life produced the most vivid sense of the great beauty, but to *pay attention*, to "listen up" to where it appears *now*. To exercise and strengthen *these* connections. To leave old ones courageously, grateful for them, but not clinging to them. To *go on*, not to go back. No hanging on by fingernails to a method useful in the past, but recognizing what was revealed, namely, the real ubiquitous existence of the great beauty. Once you have "the hang of it," you see it everywhere. You learn to perceive *as* beauty. But you're pretty much on your own. Although there are clues everywhere, there aren't many self-help manuals for recognizing her; there aren't many books about imagining the real.

Augustine experienced the great beauty. Perhaps he learned to recognize it from Plotinus, who learned it from Plato. Augustine wrote:

> *Late have I loved you, Beauty so ancient and so new, late have I loved you! And see, you were within me and I was outside, and there I searched for you and in my deformity I plunged into the beauties that you have made. You were with me, and I was not with you. . . . You called, you cried out, you shattered my deafness; you flashed, you shone, you scattered my blindness; you breathed perfume, and I drew in my breath and I pant for you; I tasted, and I am hungry and thirsty; you touched me, and I burned for your peace.* (10.27)

Augustine described his experience of the great beauty in the language of the senses. In his treatise "On the Beautiful" (*The Greater Hippias*), Plato sought to determine "not what is beautiful, but what is the beautiful." He was forced to end with the very modest conclusion, "The beautiful things are difficult."[4] Augustine learned from Plotinus to identify beauty by a particular *feeling*. Plotinus wrote:

> There must be some who see this beauty . . . and when they see it they must be delighted and overwhelmed and excited much

---

4. Plato *Greater Hippias* 304e, 359.

more than by these beauties we spoke of before, since now it is true beauty they are grasping. These experiences must occur whenever there is contact with any sort of beautiful thing, wonder, and a shock of delight and longing and passion and a happy excitement. . . . you feel like this when you see, in yourself or someone else, greatness of soul, a righteous life, a pure morality, courage . . . he who sees them cannot say anything except that they are what really exists. What does "really exist" mean? That they exist as beauties.[5]

Like Augustine I recognize the great beauty within the many beauties: art, music, the faces of strangers, in religion and sex, in books, in growing things, in smells. But the great beauty is chaste, revealing itself only to its committed lovers. Attentiveness is necessary. And a trained and disciplined eye.

---

5. Plotinus *Ennead* 1.6.4.

11 *The One Thing*

Publication is not all it's cracked up to be. But writing is.
—ANNE LAMOTT[1]

BERRYMAN

I had hardly begun to read
I asked how can you ever be sure
that what you write is really
any good at all and he said you can't

You can't you can never be sure
you die without knowing
whether anything you wrote was any good
if you have to be sure don't write

—W. S. MERWIN[2]

IN BOOK 11, AUGUSTINE CONSIDERS the mystery of time and eternity. Although he is pressured by a shortage of time (*the drops of my time are too precious*), he begins Book 11 with a long prayer for guidance and

---

1. Lamott, *Bird by Bird*, xxvi.
2. Merwin, "Berryman," 256.

insight: *Give me what I love, for I do love it, and that love too was your gift.* He says that he understands the *words* of Scripture well enough, as anyone can who knows the language, but he seeks to grasp *the inner secrets of your words* (11.2).

Again he questions created things: *It was you, Lord, who made them, you who are beautiful (for they are beautiful), you who are good (for they are good), you who are (for they are)* (11.4). But the very existence of created objects raises the question of how and when they were created. Puzzled, he proposes the idea of an eternal word by which God spoke creation.

> *Can we not hold the mind and fix it firm so that it may stand still for a moment and for a moment lay hold upon the splendor of eternity which stands forever, and compare it with the times that never stand, and see that no comparison is possible?* (11.11)

Augustine has experienced his *fluttering* mind briefly standing still, and he contrasts those experiences with measurable, conscious time. He describes two experiences of mentally arriving at *That Which Is*, eternity. *But I had not the power to keep my eye steadily fixed; in my weakness I felt myself falling back and returning again to my habitual ways* (7.17). Augustine and his mother had a similar experience shortly before she died: *We two had, as it were, gone beyond ourselves and in a flash of thought had made contact with that eternal wisdom which abides above all things.* Once again normality quickly intervened, leaving Augustine and Monnica sighing for the return of the *moment of understanding.* It didn't work; thrust back in time, they try *to taste eternity while their mind is still fluttering about in the past and future movements of things, and so is still unstable* (9.10).

Augustine was fascinated by eternity, in which *nothing passes by; everything is present* (11.11), but his first project is to understand ordinary time: *What is time?* He follows a painstaking route to the answer he offers: *There are three times—a present of things past, a present of things present, and a present of things future.* Finally accepting *custom*—usually so reprehensible to him, he shortens his answer: *There are three times—past, present, and future,* even though *it is an incorrect use of language* (11.14). Like my father, he deplored imprecise language. *It is not often that we use language correctly; usually we use it incorrectly, though we understand each other's meaning* (11.20).

Unlike Augustine, I am interested very little in conscious time. Augustine described himself as "on fire" to solve the enigma of conscious time (11.22). For Augustine, time and eternity are not two different entities. Rather, eternity is "ecstatic time."[3]

What Augustine called eternity, I call *unconscious* time—time that stands still, time that can't be measured, in which one is always at the same place in the psyche, whether ten years old or eighty. I have experienced this kind of time several times. The first was when I was ten years old, afraid to go to sleep for fear I'd die in the night and go to hell; or, when I was thirty, naked and cold under a sheet outside the operating room door. At the age of ten I knew that death was with me, always *there*, waiting. I entered that place also in several sexual experiences, and as a student, in several drug experiences. Freud wrote:

> [U]nconscious mental processes are themselves timeless. This means in the first place that they are not ordered temporally, that time does not change them in any way and that the idea of time cannot be applied to them.[4]

Unconscious time is not merely the negative of conscious time. It is experienced as "traumatic stimulation against which protection is needed." In fact, "Conscious time itself may be a defense against the tension of unconscious time,"[5] a "primal repudiation" of the terror of unconscious time. "Such tension-raising time can appear to be nonexistent once conscious time is conflated with time itself."[6]

Unconscious time "is the time of Eros, and primary narcissism—tension-raising, libidinal—self-preservative, *vital* differentiating time."[7] Sylvia, my 93-year-old hospice patient said to me several times: "Time is just a place." I tried to understand, but couldn't until I had the concept of unconscious time. The *feeling* of unconscious time is, oh! I've been here before; I know this place! This is *my* place.

---

3. Manchester, "As long as that song could be heard," 59–70.
4. *Beyond the Pleasure Principle*, quoted by Bass, *Difference and Disavowal*, 84.
5. Ibid.
6. Ibid., 85.
7. Ibid.

The One Thing

∽

Fundamentalists' primary interest in time comes from the belief that what an individual does in time has consequences in eternity. Heaven and hell, reward and punishment loom large in fundamentalist preaching. As a child I tried to image what it would be like to be rewarded or punished *eternally*: In the words of "Amazing Grace," "When we've been there ten thousand years / bright shining as the sun / we've no less days to sing God's praise / than when we first begun." Unimaginable eternal reward was bewildering, and even more mind-boggling, eternal punishment seemed overkill for a few lies and some disobedience. As I grew up I liked better to think of God as understanding all, and therefore forgiving all. A verse from "The Prayer of the Reverend Eli Jenkins" in Dylan Thomas's epic poem, *Under Milk Wood*, astonished me when I first read it as a young adult:

> We are not wholly bad or good,
> we who live under Milkwood,
> and Thou I'm sure will be the first
> to see our best side, not our worst.[8]

I could not conceptualize a God who did not strain every nerve to notice, record, and punish my sins.

Augustine did not interest himself in the fundamentalist's terrifying and terrorizing understanding of time and eternity. In the *Confessions*, there is no mention of hell. Augustine's God operates in *this* life; Augustine understands "rewards" and "punishments" as life lessons. He explores time and eternity simply as intriguingly complex philosophical concepts. But this does not account for his feverish anxiety to understand time. Why such anguished appeals to God to allow him to understand? What is at stake for him? I suggest that Book 11 should be read as a sequel to Book 10. In Book 10, he finds the self in memory. He found the *power of memory terrifying . . . and this thing is the mind, and this thing is myself* (10.17). In Book 11, he locates the self in time. Memory and time are intimately connected; memories occur in time but remain, across time, in some form, however diluted or distorted, form.

> Will the self, lost, be found again? In form?[9]

> The past only comes back when the present runs so smoothly that it is like the sliding surface of a deep river. Then one sees through the surface to the depths. In those moments I find one of my greatest satisfactions, not that I am thinking of the past; but it is then that I am living most fully in the present. For the present when backed by the past is a thousand times deeper than the present when it presses so close that you can feel nothing else. . . . But to feel the present sliding over the depths of the past, peace is necessary.[10]

I am ambivalent about the time I spend working. On the one hand, time disappears when I am absorbed in thinking something through and writing about it. However, time does not disappear, but keeps running, whether I notice it or not. I suddenly glance at the clock, realize

---

8. Thomas, *Under Milk Wood*, 87.
9. Roethke, *Collected Poems*.
10. Woolf, *Moments of Being*, 98.

that I have been "away," and am alarmed at how much time has gone by—bits of my lifetime of which I have not been aware. And so I feel that I have *lost* time. Yet I also loved being "out of time."

At present, "universalizing" is considered bad. We used to think that the person who could see the world most accurately, and thus whose experience and perspective could be universalized, was someone—well, a man—with the best education, freedom from necessity (financial and physical), and leisure to think. From the most privileged members of society we *can* perhaps learn about what is working well in the society, but we will not, by listening to them, learn much about the lives of people who are disadvantaged, marginalized, or oppressed. So now academics are learning to listen to myriad voices whose views of "reality" have formerly been ignored; these are the people who have privileged information about how the society is *not* working.

Nevertheless, the discovery of "universality" was very important for me when I was a young, uneducated, poor, wife and mother. The concept meant quite simply, *me too*. It meant that I, even I, could participate in the human passion to understand, to experience, and to describe. It meant that no one had greater access than I to "humanity" and its projects, longings, and satisfactions. At first, it did not occur to me that universalizing *my* perspective was as much a problem as when educated white men did it. And it came as a shock to discover, much later, that universalizing white middle-class women's perspectives did not work for women of all classes, all races, all geographical locations and cultures.

Imagination is a very complicated topic. On the one hand, imagination is important, even necessary, for making intentional choices. I had to imagine myself teaching large classes at Harvard University before I could do it. I used to advise doctoral students facing comprehensive exams and dissertation defenses to imagine themselves in the room where the exam will occur, answering questions and engaging in conversation with *colleagues* (not teachers) with intellectual excitement and force of mind. I cannot do anything that I cannot first imagine myself doing.

On the other hand, there is a destructive imagination—for example, the imagination that collects from memory medical horror stories when the slightest medical problem appears. Of this kind of imagination, the editor of a collection of Ernie Pyle's war stories wrote, "Cowardice is failure to stop the imagination." This kind of imagination is also the stuff of jealousy, insecurity, and it is the basis of the culture of fear in which Americans presently live.

Back to the fruitful imagination: I begin by imagining myself as complex, not reducible to the fundamentalist "good" or "bad" person. I go back in memory to family, friends, events, and circumstances with the express purpose of identifying and revealing the richness, the conflicted, contradictory, glorious richness. Am I lazy, or am I hardworking? Yes, both. Memoirs are especially susceptible to simple interpretations of complex occasions. Yet, maybe it is *only* in retrospect that one can begin to imagine people richly enough; at the time one may be focused on what action is appropriate. Perhaps when it is not necessary to decide upon an action, it is possible finally to be more generous.

Next, imagine the person one sees, her body's brief or long history, the unseen and seldom reflected-on interior of her body—the heart beating rhythmically, the blood coursing through veins, digestion, and breath. All this happening now in a body that will one day no longer perform all these precision tricks. Imagine the child who was *in fact* transformed day by day into the person one sees.

Imagine the real in relationships. Often I have not imagined people richly enough; I content myself with the cynical interpretation of their behavior. For example, I have thought that a friend uses my home as the "Berkeley hotel," a place to stay when she comes here. A more richly imagined account would recognize that she also loves me and likes to see me. "The real" is that people love me *and* they often need or want something from me. Can I seek the richness *instead* of the foreshortened cynical "truth" in relationships?

༄

There is common agreement in American culture that relationships *must* go on to the next step, the next level of commitment. This unquestioned assumption masquerades as simply "the way things are." Like any ideology that *works*, it is never questioned. "An ideology is really 'holding us,'" Slavoj Žižek wrote, "only when we do not feel any opposition between it and reality—that is, when the ideology succeeds in determining the mode of our everyday experience of reality itself."[11]

Perhaps this ideology is at least partly responsible for the fact that marriages become boring. If a couple is no longer on a socially recognized trajectory, if there is no further commitment to be made, then what? This ideology can be countered with a *discipline of attentiveness to the present*. Neither past nor future should be allowed to overwhelm and obliterate the present, but both can be brought to bear on being fully in the present. The past is present, gathered up into the present. The future is here too, as possibility that one "awaits with confidence and accepts with gratitude." Quietly. Not rushing to get somewhere else than the present. Presence in the present. The present of the present.

Imagine the real on a broader stage than that of one's acquaintances and relationships. As Iris Murdoch pointed out, we don't habitually live in the real world. We live in worlds we construct for our comfort and safety. Do I make myself accountable for the whole, for what is done in my name, as well as for what I do directly? In *My Dinner with André*, Wally Shawn put it this way:

> I think of myself as a very decent, good person simply because I think I'm reasonably friendly to most people I happen to meet every day. I mean, I think of myself quite smugly, and I think I'm a perfectly nice guy, so long as I somehow think of the world as consisting of, you know, just the small circle of people I know as friends—or just the few people that we know in this little world of our hobbies . . . and I'm really quite self-satisfied. I'm happy with myself. I have no complaint about myself . . . . But the thing is, let's face it, there's a whole enormous world out there that I don't ever think about, and I *certainly* don't take responsibility for how I've lived in *that* world. I mean, if I were actually to confront the fact that I'm sort of sharing this stage with the starving person in Africa somewhere, well then I wouldn't feel so great about myself. So naturally I blot those people out of my perception . . . . In other words, we all have every reason to hide from reality. . .[12]

11. Žižek, *Sublime Object of Ideology*, 49.
12. *My Dinner with André*, 83.

Augustine and the Fundamentalist's Daughter

∾

In order to explain the worldview I have come to trust I need not only to describe the ideas of Augustine that have intrigued and shaped me, but also Plotinus's worldview and values. Without Plotinus, Augustine is oppressively doctrinaire and obsessively preoccupied with the self. Thus, though perhaps not immediately recognizable as such, the sections that follow are autobiographical. In discussing Plotinus, I present an important feature of my orientation to the universe, as Augustine did in the later books of the *Confessions*.

Through Augustine, Plotinus's philosophy had a long and rich history within Christianity. Augustine learned from Plotinus to cultivate an interior life, a subjectivity.[13] But, still in search of reality, Augustine went *in* and then *up*, while Plotinus pictured a direct connection from his own center to all living beings and to the impersonal center of the universe. Christian mysticism owes a large debt to Plotinus.

What does it mean to say that an author is "influential?" The usual meaning is that we can find traces of his thought in later authors. But we seldom consider that, in fact, "influence" also moves backwards, as later authors reinterpret an earlier author according to the later author's perspectives and commitments. Western Christians understand Plotinus through Augustine's eyes, even though there are dramatic differences between them.

Ironically, after Augustine, Plotinus became the villain of Christian authors (with some notable exceptions). Seeking to protect Christianity from allegations of dualism, hatred of bodies and the natural world, and preference for abstractions, has led Christians to attempt to ascribe blame for these flaws to "NeoPlatonism," represented by Plotinus. Frequently used as a foil for Christians' religious or philosophical positions, his magnificent conception of the universe and the intimate interdependence of its parts is misunderstood by most contemporary Christian authors. Because he did not found a church or a religion, he left no followers to insist that his thought be carefully and accurately interpreted.

According to Porphyry, Plotinus's student, friend, and biographer, Plotinus was one of the most eccentric and thoughtful people of

---

13. Cary, *Augustine's Invention of the Inner Self*, chap. 5.

his—or perhaps any—time. Porphyry gives a wonderfully odd, closely observed, and personal account of his teacher.

> There was always a charm about his appearance, but [when he was teaching] he was still more attractive to look at: he sweated gently, and kindliness shone out from him, and in answering questions he made clear both his benevolence to the questioner and his intellectual vigor.[14]

Moreover, anyone would envy Plotinus's remarkable ability to concentrate; he was able, Porphyry reported, "to be present at once to himself and to others."

> Even if he was talking to someone, engaged in continuous conversation, he kept to his train of thought. He could take his necessary part in the conversation to the full, and at the same time keep his mind fixed without a break on what he was considering. When the person he had been talking to was gone . . . he went straight on with what he had been thinking, keeping the connection, just as if there had been no interval of conversation between.[15]

Plotinus taught that no one can understand the world who has not been startled and instructed by its beauty. Recognizing beauty is a transformative experience. Beauty's message, he said, is the unity of life, gift of the impersonal source he called the "great beauty." A person can recognize beauty by her kinship with it, for her life is one with universal life. Like Plotinus, Augustine recognized beauty by its physical and emotional effects: "a shock of delight and longing and passion and a happy excitement."[16]

Augustine was especially attracted to this Plotinian idea, but he focused more directly than did Plotinus on sensory apprehension of beauty. Augustine wrote: *You called, you cried out, you shattered my deafness: you flashed, you shone, you scattered my blindness; you breathed perfume, and I drew in my breath and I pant for you: I tasted, and I am hungry and thirsty: you touched me and I burned for your peace* (10.27).

Beauty was not, for Plotinus, an aesthetic category. To notice beauty is not to make a judgment about a quality of a particular object.

14. Porphyry *Life* 13.
15. Ibid. 8.
16. *Ennead* 1.6.4.

Rather, to perceive beauty is to see an object *in its life*, that is, to grasp the interconnections that give it existence. Plotinus said that those who do not see this beauty are clueless. But no one is born with a natural capacity for perceiving beauty; it is not inherited in the genes, or automatically acquired in the process of socialization or education. Rather, the perception of beauty must be trained by the practice of contemplation. In short, what you (can) see is what you get—either broken shards, scattered randomly, or the unity of "richly varied" (his term) life.

> When we ourselves are beautiful, it is by belonging to ourselves, but we are ugly when we are ignorant of ourselves.[17]

Plotinus described an intricate and complex universe in which life circulates from a source he usually called "the One." Life is the fundamental element of the universe, intimately connecting all who share it. He thought of "life" very inclusively; even rocks and soil have life. But, "in the bad, life limps."[18]

Both Plotinus and Augustine had alternative languages for ultimate reality. Plotinus, acknowledging the inevitable distortion of using only one term for the source of reality, usually referred to "the One"; but he also used the "great beauty," and even on occasion, "Father." Augustine said that anyone who thinks of God as anything other than "life itself" has an absurd notion of God.[19] He also quoted 1 John 4:16, "God is love," adding, *That is all you need to know about God*. Also Augustine named God *beauty so old and so new* (pulchritudo tam antiqua et name nova) (10.27).

In his poem "Of Being Numerous," George Oppen wrote, "A man must not come to feel that he holds a thousand threads in his hand; he must somehow see the one thing." "The One thing"—life—is invisible precisely because it is so ubiquitously visible. It is distributed in everything one looks at, but seldom sees. A person can utterly miss it because of its visibility. Thus Plotinus's exercises; contemplation is for getting past the words, the definitions, the categories through which we usually look at the world. So that we can see what there is. Plotinian prayer is contemplation that redirects a person's attention from personal concerns toward the whole. Plotinus gives detailed instructions

---

17. *Ennead* 5.8.13.
18. *Ennead* 1.7.3.
19. Augustine *On Christian Doctrine* 1.8, 12.

in the practice of contemplation by which a person *imagines the real*, the whole that we seldom recognize due to our fascination with our own bit part.

Unlike modern philosophers who largely neglect body, Plotinus treated body as a subject that deserved sustained reflection, focusing on it in several treatises.[20] It is not an exaggeration to say that he was preoccupied with body. He was especially struck by the simultaneous fragility and preciousness of body. Plotinus argued that as long as we do not expect bodies to be flawless and permanent, they are *wonderful*. He condensed his argument into a parable: Hatred of body, he said, is

> like two people living in the same fine house, one of whom reviles the structure and the builder, but stays there none the less, while the other does not revile, but says the builder has built it with the utmost skill, and waits for the time to come in which he will go away, when he will not need a house any longer: the first might think he was wiser and readier to depart because he knows how to say that the walls are built of soulless stones and timber and are far inferior to the true dwelling place.... While we have bodies we must stay in our houses, which have been built for us by a good sister soul which has great power to work without any toil or trouble.[21]

However, it is not philosophical ideas but one's own body that supplies the strongest incentive for thinking about bodies. The knowledge that one must die is the most evident of pressures. Centuries after Augustine lived, Samuel Johnson remarked that "nothing concentrates the mind like knowing one is going to be hanged in a fortnight." Constant vulnerability to disease and accident, especially in a time before antibiotics and anesthetics, also prompted Plotinus and Augustine to think seriously about bodies. Yet their statements about bodies have confused generations of readers. While addressing different audiences and interests, they spoke about body differently, sometimes praising bodies—human, animal, plant, and celestial bodies—as perfectly and beautifully *what they are*. Sometimes, however, in the context of urging

---

20. Sheets-Johnstone is an exception. Her books, especially *Roots of Thinking* (1990), *Roots of Power* (1994), *Roots of Morality* (2008), and *Corporeal Turn* (2009) all establish body as the origin of all human activity.

21. *Ennead* 2.9.17.

their readers to pay attention to the cultivation of their souls, they spoke quite disparagingly of bodies and the sensible world.

If one expects a philosophy to be systematic, then such contradictory statements are confusing. But when the subject is as variable as bodies, it makes sense. Bodies are the source of both the greatest pleasure and the greatest pain of human life. When we dance, lie in the sun, or listen to music, we are immensely grateful for our bodies. In the hospital with an undiagnosed and painful disease, during dental surgery, or struggling to walk on crutches—in these (and similar) circumstances we might be inclined to feel that body is not an unmitigated boon. Plotinus's most disparaging statements about bodies occur in his last (chronological) treatise, when he lay dying of a disease so repugnant that his friends and students—to a man—abandoned him.

Eventually, inevitably, Plotinus said, life will lift off from the used up body and go on to other forms. When a person dies, the life she had is not destroyed; "it is simply no longer there."[22] It can readily be seen that in Plotinus's concept of the rushing circulation of life through living bodies of all sorts, there is little room for last judgments and eternal destinies for individuals.

Plotinus insisted that there *is* providential care. But it is addressed to the *whole* universe, not to individuals; "the universe lies in safety."[23] This means that individuals can enjoy the safety of the universe only if they accept utterly and to the core, even while they enjoy its gifts, that these gifts, including the gift of life, will sooner or later pass on to other forms of life. But, Plotinus said, isn't this what there *is*? So why not acknowledge and accept it? Why all this special pleading, why all this me, me, me? Why not recognize that I am not singled out for special treatment no matter what I believe or how virtuously I act, or—for that matter—how carefully I eat or exercise? If we understand the nature of the universe we will enjoy and/or bear what is provided uncomplainingly.

We should not take personally a very broad range of the things that occur to us, for "the life of the universe does not serve the purposes of each individual but of the whole." [24] If my choices have not brought about my sufferings, then I suffer by chance. But even then,

22. *Ennead* 4.5.7.
23. *Ennead* 3.4.4; 6.4.5.
24. *Ennead* 4.4.39; 4.5.3.

The One Thing

I can choose how to respond to whatever happens. The "provision" is ambiguous—evil and good, pain and gift. One can, however, cultivate a perspective from which the universe is seen as dazzling and trustworthy beauty, as perfect safety.

No third-century person could have predicted twenty-first-century concerns over polluted air and water, endangered species, vanishing rain forests, and a threatened ozone layer. On this topic, Plotinus's suggestions did not respond to a perceived threat, but resulted from his vision of the universe as an intimately interconnected whole. Until the second half of the twentieth century, it was impossible to identify and map with scientific precision the effects living beings have on one another even across long distances. Plotinus's description of an interdependent web of living beings was intuited rather than demonstrated.

Throughout the history of Western philosophy there have been authors with similar intuitions, but they have been labeled romantic, "soft," or nature worshippers by "hardheaded" philosophers. Presently, however, scientists can measure and prove the tangible effects of environmental crises like the disappearance of rain forests, extinction of animal species, and pollution of air, water, and food. This information is no longer intuited or romantic, but concrete and well documented, a fact of life in the twenty-first century. Plotinus said it first:

> The All is a single living being which encompasses all the living beings within it . . . . This one universe is all bound together in shared experience and is like one living creature, and that which is far is really near . . . . And since it is one living thing and all belongs to a unity nothing is so distant in space that it is not close enough to the one living thing to share experience.[25]

This worldview, once Plotinus's mystical vision, now has obvious implications for practices that damage the natural world and kill people. Plotinus's worldview can inspire action based on the awareness that the community of human responsibility is not limited to humans, but extends to all living beings.

> Men build bridges and streets when there is already an amazing gold electric ring connecting every living being as surely as if we held hands, flippers, and paws, feelers and wings.[26]

25. *Ennead* 4.4.32.
26. Kingston, *China Men*, 92.

Bodies' exigencies concentrate the mind, making time real and creating a longing to "have it all now." For although life itself is trustworthy, utterly safe, the particular configuration that comes into focus as my life will eventually lose focus and slide into the ocean of life. Mortals do not have the luxury of banqueting at ease on Olympus with the blessed immortals. To wish, to imagine, or to act as if one does, Plotinus said, to be shocked when confronted by old age or death—whichever comes first—is to miss the greatest opportunity we have. That is the opportunity of realizing our connection to the All, of training ourselves through contemplation to see the great beauty, the beauty of the whole circulation of life. Plotinus described an ethic in which the perception of beauty—the beauty of the connectedness of the All—grounds responsibility for the well-being of all living beings.

Who are we really? A human being, Plotinus said, is double; on the one hand, we are what you see. Bodies capture and contain the life circulated by the One source, but bodies are not all of what it means to be "us." We also exist simultaneously "there," at the heart of the universe. And this is most essentially who we are. In our self-imposed isolation, senses fatigue, boredom dulls vision; we constantly long for some wonderful new stimulus to freshen our lives. We fall in love; we seek entertainment; we forget to look at one another, and above all we forget ourselves—our real selves and the amazing glory of the life we share with the company of living beings. Plotinus urged his readers to do the daily, disciplined and rewarding work of remembering who we are.

As I proceed further and further with my recitation, so the expectation grows shorter and the memory grows longer, until all the expectation is finished at the point when the whole of this action is over and has passed into the memory. Augustine compares the recitation of a Psalm, or the singing of a hymn, to *the whole of a man's life* [and] *the whole history of humanity* (11.28).

Augustine's poignant account of his experience of the self in time:

> My life is a kind of distraction and dispersal. [I pray that] *I may be gathered up from my former days to follow the One . . . not wasted and scattered on things which are to come and things which will pass away, but intent . . . no longer distracted but concentrated*

> .... *But I have been spilled and scattered among times whose order I do not know; my thoughts, the innermost bowels of my soul, are torn apart with the crowding tumults of variety, and so it will be until all together I can flow into you, purified and molten by the fire of your love. And I shall stand and become set in you, in my mold, in your truth.* (11.29–30)[27]

The strong images in this passage bring to a virtual climax, as it were, Augustine's description of his conversion to continence, the theme of his *Confessions*. Male sexual experience is heavily—not subtly—referenced in the contrast he draws between being *spilled and scattered* and being *purified* and *set in you, in my mold*. His most intimate social experience, together with his most concentrated intellectual, emotional, and spiritual experience mirror and reveal the structure of his life. Occurring as it does at the conclusion of his anguished search for an understanding of time, sexual experience, unacknowledged as such, represents Augustine's best effort to explain what a lifetime feels like, more specifically what Augustine's experience tells him that a *Christian* lifetime feels like.[28] He pictures the rushing painful disorienting excitement—physical, intellectual, and emotional—of youth (*crowding tumults of variety*) brought to a moment of decision and turning (*until all together I can flow into you . . . and become set in you*), followed by ever-lengthening memory and ever-decreasing expectation.

Augustine fleshes out his metaphors of flowing and congealing with the verbs *turgeo* and *tumeo* to describe his youthful condition of (swelling or swollen) prideful arrogance. Tumescent body parts represent pride: *I was separated from you by the swelling (tumor) of my pride. It was as though my cheeks had swollen up so that I could not see out of my eyes* (3.5; see also 7.7).

Gathering, containing, recollecting: these are the activities that must replace dissipation, spilling, and scattering, *both literally and symbolically.*

> *The Word itself calls you to come back . . . you will lose nothing. What is withered in you will flower again, and all your illnesses will be made well, and all that was flowing and wasting from you*

---

27. Compare *Confessions* 2.2: *I was tossed here and there, spilled on the ground, scattered abroad; I boiled over in my fornications.*

28. Miles, *Desire and Delight*, 95.

> will regain shape and substance and will form part of you again. (4.11)

Augustine's vast influence has contributed to the present ecological crisis. His exclusive attention to *God and the soul* did not direct Christians to care for the natural world. Of course, in his time the resources of nature seemed inexhaustible. Plotinus's teaching that there is a direct connection from one's own center to all other living beings—to life itself—urges attention, concern, and care for the beings with whom we share the world. Of course, Christian doctrines of creation, incarnation, and the resurrection of body could provide a similar incentive to care for the life that populates "our island home." But these doctrines, presumably so central to Christian faith, have not been fully applied, developed, emphasized, and advocated. I think we must acknowledge that Augustine's finger, insistently pointing in, then *up*, has been *one* of the encouragements to Western Christians to neglect the needy world of living beings.

Augustine's model of spirituality, withdrawal and centering, should not be the only model for spirituality. Plotinus's idea of our *connection* to the center of the universe and all living beings through sharing life suggests a spirituality that features concern and action on behalf of our interdependent world.

For Augustine, a happy ending to his sexual frustrations. For me, the long-term and intimate effects of Augustine's powerful exposition of continence, in which he contrasted and opposed spiritual and sexual experience, have been difficult to eradicate. Augustine's view of sex was woven into my psyche from an early age and on the unexamined and foundational level of assumption. It should be considered a deadly sin to separate body and its most intimate and pleasurable activities from spiritual insight. The medieval "seven deadly sins" are so called because they *deaden* a person's life, prompting him to choose deficit satisfactions over real pleasures. (The seven deadly sins are: pride, covetousness, lust, envy, gluttony, anger, and sloth.) There is no mention in this list of the deadening effect on both something labeled "sexual" experience and something labeled "spiritual" experience of neglecting to feel gratitude for "the grace of the creator in giving us a body."[29]

> If the truest life is life by thought, and is the same thing as the truest thought, then the truest thought lives, and contemplation and the object of contemplation . . . is living and life, and the two together are one.[30]

---

29. Evagrius Ponticus, *Praktiko*, 53.
30. *Ennead* 3.8.8.

12   *A Sharp Quick Sense of Life*

My point is not that everything is bad, but that everything is dangerous, which is not exactly the same as bad. If everything is dangerous, then we always have something to do.
 —MICHEL FOUCAULT[1]

The object was to learn to what extent the effort to think one's own history can free thought from what it *silently thinks,* and so enable it to think differently.
 —MICHEL FOUCAULT[2]

HAVING TACKLED AND ADDRESSED MORE or less to his satisfaction the immense question of time and eternity in Book 11, Augustine takes on the topic of the creation of the world in Book 12. The topic lands him immediately in bewilderment and ambiguity. In fact, he has introduced each of the massive queries of his later books with protestations of puzzlement, of *not knowing*. Both his anxious uneasiness and his declarations of ignorance indicate that his search is an honest one. He writes in the style of a Platonic dialogue in which real questions are explored, often concluding with answers that are not fully satisfying. His earliest Christian writings, the Cassiciacum dialogues, testify to his preference

1. Foucault, "On the Genealogy of Ethics," 231–32.
2. Foucault, *Use of Pleasure,* 9.

for Platonic dialogue. Platonic dialogues are unlike Aristotelian essays, in which the conclusion is already known to the writer, and the essay argues from a starting point dictated by the conclusion.

Augustine admits that *when the mind of man questions itself in this way, it must aim either at knowledge through ignorance or at ignorance through knowledge* (12.5). The creation of the universe has never been an issue for me; I am, however, interested in how Augustine argues, in what he considers important, and in his attitude toward those who disagree with him.

Augustine's first point was that God did not create the universe out of Godself, but *out of nothing. Before you gave shape and variety to this formless matter, there was nothing—no color, no outline, no body, no spirit. And yet not absolutely nothing; there was a kind of formlessness, lacking all definition* (12.3). He speculates: God *created this beautiful world* out of something called *formless matter* (12.4). Unexpectedly, the fact that the earth is *lowest of the low* in the universe leads him to marvel at how beautiful, nevertheless, the earth is.

This is not philosophical but theological exploration, leading to God who has *called* [him] *back*, who speaks to him *in my inner ear . . . loud and clear* (12.11). Still intent on establishing that God and the world are radically separate, Augustine repeats that he knows what he needs to know; he knows that *the changes that take place in the last and lowest creatures* do so because they exist *in a kind of formlessness* and are thus subject to change, while God *suffers no change in time* (12.15).

Finally, Augustine closes his complicated speculations by acknowledging that matters so imponderable might be allowed more than one interpretation. *What harm can it do me if my view of what Moses meant is different from someone else's view?* Augustine's generosity to others' intentions sets him apart from the fundamentalists of my childhood. He acknowledges that *all of us who read are endeavoring to find out and to grasp what the person we are reading meant to say* (12.18).

After further laborious argument, Augustine concedes grudgingly that *the material out of which a thing is made can, in a certain sense, already bear the name of the thing that is made from it; thus any kind of formless matter out of which heaven and earth were made can be called heaven and earth* (12.19). Similarly, in Book 11, after long and complicated argument, he conceded that time could actually be called past, present, and future, rather than the more accurate but strained, *present of times past, present of times present, and present of times future* (11.20). On both subjects he has explored in detail the semantic problems and finally conceded that the common expressions are fundamentally accurate.

∽

Augustine provides context for his argument about creation by imagining a debate with opponents. Debate can take several different forms. In one model, the speaker caricatures others' interpretations and arguments, using them as a foil to exhibit the greater accuracy and beauty of his own. If all else fails, *ad hominem* comments are likely to occur. Discourse can also be cooperative; participants can *think together*, learning from other perspectives and modifying their own arguments accordingly. In Book 12 Augustine exemplifies both competitive and cooperative discussion. In a competitive mode he assumes the worst of his imagined opponents, saying,

> *They are not speaking because they are divinely inspired and have seen what they say in the heart of your servant; they are speaking out of pride; they do not know what Moses thought, but they love what they think themselves, and they love their own opinion not because it is true, but because it is their own.* (12.25)

Augustine, of course, claims to be divinely inspired—God whispers in his ear—*and* he claims to love truth because it is true, not because it is his opinion. He goes further: Even if his opponents should, by chance, get it right, *nevertheless, their temerity in making the assertion comes from arrogance, not from knowledge; it is born not of vision but of swelling pride.*

Switching to a cooperative mode, he acknowledges that indeed, truth is not Augustine's but God's; it is the common possession of everyone. At this point he is willing to allow that there may be an *abundance of perfectly true meanings*, and he stigmatizes those who insist on one version of the truth. He advocates avoiding *pernicious quarrelsomeness* that *offends charity*. I wish that he could have pictured a conversation in which each perspective had something important and worthy of serious consideration to contribute. Alas, he castigates *people who are used to thinking in material terms*, calling them *feeble little creatures* (animalibus). Like generations of theologians after him, Augustine takes a meta-position, placing himself above the fray of argument, enjoying a God's-eye view.

∽

Is it possible to conceptualize a cooperative, rather than a competitive, learning process? To imagine truth as *distributed* among the several positions that are advocated? To recognize and acknowledge the perspectival aspect of all interpretations? Which of these models of truth-seeking conversation has the greatest possibility of finding the truth of a text or an event? In seminars I raised these questions as a central and substantial part of our engagement. The *style* of a discourse is as important as the facts or insights we glean. According to his student Porphyry, Plotinus was the ideal—and rare—teacher; "in answering questions he made clear both his benevolence to the questioner and his intellectual vigor."[3] In other words, he sacrificed neither accuracy nor goodwill toward the student.

∽

Scholars tend to take themselves very seriously. Yet most of us became lifelong students because, as children, we liked to read. Scholarship is a luxury and a privilege. To get a quick sense of this, imagine a society that had to choose between retaining its scholars *or* its garbage collectors. Because scholarship is a luxury and a privilege, it should be engaged in with delight and responsibility. Thus, I have wanted to understand as much as I can about how people of the past constructed religious orientations that held them in the exigencies of life and death. Our own interest in the richness of present diversities—diversities of race, ethnicity, gender, sexual orientation, and religion, to name only the most obvious—has prompted interest in the diversities of the communities and societies of the past. This means to me that as an historian of Christianity I must seek a more inclusive history than that of wars, ideas, beliefs, and institutions. Along with many other scholars I search for the history of women, of slaves, and of so-called heretics—people who had distinctive and rich religious sensibilities for which they were willing to suffer. I am interested in bodies and practices, in what people

3. Porphyry *Life* 13.

looked at and sang as well as the words they heard in church. What did they laugh at? What did they fear?

In short, I believe that it is necessary, and sufficient, to be faithful to one's deepest delight. Augustine put it this way: "Delight is, as it were, the weight of the soul. For delight orders the soul.... Where the soul's delight is, there is its treasure."[4]

⁓

The field of history has changed enormously in the last twenty years. In the 1970s feminist historians, like Joan Kelly, Gerda Lerner, and Joan Wallach Scott, began to call historical women's writings to readers' attention. And even when women's voices were lacking, we began to notice gender assumptions and social arrangements that could give a great deal of information about the conditions of women's lives in particular societies. Populist historians, like Carlos Ginzberg and Robert Darnton, sought evidence of the lives of people who did not write. More recently, "New Historicists" like Catherine Gallagher and Stephen Greenblatt, proposed that anecdotes that interrupt or even contradict the "great story" provide a less cohesive but more honest picture of past people and societies. Together, these suggestions opened the field of history beyond elitist, intellectualist history, requiring more of historians than the traditional skills of languages and hermeneutics.

Gradually, historical theology began to reflect the broader field of history's changed methods and content. I participated in the new historical interests, moving *from* intellectual history *to* a critical interdisciplinary hermeneutic. By "critical" interpretation I mean placing a text in the fullest possible context, not only the intellectual context of the author's Christian predecessors and cohorts, but also that of the social arrangements that informed his assumptions, the institutions that authorized and preserved his (usually male) writings, the personal experiences that prompted his interests, and other relevant contextual features.

My first position after graduate school was at Harvard Divinity School, where I was hired primarily to teach "History of Christian Thought" (from about 100 CE to the death of Rousseau, where others picked up with Kant and went forward). This was a two-semester

4. Augustine *De musica* 6.11.29 (355).

course formerly taught by the illustrious George Hunston Williams. This course should be taught, as it had been, by the oldest, most knowledgeable member of the faculty. Certainly nothing in my graduate concentration on St. Augustine and the later Roman Empire prepared me to lecture three times a week on Christian authors from Ignatius of Antioch to Jean Jacques Rousseau. I would not like to relive that first year of teaching! Nor, I suppose, would I like to reread those first lectures. On the other hand, that first year, and every subsequent year in which I taught the course over a period of twenty-five years, was profoundly exciting because learning *is* exciting, and my opportunities for learning in the context of that course were, quite literally, infinite. I endeavored to hold at bay feelings of inadequacy with the comforting thought that I could be confident that *someone* in that classroom was learning immensely—me. By necessity, I set out to model for students the learning experience, rather than to pose as an authority over seventeen hundred years of Christian thought.

My career as an historical theologian reflects changes in the fields of history and historical theology. When I was in graduate school in the mid-seventies, "Christian thought" was defined as the writings of a few male theologians who, until the early modern period, wrote in Greek or Latin. Although many historical theologians still focus exclusively on texts, there is new interest in social arrangements and practices, liturgies, and religious images and music. Christian "thought" irreducibly includes the music, architecture, and images that *conceptualized* and communicated Christianity to historical communities.[5] Using images and music, not as illustration but as articulations of Christian thought—as primary sources—makes for a richer, more colorful, more accurate and more persuasive picture of how a small Palestinian sect became a world religion and empire. Declining unrealistic heroization of Christian leaders by including the "tasteless historical stories" that reveal Christian movements "in the life" also contributes both to the liveliness and to the accuracy of Christian history. Moreover, the triumphal "great story" must be modified by detailed acknowledgment of the terrible damages, to individuals and communities, which are an

---

5. Miles, *Word Made Flesh*, 7–8.

undeniable feature of the past. A balanced history must insist on *both* the beauty and wealth of Christian thought *and* its abuses.

Historians enjoy the challenge of trying to understand the past. Is it something we owe to people of the past, to get their stories right? Or is it something we owe to ourselves? The latter, I think. Because it is *our* past, and if we do not find a past that leads up to our present, if we find only a past full of chaos, terminal discouragement, contradiction, and frustration, we will despair of the integrity and fulfillment of our own lives. We seek the past of the present.

∼

Robert Darnton says that our failure to "get" historical humor is a strong clue to fundamental differences between ourselves and historical people. Similarly, what aroused historical men sexually is a key to our differences. For example, early modern men delighted in parts of the female body that modern erotic tastes ignore.

> The first narrative pornographers were much more likely to linger over detailed descriptions of plump arms than to fetishize legs. Good teeth "stand out everywhere" in pornography, probably, Robert Darnton writes, "because of the prevalence of rotting jaws and stinking breath in early modern society." Moreover, early modern pornographers "fancied fat, fat in general, and fat in particular places—on arms and in the small of the back."[6]

There are also continuities. Violence seems to perennially elicit both laughter and sexual arousal. In the woodcuts for the 1596 edition of the so-called *Foxe's Book of Martyrs* the crowds of spectators at execution scenes press together; here and there one sees embraces, sometimes a man's hand is under a woman's skirt or on her breast. Or a woman leans over a balcony, the better to witness the cruel event, while a man presses on her from behind. In an illustration in one of the editions of the *Book of Martyrs*, a man beats another man with a knotted cord. The whipped man kneels with his pants around his ankles, while the persecutor has a huge codpiece/erection. Cruelty both arouses and makes people laugh. The crude, cruel jokes of childhood

---

6. Miles, *A Complex Delight*, 125; quotations are from Robert Darnton, "Sex for Thought," 206.

become slightly more sophisticated in adulthood, but remain fundamentally unchanged.

Indeed, "this wretch" (as Margery Kempe identified herself in her fourteenth-century autobiography), *this* wretch—me—a girl who was not permitted to read newspaper, magazines, or comic books, would sometimes sneak to my father's study and get *Foxe's Book of Martyrs* from the top shelf. An engraving of St. Catherine tortured on the wheel in an encyclopedia also attracted me. And in my paperback copy of *Bambi,* illustrated for me here and there by my grandfather when I was ten years old, a bloody drawing of a dog killing a small wolf is worn through the page.

An academic conversion that would change my scholarship occurred in my early years of teaching at Harvard Divinity School. In graduate school I was taught to read historical religious texts in the best possible light, seeking to identify the author's intention. Conversion to a critical eye involved asking questions of a text, not in order to diminish it, but in order to understand it "in the life," in its place in an institution, a conversation or debate, and its historical circumstances in its society of origin. I learned to notice what a text assumes and thus neglects to specify, what is *not* in a text. Reading old texts becomes exciting when the reader goes beyond seeking the author's meaning and intention to imagining (and researching) the *effects* of a text.

Challenged by students, I found it necessary to augment my historical training in several directions. Gender Studies and Feminist Theology had become important fields after my time in graduate school. By then I had also had a range of experiences that prompted me to want to understand the preferential treatment of men in public and private life. Years later, with colleagues at Harvard, I initiated a doctoral concentration in Religion, Gender, and Culture. In teaching and writing I increasingly incorporated women's history into the historical "great story," preferring to mainstream women's history rather than work within a sub-field that could easily be marginalized.

Seeking the history of women's participation in historical communities led me to study the role of religious images in forming and informing Christian communities both religiously and socially.

Gradually understanding the importance of this historical evidence, I argued in my book *Image as Insight* (1985) that scholars' preoccupation with religious texts and language has led them to neglect an important and vivid resource for historical knowledge. Using religious texts and images to augment, contest, and/or interpret one another, *Carnal Knowledge: Female Nakedness and Religious Meaning in the Christian West* reconstructed multiple messages about women's bodies and their religious meanings.

Recognizing the importance of religious images for conveying historical religious meaning led me to study the images of contemporary North American media in which values circulate to a broad popular audience. I used a sabbatical leave to read film criticism, especially feminist, Marxist, psychoanalytic, and cultural studies approaches to film. Settling on a method that combines critical and cultural studies, I wrote *Seeing and Believing: Religion and Values in the Movies* (1996). In this book I historicized popular movies, identifying a film's "voice" in a complex public conversation occurring in the social/cultural moment of its production and circulation in first-run theaters.

Reading for Life: Beauty, Pluralism, and Responsibility (1997) describes a reading method that honors both the beauty and profundity of literary works and raises critical questions relating to a text's social location, race, class, and gender assumptions and values. In *Reading for Life* I illustrate my interpretive method by "rereading" ten ancient and modern literary works that were powerfully influential and motivating at particular times in my life and career.

I taught "History of Christian Thought" for twenty years, each time revising lectures and researching new scholarship. I did not publish my lectures because once an article is published, the author must assume (incorrectly, of course) that everyone has read it, so it becomes worthless as a lecture! When I retired I decided to "write up" those lectures (that had only been "written down"), as a textbook. Immersed in this project, I noticed a jacket comment on Denys Hayes' *The Medieval Centuries* that articulated with precision my experience of writing a textbook:

> Is there a more unenviable task than writing a book like this? The author must travel fast along a well-worn track; he may not stop to explore the by-ways or admire the view; he must miss nothing, and every clause in his report must be succinct and

clear—and his reward at the end is to be told by the critics that he has said some things wrong and nothing new.[7]

The more I have invested energy in developing and exercising mind, the more I become aware that *body orders mind,* not only in the sense in which mind requires a physical home, but also in that body's physical needs and experiences—place, social location, health or disease, age, economic status, and nourishment—generate and direct thought. Although Augustine identified "something called the mind," and "something called the body," he also knew "silently" the intelligent body that cannot be dissected. Augustine's intelligent body reflected, participated in, and inhabited thoughts and emotions.

I am daunted by the challenge of loving, not just much, but well. Plagued by ignorance, weakness, and self-deception, we (humans) nevertheless commit ourselves to living richly responsive and responsible lives. We don't *know* what is generously responsible in particular situations, yet we must somehow act with confidence in the dark, by faith, in hope that love will be our best guide. The conditions under which we love are so poignant, so fragile.

> Nothing worth doing can be achieved in a lifetime; therefore we must be saved by hope. Nothing that is true or beautiful or good makes complete sense in any immediate context of history; therefore we must be saved by faith. Nothing that we do, however virtuous, can be accomplished alone; therefore we must be saved by love.[8]

A student who had an uneven record in the Masters program applied for the third time for admission into the doctoral program. My colleagues doubted that he had changed—or could change—sufficiently to make him a candidate for the doctorate. There was no doubt about his intellectual capacity, but his ability to persevere and complete coursework and a dissertation had not been demonstrated. I argued that the fact that the student had suffered in the meantime—a painful divorce and the loss of custody of two little boys—could have

---

7. Brooke, cover blurb on Hay's *The Medieval Centuries*.
8. Niebuhr, quoted by Sifton, *Serenity Prayer*, 349.

precipitated substantial change in his character. That's what it takes, I argued. Nobody volunteers to change; only pain mandates and motivates change. Pain weakens the highly fortified rationalizations and the self-deceiving psyche, making change possible—*if* it is well used. A big if, I admitted. "We wasters of sorrows," Rilke wrote.

How is life affected by having a conceptual scheme that makes sense of everything that happens? Does it even matter if the conceptual scheme is "right"? Or does any conceptual scheme effectively give the sense of privileged access to "reality"? As a child I expected the world to be a place in which the virtuous prosper. I often thought and/or said, "It's not *fair*," or "It's not *right*," as if these categories were decisive. But I have found that it is easier and more rewarding to look for beauty, rather than for fairness or rightness. What ultimately matters is that one's worldview contributes to a disposition of gratitude and generosity. To that end I have spent my adult life constructing a worldview that notices beauty, so that beauty, not wrongdoing, which so preoccupies fundamentalists, pops into my eye. A fundamentalist worldview is inadequate because it invites self-righteousness, criticism of others, and defensiveness.

> If you expect the material world to be an icon of divine beauty you may be more easily satisfied with it as it is than if you expect it to be a place in which virtuous [people] prosper.[9]

Journal entry:

> March 19, 2000 was a gorgeous day, the Marin hills neon green in the bright sun. New life everywhere. Fields of love, I thought. Cosmic love and provision, providence of the whole. Better enjoy, because *this* is what we get, not great relationships, money, success, or health. This is love; this is what we get if we're attentive, this beautiful rich world.

---

9. Armstrong, "Neoplatonic Valuations," 43.

13 *The Weight of Love*

The power of love is such that what the mind has long and lovingly thought about will stick to it like glue.
　—AUGUSTINE[1]

Thirteen books of my Confessions, which praise the just and good God in all my evil and good ways, and stir up towards him the mind and feelings of men: as far as I am concerned, they had this effect on me when I wrote them, and they still do this, when now I read them.
　—AUGUSTINE[2]

THE COLORFUL, VIVID FAMILY MEMBERS and unruly friends and students of Augustine's youth disappear in the last books of his *Confessions,* as Augustine takes up residence in his mind, rather than in his lusting, disobedient body. After he completed the *Confessions*, the people that crossed his path are evident mostly in his letters, which record interchanges on matters of doctrine and practice.

Memory, time, and creation: Books 10 through 12 are occupied with order.[3] Augustine recognized the principle of order: the way to

---

1. *De trinitate* 10.7.
2. *Retractationes* II, 32.
3. In *De ordine* 9.27, Augustine defined order: "Order is that which will lead us to God if we follow it during life; and unless we do hold to it during life we shall not come to God."

keep anything from being lost is to put everything in its place. He wrote in *De civitate dei* 19.13, "Order is an arrangement of similar and dissimilar things, assigning its proper place to each one."

> *In your gift we rest; we enjoy you. Our rest is our place . . . . A body tends to go of its own weight to its own place, not necessarily downward toward the bottom, but to its own place. Fire tends to rise upward; a stone falls downward. Things are moved by their own weights and go to their proper places. If you put oil underneath water it will rise above the level of the water; if you pour water on top of oil, it will sink below the oil; things are moved by their own weights and go to their proper places. When at all out of their place they become restless; put them back in order and they will be at rest. My weight is my love; by it I am carried wherever I am carried. By your gift we are set on fire and are carried upward; we are red hot and we go* (inardescimus et imus).[4] (13.9)

Now it is Augustine's mind that *God caresses and sets on fire*, and *we run after his odors* (13.15). Scriptural phrases tumble over each other as he describes the first moment of creation as God's *Let there be light* (13.3), thus separating light from the *watery darkness* (13.2–4), the *relics* of darkness that adhere to *our body* (13.14), because we *were made of nothing, by you, not of you* (13.33). Bodies return in Book 13 but only as evidence of creation from nothing and original sin. Creation mirrors God's separation of Augustine's light from the weighty darkness of his concupiscence. He contrasts the *brackish waters*, slippery and slimy, that characterize the human race with God's *unchangeability* (incommutabiliter)—the word is used eight times in a single short paragraph (13.16).

Yet, *all things of your making are beautiful; and see, you who made all things are yourself inexpressibly more beautiful* (13.20). So what happened? *If Adam had not fallen away from you, there would never have flowed from his loins the brackishness of that sea which is the human race,*

---

4. Augustine repeats a version of this passage in a letter (to Januarius) written at approximately the same time as his *Confessions* (Easter 400 CE): "Both holy and wicked souls love rest, but mostly they do not know how to attain to what they love, for bodies do not tend to anything by their physical mass, except what souls aim at by their love. For as a body strains by its weight, whether carried up or down until it comes to rest in its place of balance, as a quantity of oil falls down if dropped in the air, but rises if dropped in water, so souls strive after what they love, so as to find rest in accomplishment"; *Epistula* 55, 260.

The Weight of Love

so deeply curious, so stormily tossing, so restlessly flowing here and there. It was Adam's sin that created the need for *dispensers of your word to work in many waters, declaring in corporeal and sensible forms mysterious doings and sayings* (13.20). In short, original sin is Augustine's *raison d'être* as a minister. The rest of Book 13 describes the role and duties of a Christian bishop, which are to *preach, to judge (he approves what he finds good and condemns what he finds bad in the actions and way of life of the faithful)* (13.23), *to correct,* and, perhaps most importantly, to provide a model of *continence.*

Just as Augustine's people recede in the latter books of his *Confessions,* the passionate fundamentalists of my youth have grown faint in the last chapters of *Augustine and the Fundamentalist's Daughter.* Augustine wrote his *Confessions* at about the age of forty, however, and I am seventy—Augustine's age when he died. New people have come to be with me in the years since I was forty, colleagues, and former students, now colleagues. An adult daughter and son have replaced the little children I once loved. I miss their warm little bodies, soft hair, and the milky smell of their necks, but I am happy to have them as adult friends. I have a son-in-law, a granddaughter (now twenty-six years old), and my dear third husband. I have precious friends, some new, some from long ago.

> A strong egoism is a protection against disease, but, in the last resort, we must begin to love in order that we may not fall ill, and must fall ill if, in consequence of frustration, we cannot love.[5]

*Pondus meum, amor meus—my weight is my love—*is not a simple descriptive statement. It is, rather, a magnificent statement of human achievement, the only perfection that is possible for human beings. God's weight is love; "God is love" (1 John 4:16). The best people can do is to struggle *toward* that goal. As Freud pointed out, motivation—weight—also comes from fear. Freud would alter Augustine's statement to *pondeus meum, timor meus—*my weight is my fear. In pressing difficulties a person acts one way if fear dominates and motivates, another if love is the primary stimulus. To say, as Augustine did, "My weight is

---

5. Freud, *On Narcissism,* 404.

my love," is to say that he participates fully in the love that Christians call "God," with no admixture of fear.

Juan de Valdes, sixteenth-century author of *The Spiritual Alphabet*, wrote, "In everything you fear and love, closely observed, you will discover yourself." The statement echoes Augustine who said that if you want to know who a person is, you must ask what s/he loves.[6] And it anticipates Freud, who thought that to understand a person you must know what s/he fears. Fear and love are the most intensely concentrated states of the psyche; they define who a person *is*. But a person is not only defined by the *objects* of his love, but also by the relative *weights* of fear and love that motivate and direct her action. Augustine's *Confessions* recounts his movement from the extreme anxiety that made him clutch at everything that crossed his path in the fear that something would be missed, to *my weight is my love*.

I understand Augustine's statement as spelling out a goal, rather than claiming a reality. Shifting psychic "weight" from fear to love is the project of a whole life. It may be impossible fully to achieve this, but there is significant achievement in articulating the *project* with clarity. Once this "spelling out" has been done, one can begin to weave the project of love into the small and large decisions of everyday life.[7]

I am captivated by the claim that, in the human Jesus, a perfectly loving human being walked the earth. The historical existence of this perfectly loving human being is important, but only as something I believe in order to make use of the model. "Proofs" of Jesus' historicity, if they were forthcoming, would be beside the point. Between verifiable historicity and the idea of a perfectly loving being, there is plenty of room for attraction and inspiration.

I trace the life project of motivation by love to my earliest days. It was articulated in my upbringing, even though it was undermined by contradictory agenda. Karl Barth, who wrote thirteen volumes of neo-orthodox systematic theology, was once asked by a reporter if he could put his theology in one sentence. Barth said yes: "Jesus loves me, this I know, for the Bible tells me so." The reporter thought he was joking; he wasn't. That song was the first thing I was taught about God; it was the first piece I labored to play at the age of four on my quarter-sized violin.

---

6. Augustine *Enchiridion* CXVII (135).
7. Fingarette, *Self-Deception*, 38.

The Weight of Love

It is very powerful and poignant to me that the first thing my sisters and I learned as little children is, according to an important twentieth-century theologian, the essence of theology, all one needs to know about God.

The confidence that there is a loving heart in the universe and that I share in the circulation of love is precisely the truth and faith one needs for life. This confidence is, after all, (often) counter-experiential and counter-cultural, but even if a person later rejects it intellectually, having developed the habit and disposition of trust in childhood, he will probably yet continue to live *as if* it were true. Augustine said essentially "Jesus loves me, this I know," in his homilies on 1 John. Commenting on 1 John 4:16, he quoted, "God is love," adding, and that is all you need to know about God.

I am an optimist; I *silently think* that things will get better and better.[8] I still (against all evidence) silently think that I'll be prettier, thinner, smarter, stronger, and healthier next year! But at some point the tide changes and starts going out. "One must feel the washing of the tide over all that has been so meticulously etched by hand."[9] I know this intellectually, but it doesn't affect my temperament, established in childhood.

If only we could have stayed with "Jesus loves me." A severe and strict upbringing was not an adequate moral education. It was even a distraction from establishing a moral disposition. "What would Jesus do?" precludes discerning "that which I, and only I, can do in this, and only this, situation."[10] As a consequence, my moral sense tends to be sluggish. My first instinct when a situation arises that demands something from me is to say, "Not me. There's nothing *I* can do." Later, I know what I could have done. My childhood religion pretended to be hugely demanding, but it began with self-doubt and self-hatred (I *am* a sinner), not a trustworthy basis for a morality based on love.

The care of the self is not a rest-cure. Nor is it self-indulgence. It is diligence about choosing behaviors that lead in the direction of the self's best (long-term) good. Plotinus offers more subjective criteria for

---

8. Foucault's term for unexamined assumptions; *Use of Pleasure*, 9.
9. Schuld, *Foucault, Augustine, and the Hermeneutics of Fragility*, 125.
10. R. G. Collingwood's definition of "duty."

personal goodness than either "What will people say?" or "What would Jesus do?"

> How then can you see the sort of beauty a good soul has? Go back into yourself and look; and if you do not yet see yourself beautiful, then, just as someone polishing a statue which has to be beautiful cuts away here and polishes there and makes one part smooth and clears another until he has given his statue a beautiful face, so you too must cut away excess and straighten the crooked and clear the dark and make it bright and never stop working on your statue until the divine glory of self-mastery shines out in you . . .
>
> If you have become this, and see it, and are at home with yourself in purity, with nothing hindering you from becoming in this way one, with no inward mixture of anything else, but wholly yourself, nothing but true light . . . when you see that you have become this, then you have become sight; you can trust yourself then . . . concentrate your gaze and see . . . . This alone is the eye that sees the great beauty . . . . For one must come to the sight with a seeing power made akin and like to what is seen. No eye ever saw the sun without becoming sun-like, nor can a soul see beauty without becoming beautiful. You must first become all god-like and all beautiful if you expect to see god and beauty.[11]

I am confident that *each* stage of life, fully and richly lived, has its own beauty and privilege. The trick is to relax one's grip on an earlier time in order to discover the privilege unique to *this* time. Authorized by Dr. Seuss, "You're only old once," I decided that I would make a list of things I've felt I *should* do, and did, but never enjoyed and never felt that I did well. If asked to do them now, I can simply say, "I'm too old." My present list of things I will not do again is the following: climb perilous heights; ski; speak at clergy conferences; play the lute in public; consult a psychiatrist; camp; preach; take pictures.

Sick days are wasted on the sick, just as snow days are wasted on the snowed-in, and youth is wasted on the young. Old age can also be wasted on the old, but, as the bumper sticker says, "it's never too late to have a happy childhood." In old age I, who have always feared to be thought lazy, will cultivate laziness. I will listen to music, feel sun on my face, and eat brownies.

11. Plotinus *Ennead* 1.6.9.

This is what "going on" looks like at age seventy: the delight and the sense of amazing, unexpected, unearned privilege. Still the life I recognize as *mine*, my life. And surprises: "This is what getting old is all about.... You get variations of what you need. You go into the world still thinking you know what you want, and the world says: "How about considering this instead?"[12]

∽

I believe that the universe is connected, interdependent, and like Plotinus, I believe that "Providence is of the whole." The whole is sustained, though individual parts suffer because of the conflict inevitably generated by the struggle of each to hold life. I do not believe that "rewards" and "punishments," gifts and sorrows, are addressed to individuals by any design or designer, but that both circulate randomly. Chance can, however, be somewhat modified by my choices.

I am committed to a lifelong process of *becoming* Christian—that is, becoming a person who can *believe* that love is the center and origin of the universe. No other religion makes the fundamentally simple statement—so simple we complicated people can barely grasp it—of 1 John 4:16: "God is love."

Becoming Christian is about make-ing love. "As every true Christian knows, love is the *work* of love—the hard and arduous work of repeated 'uncoupling' in which, again and again we have to disengage ourselves from the inertia that constrains us to identify with the particular order we were born into."[13]

> We are not used to looking at the real world at all. Should we not ... endeavor to *see* and attend to what surrounds and concerns us, because it is there and is interesting, beautiful, strange, worth experiencing, and because it demands (and *needs*) our attention, rather than living in a vague haze of private anxiety and fantasy?[14]

Taught by Augustine, I think of God as life itself. In *De doctrina Christiana* 1.8, Augustine wrote, "Any one who thinks of God

12. McFarland, *Singing Boy*, 173–74.
13. Žižek, *Fragile Absolute*, 128.
14. Murdock, *Sovereignty of Good*, 64.

as anything other than life itself has an absurd notion of God." Life, the "One thing" is not an abstraction; it is utterly concrete—the only "thing" that *is*. Life hides in the open; a person can miss noticing life just *because* it is so ubiquitously visible. It is distributed in everything one looks at but seldom *sees*; it is everywhere—even, Plotinus said, in rocks and soil. Thus, Plotinus proposed the exercise of contemplation for getting past the words, the categories, the definitions through which we usually look at the world. So that we can finally get over ourselves ("cessavi de me paululum"), and *see what there is*.

But the "One thing" lacks *emotional* concreteness and thus needs metaphors ("father," "mother") that provide emotional accessibility, that give an experiential model of how the universe gives. Can emotional accessibility be achieved without locking the "One thing" into a narrow range of emotional experience that is limited and limiting? Contemplation, imagining the real, Plotinus says again.

Plotinus, dying alone with enough pain and isolation to crush him, with an illness so repulsive that all his friends abandoned him, considered his dying a teachable moment. "Try," he said, "to give back the all in you to the All that is in the universe." These are precise instructions in the art of dying, an art that requires lifelong preparation, "practice for dying," getting over oneself. For the "thing" I call "my life" isn't mine at all, of course. My intelligent body—"I"—has captured a piece of life for the moment, but life will circulate on without "me" someday, Plotinus said. We usually fail to recognize that our grasp on life is tenuous, desperate but weak.

Maxine Sheets-Johnstone writes:

> [T]he fear of death is tied to the body. The fear of death may in fact be manifest as fear of one's body—of what it might do or what it might become. What links morality to death, what in fact grounds morality and *makes it fully real*, is foundationally one's own body. It is one's own body that is vulnerable and ultimately impotent, that is affectively experienced as exposed, assailable, open to pain, disease, and suffering, and that is affectively experienced as out of one's control.[15]

15. Sheets-Johnstone, *Roots of Morality*, 52.

The Weight of Love

Without what Sheets-Johnstone calls an "immortality ideology," that is, "a story: a belief structure either without empirical foundations or going beyond empirical foundations," death simply *takes away*, "conclusively and absolutely, with no promise of *more*."[16] If illusions of immortality, persistent hopes for "more," undermine the present, the life I *have*, what attitude toward the nonnegotiable inevitability of death can I cultivate?

The opposite of longings for more, and more, and more, is gratitude for what I have had, and have now. Gratitude is the richest orientation for *now*, and it is an orientation that can take me all the way to death. Gratitude. Not an intellectual pose but intimately experiential. Gratitude for the sensuous richness of the world I see, touch, hear, and taste. Gratitude for the "more" I have been given, not expecting an endless provision of "mores." Gratitude for *this* life, my life.

If I don't volunteer to give it all back, it will nevertheless be taken back. Life will go on, but will no longer be "here," in me. Everything depends on *staying with it*, riding it and surrendering my life *to life*. This is the last grace, the triumph of the philosophical life. Strong drugs, childbirth, and philosophy are practice. All of these come on too fast, too strong—if only I could have a minute to center myself, to breathe, to regroup—but that minute is not given, and one must nevertheless stay with it. And even if it moves too fast and I cannot stay with it, the life in which I have participated will not be erased, for "nothing of real being perishes," Plotinus said.[17]

In some furtive corner of my mind there is a fear that when I come to die, childhood training or common sense will recapture me, causing me to die in despair for worlds I rejected that now turn out to be the *very most important thing*. The fundamentalist religion of my childhood might resurface and condemn me in various ways. Or will I, by then, have a *real* world, so durably built and reinforced, so impregnable, *that I could even die within it?* I am, right now, literally not ready to die, because I am not always *moved wherever I am moved* by love rather than by fear. I am not always able to find freedom and freshness in the face of inherited ideas. In his movie *Love and Death*, Woody Allen articulated the fantasy that I must relinquish: "I don't want to be immortal through my work," he said, "I want to be immortal by *not dying*. And I don't

---

16. Ibid., 16.
17. Plotinus *Ennead* 4.7.14.

want to live on in the hearts and minds of my countrymen; I want to live on in my apartment."

∽

Again, Plotinus has a suggestion:

> All our toil and trouble is for this, not to be left without a share in the best of visions. The one who attains this is blessed in seeing that "blessed sight," and he who fails to attain it has failed utterly. A man has not failed if he fails to win beauty of colors or bodies, or power or office or kingship even, but if he fails to win this and only this.[18]

That's Plotinus's answer: *the* only thing to regret is missing *seeing the beauty*.

∽

On her deathbed the Victorian photographer, Julia Margaret Cameron, looked out of her window at the evening sky and uttered her last word: "Beautiful."[19] I think that this requires one to be a completely loving person, so that nothing but love rushes out at the world. No fear. No regret. No grasping. Just love, "my weight is my love." This is what I aspire to, to be able, when I am dying, to see the beauty of the world.

Can I live in a way that finds such continuous delight in beauty? Plotinus's proposal is *radical and counter-cultural* because every society suggests that fulfillment lies in the attainment of wealth, power, or fame. If indeed it is the recognition of beauty that I *must not* miss, I must not expect support for *seeing beauty* and *make-ing love* from media entertainment. "Beauty *is* reality," Plotinus said.[20] Attentive looking is a start, but *imagining the real* is also essential. No amount of looking will, by itself, give one the real—the planet careening in space, *life* circulating through living bodies, growing things (cancers, plants, babies).

Ugliness is what we can't see as beautiful because of our socialized eyes. In *Wisdom, Madness, and Folly*, John Custance, a certified

18. Ibid., I.6.7.
19. Olsen, *Life*, 259.
20. Plotinus *Ennead* 1.6.4.

schizophrenic, said that in his manic stages, even dust and shit was beautiful enough to make him cry. Everything is beautiful; it's *ugliness* that is "in the eye of the beholder."

Even suffering can be beautiful, for in suffering one comes to recognize the serious. Sex also reveals beauty in a way we would not otherwise know unless we were gifted celibates. Beauty has little to do with art. That's the lesson of twentieth-century art, which often deliberately frustrates common notions of beauty.

"We never feel as grown-up as we expected to feel when we were children."[21] I reassure myself frequently that I will always be "all right." What does that mean? Clearly it does not mean that I will not grow old and feeble, or get sick, suffer, and die. However, being all right does seem to mean that I will not be on the street, a bag lady, as I always half-jokingly feared; I will have decent medical attention; and there will be people who love me. I will endeavor to avoid depression and discouragement by continuing to learn and by keeping interest in others. I will seek to reach out, to find or make the places I can be and the people I can be with in order to feel alive while I'm alive. By comparison, life has been easy so far!

> I've known a few exceptions. Old people who didn't slap the children for being slappable; who saved their strength in case it was needed for something important. A last courtship full of smiles and little presents. Or the dedicated care of an old friend who might not make it through without them. Sometimes they concentrated on making sure that the person they had shared their long life with had cheerful company and the necessary things for the night.[22]

---

21. Dinnerstein, *Mermaid and the Minotaur*, 190.
22. Morrison, *Jazz*, 11.

Augustine and the Fundamentalist's Daughter

As Augustine lay dying, Hippo was besieged by Vandals. By the time of his death, "Roman rule in North Africa [had] simply collapsed."[23] His biographer, Possidius, wrote:

> The man of God saw whole cities sacked, country villas razed, their owners killed or scattered as refugees, the churches deprived of their bishops and clergy, and the holy virgins and ascetics dispersed; some tortured to death, some killed outright, others, as prisoners, reduced to losing their integrity, in soul and body, to serve an evil and brutal enemy. The hymns of God and praises in the churches had come to a stop; in many places the church buildings were burnt to the ground; the sacrifices of God could no longer be celebrated in their proper place, and the divine sacraments were either not sought, or, if sought, no one could be found to give them.[24]

Augustine thought that his life's work was obliterated. Possidius described Augustine's death of a fever on 28 August 430 CE.

> This holy man was always in the habit of telling us, when we talked as intimates, that even praiseworthy Christians and bishops, though baptized, should still not leave this life without having performed due and exacting penance. This is what he did in his own last illness: for he had ordered the four psalms of David that deal with penance to be copied out. From his sick-bed he could see these sheets of paper every day, hanging on his walls, and would read them, crying constantly and deeply. And, lest his attention be distracted from this in any way, almost ten days before his death, he asked us that none should come in to see him, except at those hours when the doctors would come to examine him or his meals were brought. This was duly observed: and so he had all that time to pray.[25]

Dad's ninetieth birthday, September 11, 2001. My sister Dorothy had a family gathering for him at which his wife, afflicted with Alzheimer's dementia, tried to eat the centerpiece flowers. A snapshot shows

---

23. Brown, *Augustine of Hippo*, 428.
24. Possidius *Vita* 28.6–8 quoted in Brown, *Augustine of Hippo*, 432.
25. *Vita* 21.1–3, in Brown, *Augustin of Hippo*, 436.

Dorothy, a restraining hand on her stepmother's shoulder, smiling determinedly. Dad's journal recorded his horror at the events of 9/11. He attributed the disaster to God's judgment on the immorality of American society, citing drugs, abortions, homosexuality, and working mothers as evidence of this immorality. He quoted the words of a hymn he loved, "This world is not my home, I'm just a-passin' through. My treasure is laid up somewhere beyond the blue . . ."

For several years before his death, Dad regularly woke in the night, tormented by regret. Neither Augustine nor my father tells us exactly what he most regretted. Sexual sins? Intransigence? Lack of love? Lack of joy? Fear? We can't know. The similarity between them lies in the compulsion to examine, to regret, to repent.

On one of my last visits to my father, I took my son, whom he had not seen in a decade. Dad had been very judgmental of my son—not without reason—through the years. But when we came to leave, Dad clung to him, crying.

Two old men, Augustine and my father, mourning their sins, confident of heaven, and ready to go.

In one of his last sermons Augustine said,

> Whoever does not want to fear, let him probe his inmost self. Do not just touch the surface; go down into yourself; reach into the farthest corner of your heart. Examine it then with care; see there, whether a poisoned vein of the wasting love of the world still does not pulse, whether you are not moved by some physical desires, and are not caught in some law of the senses; whether you are never elated with empty boasting, never depressed by some vain anxiety: then only can you dare to announce that you are pure and crystal clear, when you have sifted everything in the deepest recesses of your being.[26]

Augustine did not shirk his duty of judging, and many occasions occurred in which he was obliged, in the ecclesiastical court, to judge anything from a boundary quarrel to homicide. But the decisions that most disturbed him were those involving fellow Christians, primarily Donatists, coerced by imperial laws.

26. Augustine *Serm.* 348.2.

> What shall I say as to the infliction and remission of punishment in cases where we have no other desire but to forward the spiritual welfare of those we have to decide whether or not to punish? What trembling we feel in these things.... What trembling, what darkness![27]

Augustine was constantly and painfully aware of encroaching darkness, in himself as well as in others: *For there is still only a little light in men, and they must walk, yes, they must walk, that the darkness overtake them not* (10.23). My father shared Augustine's anxiety about wrong decisions. Despite each man's confidence that (they) knew God's will, they both acknowledged a "trembling" fear of wrong judgments. Perhaps this fear informed the regret and repentance they felt when close to death. Fundamentalists are simultaneously sure and not sure.

How did Augustine and my father picture death? Was it the "flags flying and bands playing" imagined by my grandfather?[28] No, my father simply wanted "home." Augustine wanted *facie ad faciem*. In the last chapter of his *City of God*, Augustine wrote at length about his fantasy of the day of resurrection, acknowledging that his vision was hypothetical, an extrapolation from, rather than an exposition of, Scripture. He began with his favorite scriptural text, *We see now through a glass darkly; then, however, face to face* (1 Cor 13:12), trying to imagine what it will be like to see *facie ad faciem*. Will God be seen with *physical eyes*? he asked, deciding that

> it is possible, it is indeed most probable, that we shall see the physical bodies of the new heaven and the new earth in such a way as to observe God in utter clarity and distinctness, seeing him present everywhere and governing the whole material scheme of things by means of the bodies we shall then inhabit and the bodies we shall see wherever we turn our eyes.[29]

---

27. Augustine *Epistula* 95.3.

28. This image is from John Bunyan's *Pilgrim's Progress* (1688), in which Christian and his companions enter the Celestial City at the end of their journey.

29. *City of God* XXII.29.

I would like to be able to picture with conviction "bands playing and flags flying," "home," or *facie ad faciem*. Alas, I cannot. But Plotinus's perspective on death relaxes my lifelong, profound resentment of death, my strong sense of the radical insult to the achievement of humanity, *humanness*, humaneness, that death is. "Who consulted *me*?" I used to rage. "With whom can I renegotiate?"

Plotinus said that life (by definition) doesn't die. But at some point my used-up body will be unable to gasp-grasp life, and my particular life will be absorbed into the whole going-on of the universe. My death is simply *life moving on*. If I am strongly identified with life, rather than with "my" body, then "I" move on with it, though not as a coherent, integrated individual. Just as "life," to take whatever form presents itself. "I" become life. This is Plotinus's idea of immortality. And the problem of body—the only problem of body—is that body is so concrete, so immediate, and its needs are so pressing, that a person is strongly tempted to identify with body rather than with life.

Both Plotinus and Augustine rely on the assumption that humans *are* components: bodies and minds/souls. Plotinus's proposal is consistent; he assumes a biodegradable body, a body that has a shelf life and an expiration date. Plotinus requires that I identify my*self*, not with body, but with life, a property (thought of in his time as) unique to soul. But Augustine insists on the integrity of the person; the resurrection body, he said, will be a *real spiritual body*. He tried to resolve the apparent contradiction of thinking of persons as composed of components, yet he could imagine a future in which body and soul will be one—a third thing. He sought to avoid contradiction by strongly distinguishing the present body from the resurrection body. At present, bodies suffer, have needs, and are moribund; the resurrection body, he said, will continue to enjoy pleasure and be characterized by beauty, but will not be vulnerable to accident, disease, aging, and death.

But I seek to move the resurrection body into the present, for finally, to become a follower of the Word made flesh it is necessary to overcome the ancient distinction/separation of "something called the soul," and "something called the body." According to philosopher Maxine Sheets-Johnstone, when we analyze a human being according to components, as philosophers and theologians have done for centuries and still do, *no matter how we stack the components, we have already lost the person.* For a person is an irreducible, nonnegotiable "intelligent body."[30]

Augustine's assumption that human beings are composed of souls and bodies, exemplifies a puzzle at the heart of Christianity. For Christianity, it seems, *must have* two entities in order to transcend and unite them. Spirit and matter; divinity and humanity; soul and body; even male and female, are distinguished and placed in hierarchical order. Christian doctrines and practices assume spirit and matter in order to achieve the *frisson* of bringing them as close together as possible, yet without mixing them. Throughout the history of Christianity, conceptualizing an intimate blending of soul and body, spirit and matter, that produces a "third thing," was not tolerated.

Yet surely this is precisely what Christians believe in and hope for in the "resurrection body"—an intelligent body in which, as Augustine imagines in *City of God* 22.29, soul and body will be one, and "the bodily eyes shall *see God,* and *God will be all in all."* Augustine insisted that what he (following Paul) called the "spiritual body" is a real body, permeated throughout with spirit. He quotes Job: "I shall see God in my flesh." God will be seen, he writes, "in every body by means of bodies, wherever the eyes of the spiritual body are directed with their penetrating gaze."

> They have not been called "spiritual" because they will be spirits, not bodies . . . Why, then, is it called a spiritual body, my dearly beloved, except because it will obey the direction of the spirit? Nothing in yourself will be at variance with yourself; nothing in yourself will rebel against yourself.[31]

The doctrine of the resurrection of body places new urgency on thinking about what it *means* to believe. It challenges my credulity. If belief is something done by the rational mind, I cannot believe in the resurrection of body. But intelligent bodies *believe* in a different way than do rational minds. For me, to believe this doctrine is to commit to living *toward* it. To seek what it means to live out into the resurrection body *in the present, every day,* seems both a more realistic and a more demanding definition of belief than that of rational mind's assent. I can

---

30. Sheets-Johnstone, *Corporeal Turn,* 20.
31. Augustine *Serm.* 244. 8.11.

practice the resurrection body now by believing with my intelligent body, by paying attention to body's longings. Augustine wrote:

> I know you want to keep on living. you do not want to die. And you want to pass from this life to another in such a way that you will not rise again as a dead person, but fully alive and transformed. This is what you desire. This is the deepest human feeling; the soul itself wishes and instinctively desires it.[32]

In the dream I walk through rooms, beginning with my present house. As I walk, I recognize that I am walking back in time, back through the rooms in which my children grew up, the parsonage, the furnished apartments of the early days of my first marriage. I walk slowly, sensing that the people I had lived with in those rooms were just out of my vision, perhaps in another room; at any moment they might walk in. I don't need to see them; I know they are there, and they are overwhelmingly precious to me. I walk on, back into the rooms of my angry and bored teenage years. As I walk, my body becomes the body that had inhabited those rooms, with the physical feeling of myself at those ages.

I go back further, to the rooms of my childhood, complete with furniture, mirrors, doors, mottos and pictures on the walls, knick-knacks, and gently blowing curtains. These were the rooms in which I lay awake in a cold sweat, fearing that I was damned, and that if I died in the night I would go to hell. I keep walking, back to my grandmother's rooms on the farm in eastern Ontario, and finally, to a small house in Lancaster, Pennsylvania. I find myself in a long, narrow room with clothing hung along one wall. Under windows on the other wall, I lie on my back in a crib, kicking chubby arms and legs, looking at the light from the window. A beautiful woman with black hair comes and bends over me, smiling, and I love her back. The dream fades, and I awaken with a deep sadness. Thinking, did I love the people who lived with me in those rooms enough? My pretty young mother, myself full of longing, the little warm, milky-smelling bodies of my babies, my young husbands. Did I love them all fully, achingly, as I do now?

---

32. Augustine *Serm.* 344. 4.

> And the lost heart stiffens and rejoices
> In the lost lilac and the lost sea voices
> And the weak spirit quickens to rebel
> For the bent goldenrod and the lost sea smell
> Quickens to recover
> The cry of quail and the whirling plover
> And the blind eye creates
> The empty forms between the ivory gates
> And smell renews the salt savor of the sandy earth.[33]

Just this: I love being here, "because being here amounts to so much, because all this Here and Now, so fleeting, seems to require us and strangely concerns us. Us the most fleeting of all."[34]

---

33. Eliot, "Ash Wednesday" VI, 120.
34. Rilke, *Duino Elegies*, Ninth Elegy, 73.

Epilogue

DAILY NEWSPAPERS REPORT HORRENDOUS SUFFERING around the world created by fundamentalists of various religions. As a result many liberals condemn "religion," all religions, for beliefs that seem to support and encourage torture, suicide bombings, genocide, and wars. The central issue that divides liberals and fundamentalists is whether—or not—an individual or group is willing to be self-critical, to judge their own religion according to humanist/humane values. This was precisely what my father objected to, for no one, he said, can judge God's commands, stated with apparent clarity in the Bible.

Christian fundamentalists cite the biblical story of Abraham and Isaac as an example of a test of whether a person places human values ahead of God's demand. Abraham's willingness to kill a beloved son in obedience to God's command seems highly commendable to many fundamentalists. Examples of such costly obedience abound in both Old and New Testaments. The potential sacrifice of the persons, careers, or activities most attractive and dear to a person is required for a fundamentalist relationship with God. The contemporary secularized version of this demand is the "tough love" preached by Alcoholics Anonymous.

Augustine taught that human loves do not compete with love of God, but rather *participate* in God-is-love. In *De trinitate* 8.7, he wrote: "He who loves his neighbor must also love love above everything else. But 'God is love, and he who abides in love abides in God.'" Therefore it follows that he loves God above all else. In this passage Augustine claims that a person loves God *by* loving others.

In this book I have endeavored to sort fundamentalist characteristics that have contributed to the energy and vividness of my life from those that have constricted me and bleached life's color. Certain values inform this effort. As my father feared, I place human flourishing and respectful care of the natural world, "our island home," above the biblical value of intransigent obedience to *what one understands* as God's commands. Because of notorious and well-documented human fallibility, we must, I believe, constantly question our ability to interpret scriptural injunctions within our own circumstances, including the command to love the neighbor as oneself. The loving response is not always obvious, and a great deal of harm has been done in the name of love.

Christian fundamentalism in its contemporary American forms is rife with interior contradictions. Claiming the label "pro-life," for example, the Christian Right protests abortion but supports capital punishment. But the greatest contradiction is that fundamentalist Christianity, claiming that "God is love" (1 John 4:16), is so frequently prone to hatred, even violence against "the neighbor." Activist liberals, even if they are Christians, do not often state publicly that their efforts to build a loving society result from their commitment to the founder of Christianity who, after all, spent much of his time feeding the hungry and healing the sick. Overcoming poverty and providing healthcare, as well as addressing other pressing needs of American society, could certainly be motivated by commitment to God-is-love.

The passionate zeal so characteristic of fundamentalism could contribute to the creation of a loving society, a society in which the young, the old, and the variously vulnerable are protected by safety nets. Augustine asked, Can it ever be wrong to love the neighbor, and by loving the neighbor to promote the circulation of universal love? Perhaps if the fundamentalist, self-defined as "I am a sinner," were relaxed to define the self as "I am a child of God-is-love," it would be more evident that Christians' task in the world is love, not judgment.

Is self-critical fundamentalism an oxymoron? Perhaps it is. As I have demonstrated throughout this book, I reinterpret, appreciate, and *use* some characteristic features of fundamentalism. But I cannot imagine my father identifying the human values he held and judging his beliefs and practices by those values. Had he done so, he would not have been a fundamentalist, and I would not be, to this day, a fundamentalist's daughter.

Bibliography

Armstrong, A. H. "Neoplatonic Valuations of Nature, Body, and Intellect." *Augustinian Studies* 3 (1972) 35–59.
Augustine. *The City of God against the Pagans*. Translated by R. W. Dyson. New York: Cambridge University Press, 1998.
———. *The Confessions of St. Augustine*. Translated by Rex Warner. New York: New American Library, 1963.
———. *Enchiridion on Faith, Hope, and Love*. Translated by Henry Paolucci. Chicago: Henry Regnery, 1961.
———. *Epistula*. In *St. Augustine: Letters*. 3 vols. Translated by Wilifrid Parsons. New York: Fathers of the Church, 1951–53.
———. *On Christian Doctrine*. Translated by D. W. Robertson Jr. New York: Bobbs-Merrill, 1958.
———. *De musica*. In *The Writings of Saint Augustine*. Translated by Robert Catesby Taliaferro. New York: CIMA, 1947.
———. *De ordine*. In *The Writings of Saint Augustine*. Translated by Robert P. Russell. New York: CIMA, 1948.
———. *De trinitate*. Translated by Stephen McKenna. Washington, DC: Catholic University of America Press, 1963.
———. *Homilies on the First Epistle of John*. In *Augustine: Later Works*. Translated by John Burnaby. Philadelphia: Westminster, 1955.
———. *Sermons*. In *An Augustine Synthesis*. Translated by Erich Przywara. New York: Harper, 1958.
———. *The Spirit and the Letter*. In *Augustine: Later Works*. Translated by John Burnaby. Philadelphia: Westminster, 1955.
Bass, Alan. *Difference and Disavowal: The Trauma of Eros*. Stanford: Stanford University Press, 2000.
Bellow, Saul. *Henderson the Rain King*. New York: Library of America, 2007.
Benjamin, Jessica. *The Bonds of Love: Psychoanalysis, Feminism, and the Problem of Domination*. New York: Pantheon, 1988.
Braverman, Kate. *The Incantation of Frieda K.* New York: Seven Stories, 2002.
Brown, Peter. *Augustine of Hippo: A Biography*. 2nd ed. Berkeley: University of California Press, 2000.
Cary, Philip. *Augustine's Invention of the Inner Self: The Legacy of a Christian Platonist*. New York: Oxford University Press, 2000.

Bibliography

Cox, Patricia. *Biography in Late Antiquity: A Quest for the Holy Man*. Berkeley: University of California Press, 1983.

Damasio, Antonio R. *The Feeling of What Happens*. New York: Harcourt Brace, 1999.

Darnton, Robert. *The Forbidden Best-Sellers of Pre-Revolutionary France*. New York: Norton, 1995.

———. "Sex for Thought." In *Sexualities in History*, edited by Kim M. Phillips and Barry Reay, 203–21. New York: Routledge, 2002.

Davidson, Arnold. *The Emergence of Sexuality: Historical Epistemology and the Formation of Concepts*. Cambridge: Harvard University Press, 2001.

Dinesen, Isak. "Babette's Feast." In *Anecdotes of Destiny and Ehrengard*, 19–60. New York: Vintage, 1993.

Dinnerstein, Dorothy. *The Mermaid and the Minotaur: Sexual Arrangements and Human Malaise*. New York: Harper & Row, 1976.

Dixon, Sandra Lee. *The Scattered and Gathered Self of St. Augustine*. St. Louis: Chalice, 1999.

Dressler, Mylene. *The Deadwood Beetle*. New York: Penguin, 2001.

Eliot, T. S. "Ash Wednesday." In *Collected Poems, 1909–1935*. New York: Harcourt Brace, 1936.

Elizabeth Sifton, *The Serenity Prayer*. New York: Norton, 2003.

Feynman, Richard P. *The Pleasure of Finding Things Out*. Cambridge, MA: Perseus, 1999.

Fingarette, Herbert. *Heavy Drinking: The Myth of Alcoholism as a Disease*. Berkeley: University of California Press, 1988.

———. *Self-Deception*. Berkeley: University of California Press, 2000.

Foucault, Michel. *The Use of Pleasure*. Translated by Robert Hurley. New York: Pantheon, 1985.

———. "On the Genealogy of Ethics." In *Michel Foucault: Beyond Structuralism and Hermeneutics*, edited by Hubert L. Dreyfus and Paul Rabinow. Chicago: University of Chicago Press, 1983.

Fox, Robin Lane. *Pagans and Christians*. New York: Knopf, 1987.

Freud, Sigmund. *Civilization and Its Discontents* II. Translated by Joan Riviere. The Major Works of Sigmund Freud. Chicago: Encyclopaedia Britannica, 1952.

———. *The Interpretation of Dreams* VII. Translated by A. A. Brill. Chicago: Encyclopaedia Britannica, 1952.

———. *On Narcissism*. The Major Works of Sigmund Freud. Translated by Cecil M. Barnes. Chicago: Encyclopaedia Brittanica, 1952.

———. *On the History of the Psychoanalytic Movement*. Standard Edition of the Complete Psychological Works of Sigmund Freud 14. Edited by J. Strachey. London: Hogarth, 1914.

Futrell, Alison. *Blood in the Arena: The Spectacle of Roman Power*. Austin: University of Texas Press, 1997.

Gerson, Lloyd P. *Aristotle and Other Platonists*. Ithaca, NY: Cornell University Press, 2005.

Hay, Denys. *The Medieval Centuries*. New York: Harper & Row, 1965.

Hennessy, Rosemary. *Profit and Pleasure: Sexual Identities in Late Capitalism*. New York: Routledge, 2000.

Hopkins, Keith. "Murderous Games." In *Death and Renewal*. Cambridge: Cambridge University Press, 1983.

Bibliography

Hustvedt, Siri. *The Sorrows of an American.* New York: Henry Holt, 2008.
Irigaray, Luce. *Speculum of the Other Woman.* Ithaca, NY: Cornell University Press, 1974.
Kafka, Franz. "A Hunger Artist." In *Selected Short Stories of Franz Kafka.* Translated by Willa and Edwin Muir. New York: Modern Library, 1952.
Kingston, Maxine Hong. *China Men.* New York: Knopf, 1980.
Lamott, Anne. *Bird by Bird: Some Instructions on Writing and Life.* New York: Pantheon, 1994.
Langer, Susanne. *Philosophy in a New Key: A Study in the Symbolism of Reason, Rite, and Art.* Cambridge, MA: Harvard University Press, 1960.
Loy, David. *Lack and Transcendence: The Problem of Death and Life in Psychotherapy, Existentialism, and Buddhism.* New York: Prometheus, 1996.
Makari, George. *Revolution in Mind: The Creation of Psychoanalysis.* New York: Harper Collins, 2008.
Malcolm, Janet. "The Annals of Biography: The Silent Woman." *New Yorker,* August 23 and 30, 1993.
Manchester, Peter. "'As long as that song could be heard': Eternal Time in *The Trinity* of Augustine." In *The Subjective Eye: Essays in Culture, Religion, and Gender in Honor of Margaret R. Miles,* 59–70. Edited by Richard Valantasis. Eugene, OR: Wipf and Stock, 2006.
Mann, Thomas. *Death in Venice.* New York: Vintage, 1989.
McFarland, Dennis. *The Singing Boy.* New York: Henry Holt, 2000.
Merwin, W. S. "Berryman." In *Migration: New and Selected Poems,* 255–56. Port Townsend, WA: Copy Canyon, 2005.
———. "Words from a Totem Animal." In *Migration: New and Selected Poems,* 145–49. Port Townsend WA: Copper Canyon, 2005.
Miles, Margaret R. "Not Nameless but Unnamed: The Woman Torn from Augustine's Side." In *Feminist Interpretations of Augustine,* 167–88. Edited by Judith Stark. University Park: Penn State University Press, 2007.
———. "Resistance and Affirmation." *The Christian Century* (December 1, 1993) 97–98.
———. *A Complex Delight: The Secularization of the Breast, 1350–1750.* Berkeley: University of California Press, 2008.
———. *Augustine on the Body.* Missoula, MT: Scholars, 1979.
———. *Desire and Delight: A New Reading of Augustine's* Confessions. New York: Continuum, 1992.
———. *Plotinus on Body and Beauty: Society, Philosophy, and Religion in Third Century Rome.* Oxford: Blackwell, 1999.
———. *The Word Made Flesh: A History of Christian Thought.* Oxford: Blackwell, 2005.
Miringoff, Marc, and Marque-Luisa Miringoff. *The Social Health of the Nation: How America is Really Doing.* New York: Oxford University Press, 1992.
Miringoff, Marc, Marque-Luisa Miringoff, and Sandra Opdycke. *The Social Report: Assessing the Progress of America by Monitoring the Well-Being of Its People.* Tarrytown, New York: Fordham Institute for Innovation in Social Policy, 2001.
Monk, Ray. *Bertrand Russell: The Ghost of Madness, 1921–1970.* New York: Free, 2001.
———. *Ludwig Wittgenstein: The Duty of Genius.* New York: Free, 1990.
Morrison, Tony. *Jazz. New York:* Knopf, 1992.
Munro, Alice. *The Progress of Love.* New York: Knopf, 1986.

Bibliography

Murdoch, Iris. "Against Dryness." In *Existentialists and Mystics: Writings on Philosophy and Literature*. New York: Penguin, 1998.

———. "T.S. Eliot as a Moralist." In *Existentialists and Mystics: Writings on Philosophy and Literature*. New York: Penguin, 1998.

———. *Metaphysics as a Guide to Morals*. London: Chatto and Windus, 1992.

———. *The Sovereignty of Good*. London: Routledge, 1971.

Neiman, Susan. *Evil in Modern Thought: An Alternative History of Philosophy*. Princeton: Princeton University Press, 2002.

Nussbaum, Martha C. *The Therapy of Desire: Theory and Practice in Hellenistic Ethics*. Princeton: Princeton University Press, 1994.

———. *Love's Knowledge: Essays on Philosophy and Literature*. New York: Oxford University Press, 1990.

O'Connell, Robert J. *Augustine's Early Theory of Man, 386–391*. Cambridge: Harvard University Press, 1968.

Olsen, Victoria C. *Life: Julia Margaret Cameron and Victorian Photography*. New York: Palgrave, 2003.

Phillips, Arthur. *Prague*. New York: Random House, 2002.

Plato. *Greater Hippias*. In *The Roots of Political Philosophy*. Translated by David R. Sweet. Edited by Thomas L. Pangle. Ithaca, NY: Cornell University Press, 1987.

Plotinus. *Enneads. Plotinus*. 7 vols. Loeb Classical Library. Translated by A. H. Armstrong. Cambridge: Harvard University Press, 1966–88.

Ponticus, Evagrius. *The Praktikos*. Translated by John E. Bamberger. Kalamazoo, MI: Cistercian, 1970.

Porphyry. *On the Life of Plotinus*. In *Plotinus*. Loeb Classical Library. Translated by A. H. Armstrong. Cambridge: Harvard University Press, 1966–88.

Ribuffo, Leo P. "Confessions of an Accidental (or Perhaps Overdetermined) Historian." In *Reconstructing History: The Emergence of a New Historical Society*, edited by Elizabeth Fox-Genovese and Elisabeth Lasch-Quinn. New York: Routledge, 1999.

Rilke, Rainer Maria. *Duino Elegies*. Translated by J. B. Leishman and Stephen Spender. New York: Norton, 1939.

Robinson, Marilynne. *Home*. New York: Farrar Straus & Giroux, 2008.

Robinson, Roxanna. "The Truro Accord." *The New York Times Book Review*, August 16, 2009, 7.

Roethke, Theodore. *Collected Poems*. New York: Doubleday, 1966.

Rorty, Richard. "Is Derrida a Transcendental Philosopher?" *Yale Journal of Criticism* 2 (Spring 1989).

Roth, Philip. *Exit Ghost*. New York: Houghton Mifflin, 2007.

Schlink, Bernhard. *Homecoming*. New York: Pantheon, 2008.

Schuld, Joyce. *Foucault, Augustine, and the Hermeneutics of Fragility*. Notre Dame: University of Notre Dame Press, 2003.

Shawn, Wallace and André Gregory. *My Dinner with André: A Screenplay for the Film by Louis* Malle. New York: Grove, 1981.

Sheets-Johnstone, Maxine. *The Corporeal Turn: An Interdisciplinary Reader*. Exeter, UK: Imprint Academic, 2009.

———. "Existential Fit and Evolutionary Continuities." In *The Corporeal Turn: An Interdisciplinary Reader*. Exeter, UK: Imprint Academic, 2009.

———. *The Roots of Morality*. University Park: Penn State University Press, 2008.

———. *The Roots of Power: Animate Form and Gendered Bodies*. Chicago: Open Court, 1994.
Spitz, René. *The First Year of Life: A Psychoanalytic Study of Normal and Deviant Object Relations*. New York: International Universities, 1965.
Strauss, Gerald. *Luther's House of Learning: Indoctrination of the Young in the German Reformation*. Baltimore: Johns Hopkins University Press, 1978.
Theodore Roethke, *Collected Poems*. New York: Doubleday, 1966.
Thomas, Dylan. *Under Milk Wood*. New York: New Directions, 1954.
Toner, J. P. *Leisure and Ancient Rome*. Cambridge: Polity, 1995.
Walker, Alice. *The Color Purple*. New York: Simon & Schuster, 1982.
Wiedemann, Thomas. *Emperors and Gladiators*. New York: Routledge, 1991.
Williams, N. P. *Ideas of the Fall and of Original Sin*. New York: Longmans Green, 1927.
Woolf, Virginia. *Moments of Being*. San Diego: Harcourt Brace, 1985.
Young, Iris Marion. "The Ideal of Community and the Politics of Difference." *Social Theory and Practice* 12 (1986) 1–26.
Žižek, Slavoj. *The Fragile Absolute*. New York: Verso, 2000.
———. *The Sublime Object of Ideology*. London: Verso, 1989.